Toon, Toon, Black 'n' White Europe
Toon, Toon, Black 'n' White Europe
Toon, Toon, Black 'n' White Europe

CW01067082

Toon, Toon, Black 'n' White Europe
ISBN 9780954835736
© 2014 Barry Robertson & Peter Cain

Limited Edition (well we couldn't afford to have more copies printed!)

'Not another book about football?' 'No, another book not about football!'

By the same authors:
Toon Tales – *a Euro-Geordie pilgrimage*
ISBN 0-9548357-0-0
© 2004 Toon Publishing Ltd

Toon Odyssey – *the pilgrimage goes on*
ISBN 0-9548357-1-9
© 2005 Toon Publishing Ltd

Lordenshaw
ISBN(10) 0-9548357-2-7
ISBN(13) 9780954835729
© 2007 Toon Publishing Ltd

Photographs
Cover photos: Barry Robertson & Peter Cain
Centre photos: courtesy of Sarah Wilkie, Chris Wilkie, Paul English, Ian Rosenvinge, Michael Kromwyk, Clive Swinsco, Philippe Perbos & the authors

Toon, Toon, Black 'n' White Europe

by

Peter Cain

and

Barry Robertson

First published in Great Britain in 2014

e-mail: toonpublishing@yahoo.co.uk
https://www.facebook.com/toontooneurope

1 3 5 7 9 10 8 6 4 2

A CIP catalogue record for this book is available from the British Library

ISBN 9780954835736

Printed and bound in Great Britain
by Biddles, King's Lynn, Norfolk

Contents

Introduction

We thought it would be a good way to start.

> *Davies was jostling with Charlton as Sprake was going mad before the Gallowgate goal and the crowd surged forward. The old black scoreboard said nowts apiece and the Leech's home flag was long down, hiding from a Big Lamp brewery sunset still warm and yellow-red on a late ham and pease-puddin' afternoon going into an early pint of Fed Special or two.*
>
> *Quiet all of a sudden. Gibbo takes the free kick in front of the Paddock two yards from the touchline, half way into their half. Revie's cheats are expecting it to go to Wyn, who'll nod it down on to Pop's right, but no! Moncur, standing free like a miracle, gratefully stops it dead and lobs it ower from the Popular to float over the six yard box.*
>
> *Davies rushes, leaps. A tangling of arms but Wyn rises supreme above gangling, loopy Jack and it's a bullet header that scorns a full-stretch Sprake and bursts through the back of the tunnel to the tune of a deafening Geordie roar.*

Out we speed reborn and blinking into the expensive Swiss Alpine sunshine and we're off on another European adventure.

'Mind, that Kronenbourg's a steady pint. Cheers, Kidda, Ya sure yiv got them tickets, Barry?'

'Wheyaye man.'

'Hev another look, will ye?'

'Aalreet, tha here, man. Wor tickets for the Europa League Final. The San Siro here we come.'

***

Well, that was how we imagined it might work out, and quite how that game against Leeds got in there, nobody really knows. And the final would be in Amsterdam, not Milan. But strange forces are at work wherever Newcastle United make an appearance, and the mists of time have a habit of clouding the ebb and flow of reality.

But remember that if you were born in or before 1953, your life has already lasted longer than Newcastle United had been in existence before you were born! How's that for a clouded reality born of absurdity? Be that as it may, there is a certain timelessness about the Toon Army that means it doesn't really matter which particular season you write about. This one happens to be the 2012-2013 campaign and adjacent pre-season tournaments. And we invite all our readers to hop on board for another roller-coaster European adventure. A Toon Euro trip is only ten per cent the match itself. There is so much more to it, and this is what this book attempts to bring you. Our hopes soared and plummeted in time-honoured fashion as we once again embraced and enriched the continent's breathtaking cultural and linguistic traditions (and watched some matches while we were about it).

***

A new cyber-friend of ours in Australia, Michael Kromwyk of Adelaide, told the worldwide web that he re-read Toon Tales by way of preparation for the season we are about to describe. Here's what Michael said:

*http://charmike4.hubpages.com/hub/Why-Newcastle-United-Are-Back

'My home town team – Port Adelaide (in the SANFL & AFL) are black and white – so it runs in my blood as well! ... It's gonna be great having Newcastle back where they belong in Europe!

Finally, you may want to pick up a copy of Peter Cain & Barry Robertson's book 'Toon Tales' which recounts the 2003-4 Newcastle European campaign. These guys went to all the away games and if I recall rightly we got knocked out in the semi-finals. I'm going to read this book again in preparation for next season!'

Well good on yer, Michael, mate. In fact, it was your posting that finally convinced us that we should hit the keyboard and write at least one more Toon book for posterity. So thanks again, Michael!

And on our trips to Bordeaux and Lisbon we bumped into young Andrew Thompson, who told us his Dad had given him Toon Odyssey one Christmas when he was little, and that had got him hooked on the Euro-Toon idea.

We want you to join in the fun and relish the whole Euro-Geordie experience. Newcastle United are woven inextricably into the very fabric of the Geordie nation's collective being and underlying psyche. We don't call ourselves 'the Toon' for nothing.

An Irish friend of ours happens, for black-sheep-in-the-family reasons, to be a mackem supporter. When pressed on the subject of loyalty, he conceded that, given the choice between Ireland reaching the finals of the World Cup or sunderland getting promotion, he would come down in favour of the Paddies every time (and quite rightly so – well done, John!). It was immediately clear to us, however, that given, say, the choice between England actually winning the World Cup, or Newcastle reserves winning a meaningless friendly with a Cramlington pub team, well … there would actually be no choice to make: it will always be the Black and White. No disrespect meant to the Black Ox eleven, mind. If the choice in turn were between the Black Ox, Cramlington, beating Sutton United reserves in an equally meaningless friendly on the one hand, or England winning the World Cup on the other, well … Howay the Collier Lads! And we all know that even a Large Hadron Collider is no match for a Large Hardon Collier.

In other words, Newcastle United are to all intents and purposes our national team, whereas England is a southern club that plays all its home games in London, and the majority of whose supporters speak with a strange cockney twang. By now you should be getting a rough idea of where our loyalties lie. And if not, here's a clue: they extend no further south than Gateshead and selected parts of County Durham.

The characters and their adventures and opinions as expressed in the book do not always coincide with those of the authors, but that's what always happens when you let characters loose on the blank page; all the better to consume you, my dears. And ultimately, as we mentioned above, this book is essentially written for posterity. And we really hope posterity enjoys it! Howay the Toon.

Atromitos away – 23rd August 2012

Europe, we've missed you, but now we're back.

The long wait is over. Like the Curiosity Mars Rover, we've crossed a void. In Curiosity's case it was around 350 million miles of, well, rather empty space. In ours it was six seasons without European football. Alkmaar seems aeons ago. In fact, it was 15th March 2007 – a two-nil away leg after a four-two home win meant we went out on away goals. But now we're off to Athens again to visit Atromitos, who in fact don't play in Athens at all but in the adjacent suburb of Peristeri.

Well, here goes. Another European adventure!

'All set, Pete?'

'You bet, Barry. There's nowt better. Well, almost nowt … Where are you, by the way? I won't get away till after work this afternoon.'

'In the departure lounge at Gate 46 of Zaventem airport …'

… And as I sit here waiting for the Aegean Airlines morning flight from Brussels to Athens, I am wondering where this season will take us. It's so easy travelling around now, what with internet booking of planes, trains and accommodation, and the euro accepted just about everywhere we would hope to go in the Europa League. Hope being the operative word, as I hope we get to go to countries such as Greece, Spain, Italy, Denmark, Holland, Germany, Portugal, France and so on, rather than Georgia, Ukraine or Azerbaijan, though if needs must … If the doom-mongers are proven correct, and let's sincerely hope not, maybe it could be the end of the euro before the Final of the Euros as in Europa League?

On earlier trips to Greece and elsewhere we would often remark on how convenient it was for so many different countries to have the single currency. The euro zone really does cover a huge geographical area – from the top of Finland (a village called Määppötuulälupppsltärärrä, which apparently translates as 'place where reindeer like to crap when they can't be arsed to go behind those bushes down by the river when it's thirty-five degrees below zero)' to the Canary Islands, where the tourists behave like those reindeer, not to mention far-flung outposts of the French 'empire' such as Martinique in the Caribbean or Ile de la Réunion (birthplace of Laurent Robert) in the Indian Ocean. Fantastic, we thought, no more messing about changing money at every border you cross and coming back home with a pocket full of useless change.

These days, however, a lot of other people are thinking: 'Oh, s#1te. For how much longer is this house of cards going to hold steady? Here we are stuck with the euro doing its amazing value-disappearance act.' And this time round we are also thinking 'Let's hope there won't be any of those riots on the streets of Athens while we're there!' We have all seen the scenes on the telly. Look at the mess they made of the Parthenon that time they had a really big riot a couple of thousand years ago.

We're no economists, and hindsight is a great thing of course. But hey, surely the guys who are running the show could have intervened at some stage earlier on and handled the whole shooting match a wee bit better than this. And it really is no joke in Greece, with people losing their jobs or having their salaries or benefits radically cut. And all those miserly Germans have done about it is injected countless billions ... of euros. And what have they got in return? A time share in all the Greek banks.

By the way, I wonder where the Final will be held next May? Our regular readers will recall that Toon Odyssey ended with us having optimistically bought final tickets before the quarter-finals, in Sporting Lisbon's own home ground, where the gallant CSKA lads overcame the huge and unfair home advantage of Sporting to win the UEFA Cup as was. Let's look up this year's 'final' destination, shall we? A quick look at uefa.com tells us that it's going to be at the Amsterdam Arena, Ajax's home ground, the one where the pitch is wheeled in and out from under the stands on a huge trolley contraption. Those Dutch – they turn the sea into land, and then they move the land around according to their whim.

Well done to those nice UEFA people for picking Amsterdam. Canny, eh? Perfect for the DFDS ferry trip across from Percy Main to nearby Ijmuiden. And for those taking that boat it'll be two nights out at the maritime equivalent of Percy Main Social Club. Anyway, I can hardly wait for the fifteenth of May 2013. I wonder whether the team will be with us at the final this time? And will we win it? And will we have to beat home team Ajax in the final if they get booted out of the Champignons League into the Europa version? Mind, it will take a lot of vim to beat Ajax. Yes, this is a time of wonder.

It was on the news leaving the house this morning that some banking big-wig is on his way from Frankfurt to Athens today too. Maybe he'll be on the same plane as Pete, who is also flying from Frankfurt – but hold on, Pete's flight is not till tomorrow morning. Bet the banker won't be watching Atromitos training for tomorrow's game, or at least not until after he has first had a few choice words with the latest Greek Prime Minister and closet Atromitos fan Mr Samaras. Well he might be – who knows? Any relation to the shot-shy Celtic striker of the same name, I wonder? They certainly have plenty of strikers to choose from in Greece, don't they? And last night he helped Celtic to a two-nil win in the first leg of their Champignons League qualifier over Helsingborgs IF, from the little Swedish town of Helsingborg which looks across the mile-wide Øresund straits to the castle protecting the Danish town of Helsingør, better known to us Geordies as Elsinore, Hamlet's hoose, or *hus* (pronounced hoose) as they say in Danish too. If Helsingborgs IF lose, I think they drop down into the Europa League, so sometime we could play them too. Now that would be a good trip.

There are more questions than answers, but by the end of this book, we'll know them all. And you'll know well before you even pick up the book. But with a bit of luck you'll have forgotten by then, and that way you can enjoy it all again with us.

As a reminder: it's the first leg of the play-offs for entry into the Europa League proper. There had been talk of Newcastle asking to switch the order of the legs as we had to play cheatski less than forty-eight hours later, but in the end UEFA kept the draw as it came out of the bag, so we were playing the away leg first. Our opponents, Atromitos FC, are encamped to the west of the citadel in Peristeri, a mere Elgin marble's throw away from Egaleo football ground which we visited briefly to see them play Middlesbrough as an early-evening appetiser before the deliciously satisfying main course of Panionios v the Toon, many meals ago. Panionios is yet another Athenian suburban team, like another of our erstwhile opponents Olympiakos. We must have played nearly as many different teams in Athens as we have London teams. The place is so teeming with teams, they could even re-name Athens as the Team Valley. But enough of this Greek musing.

I wrote to the Atromitos club to see if we could have media accreditation as journalists on the basis of our two previous Toon books. In case you'd like to try our fool-proof plan, here's a copy:

To: 'media@atromitosfc.gr' <media@atromitosfc.gr>
Sent: Wednesday, 15 August 2012, 16:16
Subject: Media accreditation for 3 persons for Atromitos-Newcastle

Accreditation procedure for the UEFA Europa League play-off game between Atromitos FC and Newcastle United is now open. The media representatives who wish to attend the match should e-mail their request to media@atromitosfc.gr or fax it to (0030) 210 5774734. The deadline has been set for Friday 17th August, 18.00 (local).

Dear Sir/Madam,

We are writing the third in our series of books on the European travels and matches of Newcastle United.

Details of the first two books, Toon Tales and Toon Odyssey by Peter Cain and Barry Robertson can be found at amazon.co.uk.

The first two books include chapters on previous travels to Athens for the games against Panionios and Olympiakos, and the game of Egaleo v Middlesbrough, so we have first-hand experience of three grounds around the city of Athens.

The first chapter of the third book will describe the opening game of this new Europa League season, Atromitos FC v Newcastle United.

Here are some interesting facts that we have already started to write up and that you might also wish to draw out in your own media articles:

- the Blue Star emblem of Atromitos FC is identical to the famous Blue Star badge of world-famous Newcastle Brown Ale which was proudly worn on the shirts of Newcastle United heroes of the 1990s such as David Ginola, Alan Shearer, Les Ferdinand, Tino Asprilla and Robert Lee;

- also, did you know that Shefqi Kuqi, the brother of new Atromitos number 9 player Njazi Kuqi, was a Newcastle United player two years ago when brought in as a loan player after the sale of Andy Carroll, the Newcastle number 9? O Carroll, you were such a fool – leaving Newcastle, just to go to Liverpool;

- and last but not least, Atromitos is a dyslexic anagram of Newcastle United (and mother-in-law is a real anagram of Hitler Woman).

We would appreciate please three media tickets for the contributors to the third book, Peter Cain, Barry Robertson and Brian Robertson.

We look forward to an excellent game played in Olympian spirit and thank you for your kind attention.

Yours sincerely,

Etc.

They never replied.

To get into the swing of things and to remember some tips from Athens I read Toon Odyssey on the plane on the way there.

Since the last time we went to Athens with the Toon, it looks as if Olympic Airlines has stopped flying and instead flights are run by Aegean Airlines. I used to like Olympic. Tasty in-flight meals, stewardesses, and drinks and lots of leg-room, even in economy class. They had a nicely-scheduled plane that took off after work and got to Athens sometime around eleven o'clock so you could be in the city centre around about midnight. And at midnight in the Greek capital, the night is still young. When we touched down, it turned out that the Olympic spirit was still alive and kicking, except they now had lots of little planes lounging around the airfield which are used to fly around the islands of the Aegean Sea. If I had been in charge, I think I'd have switched the names around and let Olympic keep the international flights, because really the two Aegeans, the airline and the local destinations, fit better together.

***

Yes, a lot of water has passed under the Tyne Bridge since our forlorn Toon Odyssey trip to Lisbon in 2005 to see the UEFA Cup Final between CSKA Moscow and the hosts Sporting Lisbon who knocked us out in the Quarter Final when it all seemed to be going so well until half time. Woodgate was not playing, out injured in the first leg, and Robert was watching from the stands after having a difference of opinion with Souness. So to lose Dyer to another injury was just too much and we collapsed in the second half.

It's not even called the UEFA Cup any more. And it hasn't gone back to being called the Inter Cities Fairs Cup either. Oh no. It's now the Europa League. And like all good leagues, I don't think, it now includes more knock-out stages than it did when it was called a Cup! Hardly makes sense, does it? What kind of league is that? Well, the one we're trying to get into through the final qualifying round.

***

Atromitos – anachronistic, atypical, anaerobic, apocalyptic – none of these words have anything to do with Atromitos at all. They're all Greek to me, and everybody, but the thing is, they all begin with an 'a' which signifies 'not' in Greek. So just as anachronistic means 'not in time', Atromitos means 'not *tromitos*'. And one of our Greek friends, Yorgos, told us that *tromitos* has to do with being scared, so wonderfully, Atromitos means the 'Unscareables', the 'Fearless'. You might be wondering what happened to their local rivals, FC Tromitos, the scaredy cats. Well they got knocked out in the first round. In fact they were too scared even to turn up, and their opponents were given a bye. Bye bye FC Tromitos.

We've talked about this before: how come it's only the European clubs that have the inventive, inspiring, inyerface names? We might be 'mental', 'mad' and 'loyalest', but we could do with being 'fearless' too. Mind, at least we're not called 'Go Ahead Magpies' or 'Young Boys Newcastle'.

I would have thought that, as one of the seeded teams, we would be lined up to play one of the clubs that had fought through from the three, yes three, qualifying rounds which had begun in early July – no rest for the wicked. But no, Atromitos like us were direct entrants into the play-off round, but were unseeded. In fact we were lucky to be in the seeded half of the draw, weighing in at a lowly 25th out of the 31 seeds. Pre-draw nerves, they're almost as bad as the pre-match variety, and 10th August 2012 had been a nerve-wracking day all right. Where else could we have been off to on our travels on this year's European roller coaster?

Of the possible teams we might have played from the unseeded half of the draw, there were some highly outlandish (in the true sense of the word) outlaw places such as Neftchi Baku of Azerbaijan, Zeta Golubovci of Montenegro or Sheriff Tiraspol of Moldova. UEFA, by some process known only to themselves, made six groups of teams from the sixty-two concerned at this stage, and our group included the above-mentioned Neftchi Baku as well as FC Vaslui, Atromitos FC, Anzhi Makhachkala and Tromsø IL as possible unseeded opponents. Of these, I think you'll agree that we got off very lightly with Atromitos, with it being in Athens, one of the cradles of civilisation and financial probity, and current (ad)venture capital of Europe, and a far cry from the dubious pleasures in store for visitors to Makhachkala, capital of Dagestan, taking an ironically random example.

***

The Aegean plane is very nice, as are the hostesses who gave me a Hondos Centre biro so I could write this. Apparently the Hondos is to Athens what the Metro Centre is to Dunston. The plane even has some of those drop-down tellies that you get on long-distance flights (such as Brussels to Athens) and the map is showing that we are flying mid-way over Albania with Tirana on our right (starboard to you, Cap'n Coloccini) and Skopje of FYR Macedonia through the left port hole. I look down to see if I can spot anything of interest. Nope, nothing. No one in sight, not a sausage. Not even a path or a hut. Just parched fields and, yes, a pond. Can't wait to get drawn against either Tirana or Skopje – we'll be in for high times indeed, making a bee line for that pond and the hut. Of course we should not do Macedonia down, for was it not from there a couple of thousand years ago that Alexander the Great hailed – a taxi for Athens, just like us. The Metro was just a twinkling in some town planner's eye back then. Somehow I think I would have preferred Athens to Macedonia too. The night life, the retsina, and a wider choice of football teams to support, or so said Socrates, who never wrote a thing down (true). He left that donkey-work to Plato. You could say Socrates was a little like David Ginola or Laurent Robert – he liked doing the fun bit, but he needed someone like Robert Lee or Gary Speed in the Plato role to back him up.

This is, I think, the first time I have flown into Athens while it's still light. Usually I've taken the midnight express. What a strange view. It sprawls everywhere and it all looks the same, no variety at all. The buildings and streets all seem identically clad in a chalky white tombstone colour, picked out against the arid sage-khaki-sand shades of the hinterland. Maybe it's my imagination, but I think we flew in over Cape Sounion with its temple on the cliffs looking south to the wine-dark sea of the Aegean. A recommended day-trip out of Athens.

They still haven't finished those temples up on the hill since our last odyssey in the post-Olympics aftermath to see us play Panionios and Olympiakos. The scaffolding is still up – perhaps they had enough after building all those Olympian white elephants, which even back in 2005 were already going rusty.

Don't worry that maybe you've missed your chance to fly Olympic, because Aegean Airlines is nearly as good. Their in-flight magazine, 'Blue' is pretty entertaining. Take this for an example. In the section giving 'Guidelines for a pleasant flight', it gives the following excellent advice, 'For the sake of your fellow passengers, we recommend that you do not take your shoes off during the flight'! A touch of class that you just don't get on Ryanair or Easyjet. And well, it does get very hot in Greece, as I immediately found out when I left the air-conditioned shelter of the Eleftherios Venizelos terminal building. Phew, what a scorcher! How's that for a headline for the Sun? It was over forty degrees, enough to boil your brain to the point where you begin to believe that we're going to win this thing this year.

***

The best way to get into Athens is definitely on the new(ish) Metro system which was built for the 2004 Olympics. It's not quite as sparkly-clean as it was the last time we were here in 2005, a fact that is probably testimony to its popularity. The only thing you have to watch out for after you come out of the terminal, cross the road full of taxis, take the long people-mover flyover lined with Johnny Walker whisky, not DJ, adverts and buy your eight euro ticket from the relaxed and friendly ticket booth, is that you need to click your ticket in the post at the top of the stairs before you get on the train, otherwise you might end up with a hundred and sixty euro fine. They don't tell you that until you're nicely settled down with your luggage on the racks and the train's moving out of the station and you happen to read a very small sign on the wall. I sat there clutching my pristine, un-punched ticket, thinking forlornly about all those euros that would soon be going to solve the Greek debt crisis, and thinking it would have been much cheaper in a taxi, even one driven by a Greek with the standard-issue built-in fantasy fare generator. But luckily no inspector was on the train. Maybe that's their trouble – they come up with money-making ideas, but don't follow through (tax collection being a topical case in point). If they got in a team of tenacious Toon traffic wardens to patrol their corridors they could soon be milking all the tourists and businessmen to the tune of a hundred and sixty euros a shot. Whilst at the same time making Greece even more unpopular, which is probably why they don't bother to check anyone's tickets.

The Blue Metro line takes you the three-quarters of an hour trip down to Syntagma, the Constitution Square, where I swapped onto the Red line in the direction of the Acropolis stop, which was the one closest to our hotel at Syngrou Fix. Trusting my innate sense of direction, I wandered around, eventually covering all points of the compass without any noticeable progress. It was so steaming hot that there was nobody around to ask, but then mirage-like through the shimmering air appeared some student-summer-job types giving out free ice-cold cans of a breed of disgusting (as I later found out) energy drink off the back of a flat-bed Ford. I can't stand those things, the drinks not the lorry, but the can worked well as a makeshift roll-on, to cool my brow and kept me upright until at last I finally stumbled upon the right street and staggered, sweating like an Eengleesh peeg, into the welcomingly cool foyer of the Athenian Callirhoe Hotel. Callirhoe apparently means 'beautiful stream' – a veritable oasis on this blistering day, to be sure.

The reception fellers were so welcoming and smiling, no doubt to see the nth boiled beetroot to have rolled in that afternoon. I got up to the room and there was son Brian, sensibly sheltering from the heat. He'd just come across from one of the Greek islands, where he'd been for a reunion week with his old school friends. They are all at universities scattered all over Europe now. His island, Ios, had turned out to be overwhelmingly populated by Australians rather than Greeks – a kind of Van Diemen's Land moored some distance from the mainland and where 'Strine was the local lingo not only of the beach-dwellers but also of all the barmaids and barmen.

After a very necessary shower it was out into the mid-afternoon cauldron again and a slow meander along the shadowy side of the dusty streets until we came within welcome sight of the air-conditioned cool of the recently-opened Acropolis Museum, which was doing a roaring trade as a shelter from the sizzling paving stones. It's worth a visit at any time, but even more so when you need a break from this oppressive heat.

The Greek locals really are a very pleasant and friendly bunch. And that goes for just about everyone we met – from the hotel receptionists to the staff in the tavernas and at the ground and the Atromitos club shop, to the sports journalists we bumped into. And so obliging. Get in the back of an Athenian's car when they have stopped at a junction and they'll drive you anywhere you want to go – at least that's what they did the last time we were here, when the Don (may he be ever held in the highest esteem and his name mentioned only with the deepest respect) did a spot of impromptu car-jacking, ... er, I respectfully meant to say car requisitioning, Toon Army for the use of. But for many people, of course, the first impression they get when they walk the streets of Athens is that those legendary Nana Mouskouri and Vicky Leandros cloning programmes have been very successful indeed. And there are always one or two Demis Roussos look-alikes knocking about too. Not to mention all those cousins of the Duke of Edinburgh (local Greeks and German tourists).

It has to be said, however, that you must always watch out for the taxi drivers and their ever more inventive ways of relieving you of as many euros as possible by driving round in circles and finding new routes which challenge the very existence of the concept of travelling as the crow flies. Or maybe they travel as the Athenian owl flies when its night-vision capability is on the blink. Blinking owls – they even have them on the back of their euro coins.

In what should have been the cool, cool, cool of the evening but in fact still felt like the heat, heat, heat of mid-afternoon, Brian and I made a recce of the ground. We took the short taxi ride from Aghios Antonios, the nearest Metro station on Line Two. It was just too hot to walk. We tried to get into the training session, but we learnt from the nice folk at the club shop that NUFC had asked for a closed session, so all we could see were some knees and socks through cracks in the turnstile doors. It turned out that we could have seen the training if only we'd known that over on the far side of the ground there was the Blue Star bar which had windows opening out onto the pitch. But we didn't find out about that until the next night when two lads told us they'd been in there and seen the whole session before heading off to the city's evidently quite notorious Gafi district, where they said they'd had their drinks spiked. We'd never heard of Gafi, only Gaddafi, and tried to forget it as a possible destination. Though when some of the lads heard about it at the match, they decided they would go there on the grounds that having your drinks spiked meant you could get bladdered on a lot less money. Fair point. It now turns out that the place was actually called Gazi, named after its old gas works, and is pronounced Gazzi, but if you pronounce it Gay Zee you get a better idea of what it's known for.

On the off chance, I rang the number I had for Steve Storey, who is NUFC's smiling, friendly and efficient head of security. He'd kindly agreed to bring our tickets out with him, as there'd been too little time and too much risk involved in having them posted out from the Box Office to either Brussels, Trier or our hotel in Athens. We would get to know Steve quite well through our many reunions over the coming months, each time greeting him more and more like a long-lost friend. Definitely a credit to Newcastle United Football Club. They should recruit more people like him, and relations with the supporters would improve by a factor of several thousand. I got through, and Steve knew exactly who we were and explained that the tickets were back in the team hotel, but he'd be more than pleased to see us before the match tomorrow night.

***

Wonder how Pete's doing. He said he'd be heading off after work, didn't he? So he should be in Frankfurt by now.

'I'm doin' just grand, Barry. Thanks. Sounds like you've got everything nicely under control down there. That heat must be really something, though but. It's actually been quite warm in Deutschland all day as well. Warm enough to boil a monkey's bum in fact. And of course you're an hour ahead in Athens, aren't you? That's two hours ahead of British Summer Time. But hey, I must still have time for a couple of jars before turning in. And I've ordered supper anyway. Guess what I'm having. … That's right – once again, the *wurst* is yet to come …'

… And as I wait patiently for my *Currywurst mit Pommes Frites* in the pseudo-English-pub-type bar of the Holiday Inn Frankfurt North, I can catch my breath after the hectic drive from Luxembourg (possibly still the best-run Grand Duchy in the world) and reflect on the helter-skelter logistical developments of the past few days.

There would normally have been ten or so of our usual suspects making the trip to Athens, along with a good few hundred or more of the fellow Toon Army faithful. But this is the back end of the middle of a very hot August and loads of people are either still on, or have just come back from, their well-earned hols. For example, the Don (may I take this opportunity to respectfully express my profound gratitude and continuing loyalty to the Don, who has been like a Godfather to us all) has just been vacationing Stateside, where he took in a couple of rounders games. Well, rounders is after all one of the Ham Shanks' great national games, along with netball and girls' rugby. When in New York (USA, not Tyne and where?) last year, I wanted to take my daughters to see a girls' rugby game. The New York Giants, I think it was, were playing Dallas or somebody. The concierge at the hotel said he could fix us up with tickets all right but then asked if we would like him to arrange the flights as well. Excuse me, flights? But it's a home game, isn't it? 'Yes Sir, but it is being staged in Florida as a special promotion'. No thanks. Was this the shape of things to come? I asked where we could at least buy souvenir girls' rugby helmets, but something clearly got lost in translation. Anyhow, the Don wouldn't be coming to Athens but was building up a war chest for the group stage. He should have made NUFC an offer they couldn't refuse.

Fellow Cuths Old Boy, South-Shields-based Peter F., and a couple of his mates were mustard keen at first, but it turned out there were no direct flights (and I didn't even know South Shields had an airport!) and the airlines were asking really silly prices. Nor were matters helped by the Club's attempt to have the home and away legs switched around because of the league game at chelski just two days after the first leg. Well, fair enough, I suppose, but that left us all in a state of great uncertainty over the weekend after the draw on the tenth of August, which did not make it any easier to make arrangements ('er, I'd like to book a return flight and accommodation in Athens, but I don't know when exactly ...'). In the event we found out early on the next Tuesday morning that there would be no switch-around after all, and we could finally set the logistics-planning machinery into operational mode.

Chris and Sarah would not be along on this trip, unfortunately, as they would be ending their holiday on Lindisfarne and leaving the Holy Island on the very day of the match. Well, they would already be in the Athens of the North, isn't that right, Barry? And I believe you have some words of advice to would-be Lindisfarne pilgrims, something about a causeway, was it?

'I had a feeling you were going to mention that at some stage, Pete. Okay, okay, I admit it. And yes, we can definitely call Lindisfarne the Athens of the North! The family and I were so busy admiring the cradle of North European civilisation on a nice outing there that we forgot all about the tidal hazard. We definitely should have paid more attention to the tide table. In the end, we just made it back across to the mainland, and my brand new car had to splash through the water coming over the causeway for the last hundred yards or so. I stopped in Gateshead to give it a good full manual car wash to get all the salt off. The thing was we definitely had to get off the island because we had a booking for that night's North Sea Ferries crossing from Hull to Zeebrugge.'

'Yes, going to Lindisfarne without properly checking the tides on a day when you had to catch the Hull ferry sounds like a really good plan, Barry ... :-)'.

***

Hang on a minute, here comes my *Currywurst* and chips. And another pint of Radeberger please, Jackie.

Champion.

Where were we? Ah yes, logistics ... Never an easy task at the best of times – especially if there is a causeway involved – and the machinery of the Toon Army Transport Corps (European Troop Movements Division) was a wee bit rusty after such a long break. But we applied a bit of oil, turned the ignition switch and quickly went up through the gears and pretty soon we were back in business, purring along happily in the fast lane.

I for my part managed to take a couple of days off that four-letter word, work, and get a reasonably-priced flight from Frankfurt to Athens and back (via Thessaloniki on the return journey) and reasonably-priced hotel accommodation as well (or at least that was what I told Wor Lass – mum's the word). Actually, it cost an arm and a leg, but hey, as I always say, the salient design features of shrouds do not, as a rule include pockets. And hey, who knows how many more chances we will get to watch the Toon in Athens?

***

Did I mention that it was a very hot August? What I should have said was that it was a super-megablastically hot August. So hot, in fact, that even Chris, who on a three-hundred and fifty kilometre Cuths Old Boys cycle tour needs exactly one thimbleful of water a day, had broken out in a sweat watching the women's Olympic beach volleyball at Horseguards' Parade (which people assure me is near Saint James's Park, but I have never seen it on any map of Newcastle). Trier and Brussels had been sweltering on the previous Saturday, and temperatures across Germany had been reaching new record levels (it was 38 degrees centigrade in our back garden). And from what Barry was saying just now, Athens clearly had something special up its meteorological sleeve.

My colleague Yorgos had advised, in a somewhat cryptic e-mail to 'wear hats and drink plenty of water or beer (also locally available)'. He also said that if we ended up in an Athenian jail we should ring him on his mobile and he would talk to the prison guards – they were probably cousins of his anyway. Well, that was reassuring.

So anyway, there were just the three of us from the usual gang for the time being, but we reckoned we were sure to bump into some familiar faces once there. Maybe Alan from Gateshead. Or the Other Clive? Or maybe a couple of Aussies on their honeymoon looking for something exciting to do (remember Bruce and Sheila in Toon Tales?). Who knows? That's the great thing about Toon European trips – just when you're least expecting it, the unexpected happens.

It was all Greek to me.

I don't have a word of Greek. Not one *iota*. The first time in Athens, for the Panionios match, that didn't bother me at all. The second time, Olympiakos, I felt it was a great shame not even being able to order a beer and suchlike in the local lingo. Ahead of this trip, I felt it was bloody awful. Of course, communicating would be no problem. Everyone has English up to some level. And loads of Greeks have absolutely fabulous English. But it is always nice to soak up some of the local colour – including the linguistic variety – on these trips. I think I read somewhere that English words derived from Ancient Greek actually outnumber the stock of Ancient Greek words known to modern scholars. Random examples of such Greek-derived English words are *anarchy*, *apathy*, *chaos* and *lethargy*, and of course a *plethora* of medical, scientific and technical terms. Somebody said that the word *corruption* also had Greek roots, but apparently it's from the Latin word *corruptio*. And Yorgos reckoned that if we tried to learn modern Greek we would quickly recognise loads of words. Well, I said, recognise them perhaps, but understand them ...

But hey, in for a drachma, in for a eurocent. Barry and I got into the pan-Hellenic spirit of things and before long we were wondering whether the Toon were now at the perihelion or the aphelion of our orbit around Europe, and started writing some panegyrics on that very subject. But enough of this meta-nonsense...

The gods were on-side. Our side.

To whet the appetite for our Greek odyssey, Newcastle had got the 2012-13 league campaign off to a brilliant start, winning two-one at home to Spurs. I enjoyed MOTD's coverage so much that I watched it all over again on the Sunday morning repeat in order to enjoy the full benefit of a sober perspective. What a cracker Demba Ba's goal was, hooked in first time like that into the Gallowgate net. The victory cheered Alan Pardew up no end after he'd been sent up to the stands for a playful prod at the linesman and it also gained me one point in the Saint Cuthberts Old Boys' prediction league – which in turn earned me fourth place in the current ranking. Mind, it was early days I suppose, what with just one league game having been played and all. And truth to tell, I usually end up bottom or thereabouts by the end of the season. I suspect that could have something to do with my cunning prediction system. We only predict the results of the Toon and the mackems, and I always predict victory for the former and defeat for the latter. However, I am convinced that in the very long term I will one day end up top of the league, when Newcastle eventually win all of their games and sunderland lose all of theirs throughout an entire season.

Let's just fast-forward here please. Someone get that steam-driven time machine cranked up. At the turn of 2013-14 I was in second place thanks to the strategy just described. Newcastle were on an absolute roll, beating Spurs away, chelski at home, and man u away. That win against Newton Heath at old crapford near manchester means I can no longer say that I was present when we last beat man u away. That was the week after we went out to Hereford in the Cup, in the days of the three-day week and under-age drinking by candlelight. And didn't they show that Ronnie Radford goal on every FA Cup weekend Football Focus for the next quarter of a century or so, the bar stewards? It was over the Christmas period that things started turning a wee bit sour when we lost at home to Arsey Whinger's arsenal and again at home to Cardiff City in the Cup.

Atromitos, meanwhile, remained pretty much a mystery. All our Greek friends could tell us was that they were a small club in Athens (well, almost in Athens). So we were playing Greece's equivalent of West Ham. I loved the way we sang 'You're just a small club in London' at Upton Park after the Alf Garnetts had been singing 'You're just a small club in Scotland'. Hmm, I briefly wondered whether Trevos Brookingos was still playing for Atromitos or whether he now referred to it as 'my old clubos'. And was Alfredos Garnettos their most (in fact only) famous supporter? Such are the mysteries of life as pondered over a pint or two of German beer.

Time for beddie-byes, but difficult to get to sleep when considering the prospect of NUFC back in Europe. zzzzz

**

There we were, stood on the slopes of Mount Parnassos at the site of the great Oracle of Delphi, coughing up reeking, oleaginous, hallucinatory fumes, or at least the Oracle was, not us – the Toon Army resplendent in our black and white togas. Don't quibble, this is a dream, for goodness' sake. The lasses looking like Greek goddesses, the laurel leaves setting off their golden curls. The opposition were lined up on the opposite mountain, Mount Hades I believe – the one-eyed giant Jason and his argonautic hordes had challenged the Toon to a game of Herculean football, but no sooner had battle commenced than two Minotaurs locked horns and bustled onto the touchline where Alan Pardew promptly pushed them over and shooed them back into the fray, illuminated by a swirling, stifling Athenian sun. The air was thick with arrows and slingshot as Poseidon reared up out of the Leazes deep end and said that if they did another re-make he would get really angry. In his excitement he broke out in a bubbly tidal wave. Dionysus skimmed his javelin off the water and into the throng of Numidian archers who refused to pay the ferryman that was taking them across the waters of Tyne, all befogged and underpaid. The Gallowgate crowd roared its funereal approval and the harpies – half man, half harp – had a pint of lager and played a game of Elgin marbles. (That reminds me, won't Rangers be playing Elgin City instead of Celtic this season? My heart bleeds.) The Cyclopean referee blew up a hurricane-force forest fire and the Aegean waters were well roiled by a Blyth Spartan effort to understand this mythical Toon pandemonium. This surely was the Oracle speaking – the Toon for the Europa Cup!

Mark Knopfler began playing 'Why aye Man', louder and louder, straight into my ear, sounding a mobile alarm, which meant it was time to get up. There was a Lufthansa flight to Athens to catch. Just as well it wasn't a week later when Lufthansa flight attendants were threatening to go on strike. Well fair play to them, they've taken a lot of flak in their time.

***

Frankfurt airport on the morning of the match in Athens. Got there far too early as always, but hey. Once through security and all that carry-on, I thought I would text Barry. Inspired by having watched Apollo 13 for the, well 13th, time, I wrote: 'All Systems Go Flight. Am airside in Frankfurt'. From the chit-chat in the waiting area at gate 32C (subsequently switched Luftwaffe-, sorry, Lufthansa-style to gate 25A at very short notice; incidentally, did you know that 'Bomber' Harris was buried at a place called Goring? Kind of ironic, that), it was clear that there would be a good few Greek-Americans on board. Some of them looked as though they had just stepped out of My Big Fat Greek Wedding – and that's exactly how they were on board too: loud, Greek-American loud. Who knows, maybe some were on their way to a relative's real big fat Greek wedding. Let's hope the crockery was not a mockery.

Leaving the air-conditioned, cheap-paperback-thriller world of Frankfurt airport's No 1 terminal cum shopping mall to walk a few steps to the bus and then a few more on the tarmac to board the plane was a very hot shock to the system. I was true to my temporary German beer boycott, however, and during the two and a half hour flight drank only red wine to treat that shock. The sight of the islands and turquoise Aegean waters during the descent was stunning and a reminder of how good it is to be back in the Europa League with Newcastle United.

The forty-degree heat that kicked in as I stepped onto the tarmac at Athens airport, however, was in a different league again. This surely is how a pizza feels when being slid into the oven. A propos, our local pizza delivery service – *La Dolce Vita*, Trier – does a brilliant Diabolo for just six and a half euros, by the way. And a nice bottle of Chianti for another nine euros goes down nicely with that, though against the flow of wino etiquette I prefer my red at fridge temperature. Athens was no fridge.

Coming through the arrivals section where people hold up bits of cardboard with other people's names on, I was approached by someone official-looking holding a clipboard. Had I come from Germany, he asked. Why? Is-a for-a statistic-a purposes, do you-a live in-a Germany? Yes, but you're not getting any more of my money.

Text message from Barry: 'It's like an oven, far too hot for sight-seeing, so we're in the new Acropolis museum. Great air-conditioning. Oh yeah, exhibits good too. Change at Syntagma and make your way to Syngrou Fix.'

A meaningless aside – let's put it down to the heat:

On the subject of interesting graves, did you also know that William Joyce, aka Lord Haw Haw, was buried in Galway's Bothar Mor cemetery? If you want to locate him, all you have to do is approach one of the gardeners and say 'We're looking for yer man'. And he will say 'Sure he's right over there, going nowhere'. That's how me and my cousin Steve found him when looking for long-dead distant relatives.

**

Keeping a sharp eye on my belongings and with one hand on my wallet the whole time (paranoid that I am, but hey – only the paranoid survive!), I mastered the journey in the very hot Metro. It raced past biblical-looking bare hills then some olive groves and one or two factories including one of Boehringer of Ingelheim (not far from Mainz) before plunging into the equally oven-hot and very extensive underground section. Out I got at Syntagma to change trains as instructed. At that station I couldn't help but notice how the Greek police (at first I thought they must be boy scouts and girl guides, they looked so young) were checking the IDs of a number of people who looked as though they might well be immigrants from Africa.

Once at Syngrou Fix station I emerged into the baking, greenish-white shimmering heat at street level and promptly followed my instinctive sense of direction – I have one too – which was instinctively wrong. Trams were running down the central reservation of this busy tree-lined Athenian boulevard, and getting across to the pavement on the far side was no mean feat. Once there, I asked Nick the white van driver where the Callirhoe Hotel was and he very kindly offered to drive me there (to the hopefully cool waters of the beautiful stream). An offer gratefully accepted.

Lathered in sweat, I checked in and gave Barry a ring. He and Brian were still enjoying refuge and solace from the midday sun in the museum, so we agreed to meet in an hour or so in the hotel lobby. Plenty of time for an hour-long shower.

***

We met up and hopped in a taxi with a view to a couple of cool drinks and Greek salads down by the ancient Agora (market place). There we found a nice tavern which we thought was a bit on the pricey side but in return offered not only an interesting sideways-upwards view of the Acropolis but also – and more importantly in the heat of the day that was in it – electric fans into whose system icy water was somehow injected so as to give off a nice cooling mini-spray. What a great idea! Time passed despite the heat and before long it was definitely high time to head off for the match. And we were soon being driven by yet another Nick the taxi driver into the maze that is the Athenian network of streets. Once you are away from the out-and-out touristy area, those very streets are all pretty much of a muchness, but nice with it. Three or four storey blocks for the most part, nothing very high-rise as far as we could see. There were lots of roof-top terraces to be seen up a height, and plenty of vibrant retail activity and cosy corner cafés at street level. At one point during the ride we tried to strike up a conversation with Nick, whose English it has to be said was less than fluent. We mentioned that a few years ago we had been here to see Newcastle play Panionios. 'Oohhhh, Panionios,' Nick said. He must have thought that was where we really wanted to go because he started frantically looking for an opportunity to do a U-turn. We managed to restrain him however, and did eventually get to the Atromitos ground. Mind you, the area did look very like the surroundings of the Panionios ground, if my memory serves me well, which it probably doesn't.

***

This was definitely the right place, however, as we had just spotted the first couple of Toon shirts. Then we saw the club coach and a smaller black equipment van threading their way carefully through the pre-match crowd thronging the narrow street. The coach pulled up to allow staff and players out. We thought that this might be the best time to phone Steve Storey, but it obviously wasn't because there was no answer. We asked one of the staff if they could point Steve out to us. And there he was standing right beside the colleague we'd asked.

'Steve Storey? Great to meet you.'

'Was that you who rang just now?' Steve asked, 'I had my hands full and couldn't get to my phone.'

'Yes it was us. Sorry to bother you because you're obviously really busy.'

'Ah, no bother, lads. I've got your tickets here. I just need to see your passports please ... that's perfect. And here you are.'

'That's very kind of you. Thanks so much for taking the trouble.'

'It's a pleasure. Enjoy the game. And see you another time?'

'You bet!'

So at last we were in possession of those ever-elusive tickets. Steve told us that altogether there would be only forty-eight Newcastle supporters, nearly all of our allocation of tickets provided by Atromitos for their 10,200-seater ground having been returned. Well, we had proven our credentials and were hopeful that these exact same arrangements could be made at later stages in the competition. Though on second thoughts we reckoned it would be a better idea to collect the tickets at the actual venues of future matches and not have to come back to Athens every time, as that could conceivably complicate matters.

Soon the happy Toon Army family had gathered inside the ground, and – almost surreally – everyone shook hands with everyone else. They did, honestly! We were even located in the same end of the ground as we had been in the Panionios stadium. And there were some familiar faces about. The ubiquitous Michael Bolam, aka Biffa was there, and a fair few who had been at the pre-season matches in the Algarve.

Vilamoura – what an ideal place for a pre-season tournament, by the way. And another trophy to put alongside the countless Northumberland Senior Cups, Texaco, Anglo-Italian, Japan and Intertoto Cups, and who can forget the Dublin Challenge Trophy in our bulging post-1969 trophy cabinet. We sat beside Paul English, Stu Preacher and Alan Gibson and family – fellow fans whom I know through one of the many NUFC fans forums on the Internet and witnessed the lads coming out victorious with a possibly unique penalty shoot-out draw (yes, draw) against Olympiakos and win over Braga, featuring dubiously-chosen man-of-the-tournament Hugo Viana. The tournament was a bit disorganised with no announcements, so most people left at the end of the ninety minutes of the Olympiakos match, and it was only the faint cheers that we heard as we walked around the stadium that prompted us to run back and stick our noses up against a perimeter fence to get a partial view of the last few penalties.

Our numbers were swollen to around about eighty by a contingent of the Greek branch of the Toon Army and assorted tourists on holiday in Athens who all got their tickets locally. Just before going (well, squeezing) through the turnstile, I had asked a steward if we could get a pint inside the ground. Oh yes, of course you can, came the reply. No such thing! What you got was over-priced and tepid coke or just water, likewise over-priced and tepid. Talk about a captive market! We got talking to a couple of lads who lived locally, doing a bit of selling 'this and that' for a living and another lad who taught English at a Greek school. All three said that learning Greek wasn't too bad when you lived in the country and seriously applied yourself to the task. Sounded like a good plan, but our two and a half days in Greece probably wouldn't be enough for total-immersion learning. Some other time maybe.

The team came out into the forty degree heat and humidity and lined up in an all-maroon strip with Steve Harper in goal, Tavernier, Perch, Williamson, and Ryan Taylor, not Steven, in defence, Gosling, Marveaux and new signings Anita and young Bigirimana in midfield and Obertan and Cissé in attack. Ben Arfa couldn't be selected in any case as he was still serving a European ban from his time at Lyon and regulars like Coloccini and Tioté were back in the Toon. The bench included first-teamers like Cabaye, Steven Taylor, Gutierrez, Krul and Santon. The match got under way still in extreme heat even though it was turning to evening time, and it couldn't fail to affect the way the game was played – at a holiday pace. We were kicking towards the goal at our end of the pitch. Mid-way through the first half, up at the far end a long ball forward evaded Tavernier and one of the Atromitos players, Epstein, got in a shot which beat the on-rushing Harper and bounced in at the far post. According to the nicely-produced free programmes that Atromitos had handed out, this was only their second ever goal in a

European competition, the first one having come in a two-one loss to Seville in 2006. The programme also told us that, a bit like MK Dons, they'd shifted their ground from the Panathinaikos district of Athens, where they just couldn't build up a fan-base in the face of the competition, to their current location in Peristeri. Until 1977, their pitch didn't have grass. Now that's something to think about.

First blood to Atromitos, against all our expectations. It looked like it was going to stay that way till the break, but on the stroke of half-time Ryan Taylor stepped up to a free kick outside their penalty area and expertly swept the ball to the right and out of the reach of their diving keeper. All square, one-one. And that was the way it stayed to the end. The game slowed down still further and chances were few and far between, perhaps the best one going to Atromitos with about a quarter of an hour to go. All in all, a draw was a fair result.

At the end, we were kept in detention as usual. Though after a while we really did think they were taking the mickey a bit, as there really was absolutely no sign of trouble from either set of fans. And why should there be? The players came back out and threw some sweaty shirts to the grateful sweaty shirt collectors amongst us. We got talking to some members of the Greek Toon Army. We think they were Greeks who were studying in Newcastle. Much was lost in translation, however.

Out of the stadium at last, we hung around on the narrow suburban street of whitewashed two and three-storey flats and houses flanking the similarly white-washed and no higher walls of the stadium. We ended up with a clump of Greek sports journalists. One of them, Kostas Orospos by name (or something like that), was a football website correspondent who told us that he'd be going over to the Toon for the return game. He'd just come out of the post-match press conference and offered to go back inside and try to get Alan Pardew to come out for a photo opportunity. He was true to his word and soon re-appeared out of a side door into the Athenian twilight with the man himself, all smiles and very approachable and affable. Alan recognised Barry from the Algarve tournament, where he'd presented him with complimentary copies of the Toon byeuks and got a very blurry photo. He was happy about our performance in the incredible heat. Chatting with him was quite a highlight in the twilight, much better than roaming in the gloaming, and a very good start to our Europa campaign. Pete couldn't resist giving Alan some advice to the effect that chelski would be no pushovers in the upcoming League match. He said 'I know they won't'. I clarified Pete's statement by adding 'Unless you push them over yourself, of course, just like that linesman last Saturday'. Alan gazed wondrously into the middle distance and seemed to be pondering that tactic as he made his way to rejoin the team coach. We had the presence of mind to stop his tactical reverie and ask him if he would have his photo taken with us, and he kindly obliged. Unfortunately some Demis Roussos lookalike barged in at the last moment and took Pete's place. It's true – honest!

The team filed out of the players' corridor and we managed to shake hands with Cissé who is surprisingly frail-looking close up, and Jonas who is quite the opposite.

'Bonne chance contre Chelsea, Papiss.'

'Merci.'

(Vive L'Europe!)

***

By now it was about a quarter past eleven, and dark. We were hungry and thirsty, so we went in search of another taxi to take us back into town ...

There were a number of yellow cars hanging around the ground. At first sight they looked like taxis, at second sight they didn't. Never mind.

No linguistic worries this time. Our yet-another-Nick-the-taxi-driver was fluent. In fact, he seemed to be suffering from some form of verbal diarrhoea. Could he take us to the restaurant where Barry and Brian had been the previous evening? Of course he could. The description was perfect, he recognised it immediately. Back we plunged into the still teeming maze of streets around the Acropolis. Nick was giving us the benefit of his local knowledge, whether we wanted it or not. Unprompted by anything we said, he told us for example that the Parthenon had been built around 500 BC. As he sped through his third red light of this particular journey, he told us that construction had taken just eight years (until they downed tools and never quite got round to putting the roof on). The Ancient Greeks were a clever lot, as we all know. So they clearly designed and supervised everything, but who did the actual hard graft? But the slaves, of course, Nick told us. Prisoners of war. Those people did all the work.

'If you were a Greek citizen, you did not do any work yourself.'

Taking the next red light at about eighty km in this fifty km zone, he added:

'You must remember, we Greeks have a long and proud tradition.' (What, did he mean of not doing any work? Surely not.)

'The Germans,' Nick ranted, a propos of nothing we could think of. 'They are the ones to blame. They have only given us two hundred billion euros. They must give us another hundred billion. That is only fair. It is a good investment. And they are so wrong if they think the problem is that Greeks don't pay their taxes and fiddled the books so they could be admitted to the euro club. They are completely wrong, I tell you. Believe me, that is only half of the problem!'

Yes, bloody Teutonic pedants, we agreed. Absolute rotters. From now on we would not be drinking any more of that horrible Piesporter Michelsberg hock. On the other hand, my temporary boycott of despicable German beer was fast coming to an end, and we hoped this taxi ride would as well. When Nick took another left at speed through a red light, Brian said, er, I think you should have gone straight ahead there, and this is the second time you have brought us along here. Barry recognised the neighbourhood and asked Nick to let us out here, the rest was walkable.

So I asked what the damage was and Nick told me it was twenty euros. Judging by other fares that day, we reckoned that seven euros would have been nearer the mark. Compared with the price of London, Brussels or Luxembourg taxis it was still a bargain, but I thought I might haggle so I said, 'No way, bonny lad. You haven't even got a meter.'

'Well how much do you want to give me?'

'Fifteen.'

'Okay.'

Let's just put it down to experience. And he was very entertaining, after all. Plus, he had taught us so much we otherwise would never have known about Germans and Greeks.

At any rate, Barry and Brian were well pleased to be back on what was virtually their home turf. Isn't that right, Barry?

'You bet ...'

27

For the second night in a row, we were headed to what is now established as our favourite Athens restaurant, and the only one whose name I know, the Philistron, on the walkway around the Acropolis. The best plan is to sit up on the roof terrace where you have an unbeatable view of the Parthenon in the foreground and Mount Lycabettus in the background. At night, it's floodlit and just magnificent. You choose a selection of dishes to share, add a couple more if you're still hungry, and wash all the meats, peppers, vine leaves and calamari (if you like faintly fish-flavoured bubble-gum) down with some cold retsina. Then float back round the rest of the Acropolis, down past the new museum and back to the city and your hotel. What could be better? It must be one of the nicest circular walks in the world. Hop on and hop off and take in all the sights of two and a half thousand years of high civilisation. From the drama of a still-in-use open-air ancient Greek theatre (called the Odeon, by the way, and which has now out-lasted its Pilgrim Street namesake) carved out of the Acropolis hillside to a twenty-first century open-air cinema, a very popular pastime for the Athenians of today, or rather tonight, or rather this morning. For we have already reached the early hours ...

So the 'evening' ended on a culinary high, and with a fantastic floodlit view of Athens. And the walk back to the hotel – during which we stopped off for a final pint of (German) beer – was mercifully downhill.

***

After breakfast the next morning, we still had time for a leisurely stroll around the government quarter, where we half expected to see some demonstrations and rioting (but thankfully didn't). We picked up a couple of the plethora of sports newspapers published every day in Athens and settled down in a cosy tavern just off Syntagma Square. How on earth do they support so many papers? Funnily enough, their titles were in English and in the Latin, not Greek, alphabet: 'Sport Day' and 'Goal News'. Goal News devoted three pages to our game and Sport Day had four pages of match details, despite competition from bigger Greek teams like the black and whites of PAOK Salonika who'd been playing Rapid Vienna and winning two-one, AEK, Panathinaikos and Olympiakos who all got four pages each too. Okay, we have to admit we couldn't really make out too much from the Greek text but we could understand all the numbers and the pictures, which told us that with seven out of ten, Perch, Taylor and Anita were our top performers with Perch chosen as our man of the match, while Epstein, their goal scorer, pipped them with seven and a half. They even gave scores for the two managers who both got six and a half!

That passed the hour or so until it was time for Barry and Brian to head off to the airport and their flight to Spain for a family holiday. After saying our farewells, I did a bit more strolling and shopping for some presents, but after another hour or so, the heat once again became unbearable and so I took refuge in the Acropolis museum as recommended! Then it was a siesta at the hotel and a light evening meal in the hotel's rooftop restaurant, also with great views, followed by another walkabout.

Got back to the hotel about midnight, but it was still so hot that I had to sit out on the balcony and get some notes written. That's what I was still doing at two in the morning, and it was still warm, but bearable. Looking back over the previous twenty-four hours, I noted that the highest temperature had been forty-three degrees Centigrade at two o'clock in the afternoon. Thank goodness for air-conditioning. I had at least managed to learn the Greek for 'it is very hot': *zesti*. It was *zesti* all right, bloody *zesti*.

All in all, then, it had been another great trip to Athens, by now one of our favourite European haunts.

Atromitos at home – 30th August 2012 and the draw for the Group Stage

As far away from Rumania as the Europa League can take you!

The week after, back in the Toon, Haris Vučkić got the only goal of the game after twenty-one minutes. He'd only just come on as a substitute for the unfortunate Ryan Taylor, who sadly was going to be out for a long time with a cruciate ligament injury to his right knee. It was Vučkić's first goal for the club, and what a good one – he got away from his defender to collect the ball from a throw-in on the East Stand side, set himself up for a powerful left-foot shot from outside the right corner of the penalty area, and via a deflection off a defender's back, it went in off the inside of the foot of the far post. That put us through two-one on aggregate into the draw for the next round. Before we go on, let's not forget to take our hats off to a proud Atromitos who could hold their heads up high for their performances in both legs.

And who could say where the next round, or more accurately the league stage, would now take us? I was hoping our next opponent would be a Rumanian club – by the way, when did people start calling it Romania instead of Rumania? I always remember it as Rumania when they were in the World Cup or Olympic gymnastics, so what's changed? – because at the time of the next home and away games, well, I would be in Rumania.

There were forty-eight teams left in the competition and the UEFA big-wigs down in their overground bunker in Nyon on the shores of Lake Geneva had arranged them into four pots of twelve in descending order of their ranking. This is done according to a complicated formula combining each club's recent European competition form with the collective ranking of their domestic league. Seeing we have had an enforced break from Europe, our ranking relied solely on the European performance of Premiership teams, and thanks to mancityutd, cheatski and arsenal, we were upped into Pot Three along with some famous European names such as Lazio, Sparta Prague, Borussia Mönchengladbach and Partizan Belgrade and lesser lights including Steaua Bucharest, Genk of Ford test track renown, the stutteringly repetitive Dnipro Dnipropetrovsk and the, in some way, creepily named Young Boys. I asked a German colleague who used to live in Bern, Switzerland and it turns out they chose that name to distinguish themselves from the Old Boys of Basel, which sounds much more wholesome.

Spoiling this, however, and knowing that *dorf* is German for 'village', is the revelation that their home ground is the *Stade de Suisse Wankdorf*.

Being down in Pot Three meant we were going to be up against one of the top teams from Pot One, which included previous opponents Inter Milan (Inter two – Shearer two at the San Siro), Marseille (Drogba shot us down two-nil in the UEFA Cup Semi-Final), Sporting Lisbon (beat us in the following year's Quarter Final, but we beat them on the way to winning the Fairs Cup), PSV (we sat among the Dutch fans behind Kenny Dalglish in the Toon dug-out) and Bayer Leverkusen (Shola beat them to celebrate Sir Bobby's seventieth birthday) as well as Atletico Madrid, Lyon, Bordeaux, Stuttgart, Enschede and a couple of English teams we were not allowed to play at this stage of the proceedings. Any of those would be great – good teams, interesting places.

In Pot Two we would have been happy for a reunion with our other old adversaries Basel (Sir Bobby got back off the team coach to talk to us as they were leaving their plush Basel hotel) or Athletic Bilbao (they beat us even though Kevin Keegan's team had been three-nil up at one point in the first leg). We also had high hopes for Panathinaikos (another trip to Athens), FC København (wonderful, wonderful Copenhagen), Napoli, Udinese, Club Brugge, or Hannover 96, followed by erstwhile opponents Fenerbahçe. The jury was out on Metalist Kharkiv, Rubin Kazan (where are they?) and Hapoel Tel-Aviv (as long as they play in Cyprus).

In Pot Four, some good trips were on offer to the Nordic clubs of Helsingborg, Molde FK and AIK Stockholm, and the warm climes of the Portuguese Maritimo Funchal and Académica Coimbra and AEL Limassol in Cyprus while Rapid Wien would also be very welcoming as we had found when we passed through on the way to Dubnica for an Intertoto Cup game long ago. NK Maribor of Slovenia and FC Fehérvár of Hungary could be nice discoveries on the lines of Dubnica. After those prime choices lurked the unknown pleasures of Anzhi Makhachkala, Hapoel Kiryat Shmona and Neftchi Baku. We looked high and low on the map of Europe and couldn't find them anywhere. They could be an experience but maybe one we could do without, in direct proportion to how often they feature as a backdrop to reports by John Simpson and Kate Adie.

Day trips to Leverkusen, Eindhoven or Enschede from Pot One and Brugge from Pot Two would make life a bit easier. It was a long trip to anywhere in Pot Four, but Vienna would be really tasty! Anyone from Pot One would be fine really, but if we were not favoured by the gods of the balls in a bag, Pots Two and Four held some nightmare visions.

Lunchtime on 31st August 2012 with a sandwich in front of the UEFA website brought us the news: Belgium (!), France and Portugal here we come! Hope the very first match is at home, but we will know soon enough!

The 20th of September in Madeira! Not even Portugal, but the Portuguese holiday island equivalent to Spain's Majorca! Excellent! Then the 8th of November in Bruges and the 6th of December in Bordeaux. We could not really have asked for better – all beatable teams playing in really nice places, and it should be feasible to go to all of them. I hope our track record at attending European matches will give us a better chance of tickets …

Must check flights from Bucharest to Madeira! Let us hope that some Rumanian-based multi-national has a major customer or manufacturing subsidiary on the remote mid-Atlantic volcanic rocks of Madeira. Or that Madeira is the favourite winter-break holiday destination of all Rumanians. Or maybe they are twinned towns – they have so much in common, I hope. Clutching at straws, but there needs to be a reason for daily cheap flights, or else … Time to get onto Skyscanner or Trip Advisor, or my trusty travel agent.

Maritimo away – 20th September 2012

A long way away

Another day, another dollar on Newcastle to win two-nil away at Maritimo. Money well spent. A beautiful blue-sky day in Brussels as I take the three trains to the airport for the 11.40 TAP Airlines flight to Lisbon and then a couple of hours' wait before the onward flight to Funchal, capital of Madeira and home to Maritimo, our first opponents in the Group Stage. I'm assuming the weather is going to be even better in Madeira because it's further south even than parts of Africa, on a level with Marrakech but out by itself, a black volcanic rock in the Atlantic Ocean. I bet it was used for some nefarious purpose in the First or Second World War as an airbase or submarine hitching-point or spy enclave. I must look it up and let you know. The Portuguese are in a number of strategic spots – their Azores islands are still a vital hopping-off point for American warplanes. I happened to be there a few years back when they were making daily heavily-laden flights out to Iraq and coming back a lot lighter. I've even got a few photos of them, but I don't want to end up hiding in the Ecuadorian Embassy with that Swedish gadgy, so I can't show you. I wonder if the Azores play in the Portuguese league? Now that would make a great trip for a European match – about half-way from Newcastle to America.

I wonder how Madeira ended up being Portuguese. A couple to three hundred years ago we were pretty adept at taking over far-flung islands either by force or by treaty. We couldn't have just sailed in and taken over because, after all, they are our oldest allies, the Portuguese, aren't they? That simply would not have been cricket, old chap. But surely we could have swapped them the Falklands for Madeira and avoided a lot of toil and trouble and ended up with a decent sunny holiday island an easy flight away. It does lack a sandy beach or two, though maybe even that could have been arranged with just a word in Mr Churchill's ear.

I was in the Toon just a couple of days ago to do my twelfth Great North Run, this time accompanied for their first run by daughters Sarah and Emilie, whose sixteenth birthday was this very month, so they scraped in as possibly this year's youngest entrants. I wouldn't go so far as to call ourselves competitors, as it was more a combination of a brisk walk and a relaxed jog that we managed this year, which is all that could be expected considering we'd done practically no training. Next year, we must do better.

We popped into the Box Office to see if we could find the ultra-helpful Chris who arranged for our Atromitos tickets to be brought over for us by head of security, Steve Storey for collection in Athens. On the application form for Maritimo, I'd asked if we could do the same this time, because I had not been sure I'd be able to go into the Box Office to collect the tickets, even though the forms had only been put on the internet on the Wednesday. It must be a nightmare of logistics for the two teams to coordinate ordering the right allocation of tickets and deciding how to distribute them when UEFA often only gives a matter of days between finding out who is playing each other and the match actually taking place. The travelling fans have the even bigger challenge not only to get tickets for the match but also for a plane to some out-of-the-way place where they sometimes don't even have flights every day, and where the tickets suddenly shoot up in price when their too-clever computerised price-setting system detects a burst of reservations a few minutes after the draw is announced. The things we have to contend with.

The again very helpful lady on the desk looked through the small pile of applications for us – only about a hundred fans were going, she said, and she found a message saying that our tickets were already earmarked for Steve Storey to take out to Madeira with him. So it was going to be the same procedure as last time. Except there was a new twist: in fact it was a voucher that Newcastle was giving out and we had to exchange that for a real ticket at the Maritimo ground. So I'd be making a double exchange. These days, the Box Office really is a smooth operation and the staff do a great job. I can't imagine that you'd get someone at any of the other big clubs going through all the applications for you to make sure your ticket was there.

The relatively low take-up of tickets is easy to explain. Maritimo might be in a very nice location but it's a divvil of a place to get to outside the peak tourist season. There are charter flights but often they are only weekly and no one can take that much time off from work or home, and then there are scheduled flights over which TAP has a near monopoly, and the prices are correspondingly Monopoly-money 'sky'-high. My ticket, which was for going on Wednesday and returning on Friday to get the best deal was already 460 euros (about £370) and it was easy to pay £500 or more if you were restricted on your times and days of travel. A lot of people just cannot justify paying that sort of money. But we're on a quest for silver, and we're writing a diary, and we love doing this, so for us there's no choice and we're glad of it.

They just showed the sightseeing highlights of Madeira on the droppy-down screens on the flight out of Lisbon and, like many islands around the world that I've been lucky enough to visit – Holy Island, St. Mary's and the Farnes to name but a few – it has an inhabited side and a wild side. You know what's coming next, don't you? But I'll say it anyway: I don't know if I'll have time to take a walk on the wild side, but it looks pretty wild with steep forested cliffs and ravines, waterfalls, high peaks, hiking routes and plenty of places to fall off and get lost. It reminds me a bit of the north side of Majorca, where the UEFA Cup took us nearly ten years ago to follow Sir Bobby and his team. Those were the days, eh? If I get some time and the inclination (it's pretty steep), I might try to get up to that part of the island. I hadn't been thinking about it, but when I looked out of the window and saw we were over the deep blue sea, having just left the coast of France at some point where there is a fairly large inhabited island just offshore (the French Lindisfarne), I realised that a fair bit of the first leg of the trip to Lisbon and just about all of the second leg out to Madeira is spent overseas. This is certainly the Atlantic, and possibly this particular bit might also be called the Bay of Biscay, or even better, the Bay of Gasco(i)gne. That's nice of them, they have just switched the flight map on and I can see that we crossed the coast somewhere south of Nantes and north of La Rochelle. It looks like a good place for a holiday. What do you reckon, Pete?

***

It all sounds great so far, Barry. And I am really gutted I can't be on this trip. But here I am working like a dog on this Rumanian course in Bucharest. They haven't taught us whether we can spell it with an 'o' or a 'u' yet. I looked into the possibility of getting to Maritimo from here, but the connections weren't good (one variant via Madrid, another via Zurich, yet another via Blauwewildebeestfontein as the first leg and then Lüderitz as the second), and the whole thing was going to be horribly expensive. And the time away would have been about a quarter of the ten-day course, so it would hardly have been worthwhile coming here in the first place. So given that I had arranged to book a rest in Bucharest I decided to remain here, in Rumania. Of course I could equally have gone to see houses in Seahouses.

***

Never mind, Pete, there'll be other trips, and you never know we might play Steaua Bucharest at some stage, and you'll have got the lay of the land for us, as it were. Mind, all this talk of first and second legs makes me think of this first match of the six we are going to play in the Group Stage. I am guessing a little, but I suspect that Maritimo may not be the hardest of the three away games we will play. Bordeaux and Bruges are going to be slugging it out in Bordeaux, not too far away to the south and thirty thousand feet downwards from where I am right now in this TAP plane, while we are at Maritimo. I have a feeling that the hardest game is going to be Bruges away. They're a decent football team, and we know that after twenty-five years in the doldrums, Belgian football is on the up and up, regaining some of its former vigour with some excellent players such as Kompany, Vertonghen, Lukaku and Hazard. Luckily, none of the really good Belgians plays for Bruges. They'll be hard to beat but we've heard that they'll also be hard to see as tickets will be in very short supply. The reason is that NUFC are organising an official club-approved travel-and-guaranteed-tickets deal through Thomas Cook, which means that the likes of us who do not need to travel from the Toon will be well down the pecking order. But do not fear – we have a cunning plan, details of which to be revealed later.

What? You can't wait? You want to know now? Oh well, if you insist:

Cunning plan: buy a couple of Bruges Europa League three-home-match mini-season tickets which are going on sale to non-season ticket holders on the day of the Maritimo match, so some transatlantic internet wizardry will be required while on the island of Madeira.

As for Maritimo, I am going to do some first-hand investigating when I arrive in Funchal, starting by buying the local papers for match previews. A little bit of Spanish, a little bit of Latin, and a little bit of French and you can get the gist of a Portuguese paper if you stick to known ground such as football rather than local Madeiran farming news.

Well, Barry, you and everyone else will be pleased to know that virtually the same goes for the Romanian language.

***

'What is this? Our cunning linguist in Bucharest wants to get us to learn Romanian or even Rumanian?'

***

'Definitely. Like Portuguese, it is a Latin-based language, and if you can draw on some Spanish, Italian, French and Latin, or Portuguese as well, you can very quickly get to understand a lot of Romanian, at least as far as the written word is concerned. It is totally fascinating that here in South-Eastern Europe, the Balkans, a region dominated by Slav languages such as Bulgarian, Serbian or Croat, and of course with Ukrainian and Russian to the east, but also with Greek and Turkish not that far away, you have this island of Latin-based culture and language. I was sceptical at first as to just how Latin-based the language was – after all the Romans weren't here all that long compared with other places. Dacia was a Roman province only from 106 to 274 AD. That is not a vast period of time – the Romans were in Britain a lot longer and did not leave anything like the same sort of lasting linguistic footprint. The Emperor Trajan conquered the Dacian tribes because they had been giving Rome a lot of grief. After teaching them a few lessons and leaving them alone again a few times only for them to get uppity again, he finally lost his temper and built a bridge across the Danube so that the legions could pour in and sort the Dacians out once and for all. You can see the whole story depicted on Trajan's column in Rome. He did a lot of empire expanding, did Trajan. And it was his successor Hadrian who decided there had been enough expansion and that it was time to consolidate and have secure borders – hence Hadrian's Wall.

So anyway we have modern <u>Rom</u>anian, which is very much a <u>Rom</u>ance language but with lots of Slav words, and also with Greek and Turkish and even German influences. And of course we have the modern Dacians, or at least Dacia cars, which are essentially last year's Renault cars with a Latin twist. One of the Dacia models, a smart, SUV-looking and very affordable and reliable vehicle, possibly has one of the silliest names for a car ever – the Duster. You could have knocked them down with a feather.

Bucharest is modelled on Paris, and in some of the nicest quarters you could be forgiven for momentarily thinking you were in the French capital. Indeed, many of the landmark buildings were designed by Parisian architects of the Haussmann era. It even has an *Arc de Triomphe* (*Arcul de Triumf*) and the main station is the *Gara de Nord*. The Metro system is maybe not as pretty as its Parisian cousin, but it is ultra-efficient and cheap, and the wine and beer are pretty good too.

I also had a trip by train to a place called Brașov, which was founded by Germans, and its German name is Kronstadt. The city centre there is completely different from Bucharest, only a hundred miles away, and makes you feel you were back in the Austro-Hungarian Empire. Brașov is a ski resort in Transylvania, in the Carpathian mountains, and so is really atmospheric, especially in winter and on any dark night when Count Dracula comes out to play. Yes, Romania has a lot to offer the visitor. But outside the country many people mistakenly think that 'Roma' means the same as 'Romanian'. Not at all! Many Roma have Romanian nationality, it is true, but in fact there are Roma roaming throughout eastern Europe and beyond. And if you meet a Roma in London, say, he or she is just as likely to be a Slovak or Hungarian citizen.

***

Well you seem to have the Romanian angle sorted there, Pete. If we ever play Rapid or Steaua Bucharest, FC Brașov or CFR Cluj we should be fine. Well done, an excellent scouting mission.

I was just thinking there that Maritimo must have something about them if they have managed to get themselves into the Europa League. Hmm, maybe they will be no pushover after all. But surely Alan Pardew will sort that out! By virtue of finishing fifth in the Portuguese league in 2011-12, they got into the third qualifying round of the Europa League where they beat Tripolis Arcadia, which is on the road to Sparta from Athens, on away goals after a one-one away and a nil-nil home draw. They then had the dubious honour of playing FC Dila Gori of Georgia in parallel with us playing Atromitos. I think the fates were kind to us when choosing our respective opponents. Maritimo won the home leg one-nil and they won two-nil in the away leg, which was played in Tbilisi instead of in Gori, so the Maritimo players never got to see Gori, the birthplace of Stalin, and neither did we.

We're now back over dry land somewhere on the Galician coast of northern Spain and heading for Lisbon. In next to no time, we're approaching Lisbon, flying parallel to the long straight Portuguese beach which stretches north-south like a physical line of longitude. Down there, a third of the way from Lisbon to Porto is Nazaré, where some of the mightiest surfing waves in the world come crashing in from the other side of the Atlantic. Whereas a flight into the capital of their peninsula neighbours, Spain, would remind you of a moon landing with the red-orange earth and desert all around, this part of Portugal is a dozen lush shades of verdure, testimony to all the Atlantic wind-borne rain that falls mainly before Spain, on Portugal. Disappointingly for the tree-huggers, there are winding ranks of perhaps a hundred wind turbines all at a dead stop. It's going to be a nice, calm sunny day, twenty-six degrees they say on the Tannoy. Hey! I've spotted a brace of turning windmills – the exceptions that prove the rule. On the approach to the airport I spot a classic example of the dip and slope of an escarpment. Stoker Meaken, our old RGS geography teacher, would have been proud of Portugal. Hang on a second, didn't Pete mention Dracula just there? Dracula? Bram Stoker? Hmm, spooky … (Pete: this is really creepy – one of our geography teachers at Saint Cuths was Mr Spoor – nicknamed Spooky). And we certainly fly straight into the heart of the city, with so many houses so close to our plane's wheels that some of the roofs must have tread marks. I wouldn't like to live on the flight path. It's bad enough flying down the flight path.

***

At boarding gate 15 in Lisbon Airport, a group of seven men all in identical blazers and light blue and black striped ties all appear together as I am waiting for the crowds to clear. These are the UEFA officials heading out to Funchal on the same plane as us. Of course, they all settle into business class. After all, our ticket money has to be spent on something, doesn't it, so why not splurge it on luxury travel for the ref and his pals? Like the old chant goes, most of them need specs to see. And talking of the infirm and impaired, I am surrounded by half a plane-load of tipsy French pensioners, all in nicely high spirits. Who would have thought that *La Toon Armée* would be turning out in such numbers? I checked but none of them had Cabaye or Ben Arfa or Cissé or Ba stitched on the back of their beige leisure jackets or twin-sets.

Typical, isn't it? We take off half an hour late without the slightest whisper of an explanation or apology. TAP stands for Take-off Always Postponed, after all. What a great view of Lisbon you get, though. At the start of the main runway, over to the left you see the long curving ribbon of the Vasco da Gama Bridge with its four yacht sails stretching across the Tejo Estuary, then once you are in the air you again skim over the ridges of the city-centre rooftops, over the wide, tree-lined *avenidas*, the football stadia of Sporting and Benfica (the latter being the original Stadium of Light – the *Estádio da Luz*), the *São Jorge* castle mound, the steep winding alleyways of the old town and the neat orthogonal lines of the post-earthquake new town down by the port, and then finally over the *Ponte de 25 Abril*, Lisbon's version of the San Francisco Golden Gate Bridge, before heading across the long sandy beaches to the open sea. And all in glorious sunshine. Halleluja!

I'm in row five just behind the luxury curtain separating the hoi polloi from the UEFA officials, but it's not soundproofed enough to stop me hearing them clinking their champagne glasses together and chomping on their *bacalhau* and *pasteis de nata*, possibly. The delay means it's going to be a bit of a rush to get to the hotel, drop my haversack off, and head over to the handily-placed Maritimo ground to see if they'll let us in this time for the training session, or will it be behind closed doors again, like it was for Atromitos?

At about our altitude of 37,000 feet, there are clouds, not of water vapour but of dust, dirt and sand. We descend through them and the engines keep going. Good. Far below us there are some traditional white clouds. They are wet I suppose, but somehow aero-engines keep running while they fly through them too. Suddenly Madeira and the small archipelago of islands hove into view, Port Santo first. Ruggedly handsome rocks beset on all sides by foaming white surf. More rocks and steep cliffs and then a clump of little rocky islands, one with an airstrip. Then a gap, then another scattering of steep-cliffed rocky islands, and then Madeira at last, where the sea is calm and deep blue. High overhead, a few wispy clouds and a lower bank of fluffy cumulus, but the rest of the sky is as blue as the ocean. The eastern tip of the island is very bare and brown and dusty and the airport is right on the cliff's edge and it looks as if at least part of the airfield is a concrete, artificial extension of the natural geography. When we get down on the ground, the weather disappointingly turns overcast, but it's still very warm at twenty-eight degrees.

The airport bus timetable and route have clearly been developed by the local taxi drivers' association as the buses run rarely and wind through all the villages in between, and so they take an age to get to the town. Unless you want to leave three hours early for what should be a twenty-minute trip, the only alternative is to take a taxi whose meter whirls around at such a rate that you get a bill for thirty-five euros by the time you arrive. The last Nick in Athens would have approved.

***

The team stayed at Reid's Hotel, one of the most famous hotels in the world. A posh pink Portuguese palace perched perilously precipitously on a promontory and priced to repel the hoi polloi. Which explains why the press and media bus was parked outside my very nice, but nowhere near as pricey Pestana Casino Park Hotel which at this point I must recommend highly. Stylishly designed by Oscar Niermeyer, a celebrated (so they say) Brazilian architect who amongst other buildings also apparently designed the French Communist Party's Paris HQ. But there was nothing communist about his swish Madeiran hotel. They don't go in for beaches on Madeira, because the black rock mostly rises straight and steeply out of the sea, so the hotel was set in tropical gardens on the cliff's edge. Just outside the breakfast area was a good pool which I used a few times, and very nice it was. From your seat at the pool bar as you dry off in the sunshine, you can look down on the port of Funchal where you may well see a cruise liner moored along by the jetty, spending half a day there and then heading back out onto the ocean, only to be replaced by another shortly afterwards. By the time I was installed at the hotel and had had a quick look around it was getting on for six o'clock so I asked directions from the reception and headed out to walk up the volcano to the Maritimo stadium. It was a walk of maybe half an hour all told. The stadium is built into the side of the volcano and the great touch about this design is that there is a parapet way up a height above the stadium from where you can have a perfect view of the whole pitch. It's much better, and closer, than being in Level Seven. By the time I got there, the lads were already out training on the pitch. There was no way they could make this a private training session as the parapet is a public place with cars and pedestrians going by. I could make out Ba, Shola and Sammy, Steven Taylor, Anita, Perch, Santon, Obertan, Harper, Elliott, Adam Campbell, Bigirimana, and Williamson and the others might have included Marveaux, Vučkić, and Tavernier. Alan Pardew was overseeing operations from the side of the pitch while John Carver had the players doing stretching exercises, working in pairs, close control, give and go, and dribbling. Then Alan Pardew led the team in set pieces – taking and defending corners and free kicks, long balls forward – and then they broke up again into pairs to practise long and medium-range passing.

I took the opportunity to phone Steve Storey to ask what was most convenient for him for collecting the voucher and/or ticket. When I told him I was up on the parapet, he looked up and waved, and we arranged that the easiest was if I could turn up at some time between four and six tomorrow at the orange hut on the pavement near to the main stadium entrance.

The stadium has been undergoing refurbishment but is in a state of disarray as it seems that they ran out of money and cannot finish the work off until they gather together the missing moolah. This leaves the two goal ends and the opposite side from the main stand looking like building sites, cordoned off with red-and-white-striped incident tape and boarding.

The team trained for just over an hour, till ten to seven, and then a bunch of people who might have been the UEFA referee and officials came out onto the pitch for a five-minute look around. Their hard work done, they went back to the changing rooms. The coach driver did a very good job to steer the team back up the very narrow alley way which winds down the side of the stadium from the parapet to pitch level. I have no idea how he had managed to reverse his bus down there earlier.

In the evening, I took a walk into the old town of Funchal, which is actually quite a hike from the west end where most of the hotels and the football ground are. I walked on and on without seeing much of interest and was just about to give up on the place when I got to a main street which I imagined to be the boundary of the town centre. But luckily I thought I'd just keep on going for another couple of hundred yards, just in case, and I was rewarded when all of a sudden I found myself in a much more promising narrow street full of restaurants and bars thronged with people, many of senior vintage. This was the original old town. It was a bit touristy, but with a touch of class. At the start of the street, I asked the doorman of one restaurant which had a welcoming tree-shaded garden and he explained to me where the most interesting streets of the old town were, and I assured him that I might well return later. The main alleyway had most of its doors painted like works of art which gave a nice feeling to the place. I looked around the main drag and back along the seafront, where there was a bit of a sandy beach, no doubt artificially constructed. My circling back to the first restaurant, 'Almirante' – the Admiral – was rewarded with a mixed salad for five euros and a sample of five fish of the day, which weighed in at a slightly surprising seventeen and a half euros, though it was very good. The Don's friend Kev, of Kevin Keegan signed his arm fame, turned out to be in the restaurant too. He was highly impressed by Madeira and the good deals at the hotels and he'd managed to find a flight for a bit of a bargain price compared to what some had paid.

After the meal, I wandered back around towards the seafront and was drawn to a packed-out open-air café where a local trio of very good musicians were playing some good music to while away the rest of the evening. So it had turned into a very pleasant tee shirt and shorts warm evening, especially when you think we could just as easily have been in Kazakhstan or some such other 'part' of Europe. Thank you, oh UEFA master of the balls.

Madeira has a similar feeling to other volcanic islands such as Sicily, and not surprisingly the islands of the Azores, which are also under Portuguese protection. All of them impress on you the same sense that you are clinging to the slopes of the volcano, with black lava and pumice stone everywhere you look. The pavements, walls and many of the buildings are solid and heavy, made at least in part of the local black or grey stones. Deep gulches scythe into the sides of the steep hills, and there is no flat land anywhere except where it has been artificially sculpted at the airport and the Maritimo and Nacional football grounds.

***

The day of the match began with a leisurely breakfast and a couple of swims in the hotel pool followed by a wander around the town, during which I also did some remote organisation of buying the vital pair of mini-season tickets for Bruges to be sure that we would have tickets for the NUFC away leg when tickets were going to be as scarce as rare earth metals. In the town there was an electric car show going on, which was a bit of a surprise, so I had a sit in a big Toyota Prius and a little Noddy-car-style Renault. (Didn't see any Dacian Dusters, mind.) I am not so sure anyone will buy many of these, though I hope they do for Nissan's sake, what with their strangely-shaped Leaf, which is a little curly at the edges. The Achilles' heel of all these electric vehicles is of course the battery. If someone could solve the fundamental weight, charging and lifetime problems, they would be on to a winner but it seems to be a question of trying to work against the natural laws of physics and chemistry, and there is little prospect of an acceptable solution until something really new comes along. Unless maybe cars go nuclear! Dragging myself away, the next thing I hit upon was a little barber shop and feeling a bit hot and a bit hairy, I stepped into the cool and re-appeared fifteen minutes later with a weight off my mind. It's interesting to collect haircuts from different parts of the world, just a pity they never last. Though I would think twice before getting a Kazakhstani or Azerbaijani one. Though apparently there are still quite a few ethnic Germans in Kazakhstan, so there is bound to be a teutonically efficient Herr Kutt or two about. And probably also a German rent man called Karl Bach (Karl Bach next week).

After all this and another swim to cool off, it was time to set off for the match. Huffing and puffing and taking a breather on the way up the slope, I caught up with a very nice couple from South Shields who recognised my GNR 2012 tee shirt. They were staying at the Reid's Hotel and had seen the team getting installed the day before. We wended our way steadily up the volcano's steep foothills to the Maritimo ground in the afternoon to sample the pre-match atmosphere and collect our vouchers and tickets. I suggested that they might like to try to swap their neutral-section tickets for Toon tickets and I said I could ask Steve Storey if there were any tickets available, but they preferred to stick to what they had, which were in the more comfy seats in the main stand. I found my way to the little orange hut and there was Steve and colleagues surrounded by Toon fans swapping vouchers for tickets. I've said it before and I'll say it again, what great service Steve and his colleagues give to the travelling fans.

There was a great atmosphere of very friendly locals and Toon fans mixing together in pre-match drinks in the parapeted area above the ground. The one little bar was doing a roaring trade in lager in plastic beakers and cheese and ham buns. Amongst the crowd outside the bar, I bumped into Michael Bolam, the famed

Biffa of nufc.com. It turned out he had also gravitated to the same crowded open-air music café the night before and had been similarly impressed.

It is the 102nd anniversary of Maritimo this year, and high time to replace their sun-disintegrated plastic seats, which leave blue or yellow powder streaks on your clothes if you care to sit down. But why do they have blue and yellow seats when their club colours are Portugal-flag deep red and green? I have a feeling that the two rival clubs on the island are split, or defined, by their loyalty or lack thereof, to the Portuguese mainland, with the other team Nacional being more for a Madeira nation. Or maybe it's just my imagination. In any case, you need to have at least two clubs on such a remote island if you want to have a proper game of football.

The ground is three-quarters a building site, but the Maritimos couldn't even fill the quarter that was open, while the ranks of around eighty-three travelling Toon fans were swollen by some local fans and others who paid on the gate including a fair few UK tourists wearing Derby County and other shirts, and pensioners who happened to be here on autumn breaks.

The late afternoon/early evening match was played in sunlight throughout, which is very unusual for a Europa League game as they are invariably played out under floodlights. However this year, UEFA have introduced six o'clock starts, very much for the benefit of television scheduling, and by thus allowing two matches to be shown each night they have boosted their coffers even further. With Portugal and Madeira being in the same time zone as the UK it was six o'clock here too, whereas at other games dotted around Europe the time would already be seven o'clock. And with being so far west into the Atlantic, the light held out very well throughout the whole game. For some time before the start, there seemed to be a risk that the mist which habitually clings to the rim of the volcano might descend further and envelop the ground and put a dampener on proceedings in more ways than one. Very politely, it decided to limit its descent half-way down and leave us in sunshine.

The team came out into the evening sunshine in the fluorescent yellow tops and black shorts that were to become familiar wear in our European games, even when there was no colour clash at all, such as here where Maritimo played in the maroon and bottle green of the Portuguese flag. The starting eleven had a new and unusual look in midfield and attack, while the defence looked dependable –

Elliot, Santon, Taylor, Williamson, Perch, Gosling, Amalfitano, Bigirimana, Obertan, Vučkić, and Shola – and only Steve Harper and arguably Marveaux of those on the bench could lay claim to any significant first-team experience. This was going to be an adventure on the high seas.

There may not have been any goals, but it wasn't for the want of trying, and it could have been us trailing after an early corner if not for a very good save from Elliot, tipping a powerful shot by their number seventeen, Sami, over the bar. Then after half an hour we piled on the pressure with three corners in a row. Santon nearly scored from the first, then Williamson took a pot shot which deflected off a defender then rebounded off the keeper out to Shola whose header ricocheted from the goalie onto the post and bounced off the goalie again and somehow didn't go in. Then from the third corner the ball came out to Gosling outside the D, who slammed a low shot against the foot of the post and away. It was like pinball.

In the second half, Shola broke away, bamboozled the defender with a Shola step-over and fired away a rising shot which had the goalie beaten to his left, but it went and crashed against the bar and bounced back into play straight to Obertan but he couldn't get a shot in. The Toon Army down in our little section at the end of the main stand wanted to see a real goal, not just multiple near-misses, and started up an 'Attack Attack Attack' chant like in the Dalglish Cup Final. The warmth and humidity of the evening may have affected our players and slowed their pace in the final quarter of the game, with mis-directed final balls from Obertan, Amalfitano, and Santon. But then an attack and a goal nearly came at the wrong end. Maritimo almost got a winner from a late corner which was helped on in the air by two of their players and would have gone in if Santon guarding Elliot's left post hadn't managed to head it upwards onto the underside of the bar and away from danger. It might have been nil-nil but it hadn't been uneventful. Newcomer Bigirimana had looked good and Shola had again shown promise that he could make it some day.

The next morning's Madeiran papers, the *Jornal da Madeira* (great name) and the *Diário de Notícias Madeira* were, as far as I could tell with my Spanish-based Portuguese guesswork, rightly proud of their team's performance – 'We neutralised Newcastle' – against what they kept saying was a 'top English club'. Both gave us the front-page headlines and photos and four inside pages of lavish treatment, on what they also impressed on us was the 102nd anniversary of the club's foundation. The *Diário* said that the draw had earned them an extra 100,000 euros of UEFA prize money, bringing their guaranteed Europa League total to at least 1,600,000 euros, which I suppose applied just as well to us too. A win gives a team 200,000 euros. It means a lot to a small club in mid-Atlantic. For the *Diário*, their Brazilian defender Guilherme was the man of the match, while the *Jornal* gave the honour to their forward, Sami. The *Diário* was also highly impressed by the good nature and impeccable behaviour of the Toon supporters. They also saw something that we hadn't – that at one point Alan Pardew and the Maritimo manager, Pedro Martins, had had a slight difference of opinion down on the touchline, but that it was soon resolved amicably, and at the end Alan Pardew had been very complimentary about Maritimo's performance, saying they had been a surprise package. Even the local mayor, MPs and MEPs and improbably enough, an old sea captain also gave their positive opinions on their team's performance in the *Diário*.

After the game, I walked back down the volcano with a bunch of Toon fans including John who told me that he was planning on retiring soon and heading down to the Algarve to somewhere inland from Vilamoura, which sounded as if it must have been very close to where we spent our summer holiday watching not only the Toon bringing home the silverware from the aforementioned pre-season tournament against Olympiakos and SC Braga, despite Cissé missing a series of sitters and a penalty (a portent of things to come?), but also Bradley Wiggins bringing home Olympic gold. It wasn't hard to choose which was the more exciting.

I found a nice open-air restaurant called *Jardims do Infante*, which looks down onto the main road running through Funchal. The staff were all women and very good at their work, and the food was excellent – a tomato and onion soup with an egg run into it, and then a mixed grill of fish which was truly delicious. All washed down with some *vinho verde*, freshly fermented 'green' white wine with a bit of a tang to it.

Hang on a minute ... You know when I just told you that the paper had a quote from an old sea cap'n? It didn't sound right, did it? Well, I've just read the *Diário* preview from the day before the match, and it wasn't an old sea-dog at all. No, my Portuguese let me down. It was the white-haired ex-skipper of the Maritimo team, Angelo Gomes. That makes more sense now!

After another extortionate taxi ride to the airport, heading east from Funchal and seeing another thirty-five euros go west, I joined the queue for the TAP flight back to Lisbon. I'd already checked in online to book nice window seats for both flights back as I like to have a good view of the passing scenery. You might have noticed. I can't understand all this 'Must have an aisle seat to get off quicker' palaver. Maybe they have toilet problems and considerately don't want to disturb the others in the same row. Either way, why not just choose a window seat two rows ahead and you'll have a more interesting view and still get off before the aisle-obsessives sitting aft of you. (Quick note from our man in Bucharest: well, Barry, if you were my shape, you would appreciate the little bit extra comfort of an aisle seat. I sometimes have nightmares about having to sit in the middle, as I once did on a flight from New York (USA, not Tyne and where?) – a cramped experience, I can tell you, especially after completing the marathon, half jogging, half walking).

Anyway, here I am in the queue when there is another kerfuffle. They say we can go on the earlier plane at 10.40 instead of 11.55 – sounds good to me. So I can really have a good look around Lisbon to pass the time between planes. And what is more, they're upgrading me to first class too. I ask if they can also put me onto an earlier plane to Brussels while they are at it, but apparently not. Even getting one earlier flight is almost unheard of, as they always say that if you buy a cheap ticket, you can't change it, so this is a bonus. Maybe it's an island thing. As we take off it becomes clear that the distinguished-looking old gentleman (not me, the other one) in First is some celebrity as the captain and stewardesses spend quite some time talking to him and showing obvious deference. Later when I open my local *Jornal de Madeira*, he's there on the front cover – the Governor of Madeira, who is called Alberto Joao Jardim according to the report on Page Three. No, he hadn't got his tits oot for the lads. Though maybe that was how he'd got himself elected. Did he have something to do with that *Jardims do Infante* restaurant, I wonder?

Arriving back in Lisbon Airport, I take the chance to go to the Transfer Desk to see if there is any way I can wangle myself onto the one o'clock or three o'clock planes to Brussels. Not now they say, but if I go and hang around their Gate 17 check-in desk at TAP HQ just before the 15.00 boarding time, there is some chance they might let me on that one. It's a couple of hours' wait, time that could be otherwise well-spent on the streets of Lisbon. The lady says it could be possible as even though it seems full in economy, business has some space so they might find me a seat. This changes my idea about going into Lisbon so I decide to wait in the fairly pleasant surroundings of the airport. The Harrods Café – don't ask me why they have Harrods cafés in Portugal – has highlights of Tottenham's Europa League game against Lazio, a nil-nil draw and they do a very acceptable *pastel de nata* and pot of *cha*. In case it's slipped your memory, the word char for tea is one of the rare examples of Portuguese being assimilated into the English vernacular. If it all goes wrong and they leave me stranded, I can always jump on the subway as they call it here – a not so rare example of Americanisms seeping into Portuguese – and take a short trip around Lisbon instead.

***

After waiting around for hours, I am finally rebuffed from the three-thirty flight and I then learn that my flight at five-to-eight is delayed, if not cancelled. Typical. They say they can't even give any information until after it ought to have taken off. By the time it gets back in the wee small hours, if it does, all the trains and buses from Zaventem airport will have stopped. I ask whether they will give us the price of a Brussels taxi to get back home in the middle of the night and I fill in a claim form. As you might guess, a few weeks later I got a reply saying sorry but they owed me nothing.

Well there was nothing for it but to take the train into Lisbon. I had hours to kill and it's not even a half-hour ride away. I got off at Rossio in the centre of the city and walked through the two side-by-side squares where, led admirably by the Other Clive, we'd sung long into the warmth of the night after the defeat to Sporting, and then I headed down through the straight streets of the post-earthquake new district and the ochre-coloured monumental main square to the shoreline and the columns out in the water which mark the gateway to the old Portuguese empire of Africa and the Far East. There would have been no Eusebio if there'd been no Empire. (Pete: actually there would have been, it's just that he wouldn't have been Portuguese.) Pedant! Anyway, on the way back I stopped for a cool refreshing drink in one of the street cafés and then found a well-frequented old bakery and bought a stock of *pasteis de nata* to take home.

And so back to the airport only to learn that the plane is not going to be leaving until well into the evening. To pass the time, I tour the Duty Free and pick out some Malmsey Madeira wine – I like that word, Malmsey – and a bottle of vintage port, plus an extra box of those *pasteis de nata*; can't resist them. Then to while away the final hour of aeronautical injury time, I ask the helpful staff at the TAP Information and Transfers Desk to give me a compensation form (another one – the desk officers had changed) to see if I can claim something under EU passengers' rights. You never know, TAP might pay for half of my trip. After all, if you don't ask, you don't get. So you might as well try to tap TAP, as it were. A few weeks later I found out that if you ask, you still don't get. The plane finally got away at 22.57 and I think if it had left after 23.00, we might have been due some recompense. I arrived back home at half past four in the morning. But it was well worth it.

Bordeaux, Home leg – 4th October 2012
I'll have a bottle, please

I am flying over the narrowest part of the North Sea to follow the East Anglian coast on a beautiful bright day with a few scattered clouds, giving a great view of the English cliffs, bays, river mouths and beaches. Around the bulge of East Anglia, as we approach The Wash, there is an array of maybe a hundred offshore wind turbines, some working, some still being built with just their piles jutting out of the water. And then it's the Humber and the best bridge to nowhere ever built, and then on to Kingston upon Hull. Just to the north, there is an eye-boggling range of curved escarpments, dips and slopes lapping one over the next like wavelets of solidified rock rippling over the landscape. The early-morning raking sunlight emphasises their profiles, putting the dips literally in the shade. There are still more waves a little further to the north, succeeded by a rugged brown moorscape at the level of Scarborough and Whitby and then another series of escarpments before reaching Teesside and then the sandstone cliffs of County Durham. The remnants of Marsden Rock, the Gypsy Green of the GNR finishing straight at South Shields, and then the glistening, immaculate Tyne – well, not really; in fact it's nearly as bad as the where?, spewing out all sorts of purple gunge into the North Sea. On we fly past Tynemouth, Cullercoats and Whitley Bay's St. Mary's Island – where the tide is out and people are walking across the causeway – before crossing the coast at Seaton Sluice, swooping over Delaval Hall and New Hartley and finally touching down in the parish of Alan Shearer. What a great morning cinema reel that had been. Who would ever want an aisle seat and have to miss all that? (Pete: Well there's me ...)

***

So European nights return to the Toon after too long a wait – six years in the wilderness since being knocked out by AZ Alkmaar. Tonight we are being treated to NUFC v *Les Girondins de Bordeaux*, bringing together the two favourites to qualify from the group. Bordeaux include amongst their number a decent-looking forward by the name of Yoan Gouffran.

They have brought along a boisterous set of maybe five hundred fans who have a special chant which ends with a roar of 'G - S - B'.

My brother Ian and I had bought seats in the Platinum Club especially for the European occasion and who should we bump into there but Ian Rosenvinge, who must have just dropped in, as he would later in Lisbon too.

There was a funny sign on the wall outside the Platinum toilets, or at least I thought so. I tried to take a picture without drawing attention as I did not want to be marked out as some kind of furtive toilet picture-taker, but I drew so little attention with my nonchalant clicking that the picture came out too blurred even to show you. (Pete: so what was the sign, Barry? Come on, don't keep us all in suspense like that ...)

***

We were playing in our fluorescent yellow shirts and black shorts and lined up at the start were Elliot, Simpson, Williamson, Perch, Ferguson, Anita, Cabaye, Tioté, Obertan, Shola and Cissé. We had the game under control right from the start, and it came as no surprise when, just after Yoan Gouffran had had a half-chance saved by Rob Elliot, Shola at the far post calmly side-footed in a low cross from ex-Bordeaux player Obertan who had done well to create the chance a quarter of an hour into the game. Elliot was forced into a good save from a tremendous long-distance shot but then it wasn't long before we got another when one of the Bordeaux defenders misjudged a centre from Simpson and poked the ball into his own net. Two-nil at half time and it was all looking very comfortable. Elliot had played well but had to be substituted at half time, bringing the welcome sight of Steve Harper into the game for the second half and he was soon in action pushing the ball onto the post from a back-heel by the tricky Saivet. Just after the break, Cissé put the result beyond doubt when, resisting the temptation to go offside, he expertly put in Ferguson's cross with a twisting and stretching first-time left foot shot for our third goal. We could surely afford to celebrate now, and this thought was obviously shared by a very enthusiastic fan who burst onto the pitch in the wake of Cissé's goal.

Streakers are not as common in France as they are in the UK. And I don't mean that they're higher class, I mean streaking has never caught on in France. So the Toon streaker, 'Johnny P 123' as it said in red print on the back of his white shirt caused quite a sensation the next day in the French papers. He had a perfectly good shirt on, but he'd simply forgotten his pants. He made excellent use of the extra freedom of movement this gave him and evaded numerous challenges by the yellow-caped stewards and police until he was finally trapped in a pincer movement. (Pete: mind, that sounds painful, all right, what with not having any kegs on and all ... you've got to be careful with pincers and pliers.)

In what remained of the game, David Bellion, ex of SAFC, got a tremendous reception when he came on as substitute for the last twenty minutes or so. Tremendously bad. He had what was probably Bordeaux's best chance of the night with about a quarter of an hour remaining, but true to form he fluffed it, Steve Harper saving with his legs.

(Pete: the sign, Barry, the sign ...)

***

Whenever we play Man U, in the back of your mind, no matter how hopeful you might be, you more or less expect to lose, so the occasional win or even draw is a year-long source of pride. Last year it was three-nil, including a great goal from Cabaye. This year, nil-three, so normal service restored. But that non-goal early in the second half would have brought it back to one-two and the Mags would have been flying. We had a great view from our seats in the Leazes End with the goal just to our left and everyone was convinced it had made it over the goal line, and the players were too. The crowd's support was deafening. Mind, it has to be said that the Man U fans were loud and they had a lot to shout about from the eighth minute on. But they only sing when they're winning – which unfortunately is most of the time – and they'd been a whole lot quieter last year. Our fans were resolute and raucous in their response, led by all up on Level Seven who were perched alongside the away fans. Faced with inevitable defeat, they started doing the 'Poznan', the Man City face-away-from-the-pitch pogo like the mackems did when Man U lost the Premiership in the last seconds of the 2011-12 season. You have to give the mackems that one – it was a classic. It's only a pity that for some inexplicable reason our lads had somehow lost the little extra touch of magic that they had had last year. That's not to say that we didn't have our moments – the Demba Ba shot which crashed off the bar, and Cissé headed it into the goal but did De Gea claw it out? I don't think so. Then long shots from Cabaye which last year would surely have found their target – but it was not to be this year. And little bits of bad luck when it looked like Ben Arfa, Santon, Cissé or Ba were through on goal. We were arguably on top for the rest of the first half and all the way through the second half until the sickener when that cross flashed across the goal and somehow sneaked in at the far post.

One highlight was the roar of anguish from Tioté heard all around SJP when he was penalised for winning the ball off Rooney. It must have been terrifying close up, judging by the look on Rooney's ugly mug. And did van Persie elbow Cabaye? It certainly looked like it. And what was the fourth official playing at, allowing SAF to take up position permanently outside his technical area, and only now and then half-heartedly and ineffectually attempting to get him back in his kennel. All in all, it was an exciting game and we were not humiliated and could hold our heads up despite the score line.

***

So my Toon trip had ended in a three-three draw on aggregate, a three-nil and a nil-three. Fair enough, and given the choice I'd rather have beaten Bordeaux really, because we are now back on track in our European campaign. I was actually quite surprised how easy it had been to beat *les Girondins*. And just about all of our Premiership rivals will be beaten by Man U, so it is not as if we are losing ground to anyone in particular. That's my prediction as I fly back over the North Sea to Brussels, passing over Bruges on the way. By the way, there's a nice little Belgian-inspired restaurant called Bruges in la-dee-dah Jesmond student-land where we ended up after the match on Sunday evening. It is run by a locally-born brother and sister with absolutely no connection to our next European opponents. And very nice it is too. The menu includes *carbonnades,* which is Belgian beef stew, often laced with beer, to which a dash of Tyneside has been added by plopping in a few tasty dumplings. Or they have slow-roasted belly pork, or steak-frites, with the frites nearly as good but not quite as crispy as the double-fried real ones. But excellent none the less, and even better when combined with the very friendly North-East welcome. I am sure a lot of the Belgian Bruggers will flock here when they visit in a few weeks' time.

(Pete: that reminds me of the Belgian restaurant in London – *Moules Frites* I think it was called – where Sarah, Chris and I once went, after we had played Spurs I seem to recall. Anyway, the nice waitress – who was French, but let's not quibble – informed us in a business-like way that we could order anything except 'a-dack', which was off. This was a shame because Chris and I had already been considering Haddock and Chips. Never mind, we said, we'll have the duck instead. 'But I 'ave already told you that the dack is off.' Oh sod it, let's have *moules-frites* and a fruity beer.)

Now hang on, there was a sign I was going to tell you about. Now what did it say again? ...

Bruges away – 12ᵗʰ November 2012

See Bruges and ... get arrested.

'I wrote to the Bruges club to see if we could have media accreditation on the basis of our two previous Toon books. Surprisingly, we never received a reply.'

'Plus ça change, Barry!'

What a carry-on! Weeks before the game in Bruges the inevitable ticket saga took its inevitable course. The ground there is not very big – the capacity is only around 29,000. Our opponents Club Bruges share the *Jan Breydelstadion* with local rivals Cercle Bruges. That perhaps sets a useful precedent for clubs such as Arsenal and Chelsea. And they could maybe also share with that other London club, England. Nobody would care. In fact their fans probably wouldn't even notice. But somehow I don't think this ground-sharing business will ever catch on in the North-East. For a start, what colour would the seats be?

Anyway, the hope was that the Toon would be allocated a reasonable number of tickets – 5,000 say. In the event, Bruges decided to allocate a measly 2,500. And by the time that was announced, five to six thousand Geordies had made their travel and accommodation arrangements, and that all costs money. Given this situation, the local police understandably announced that any Newcastle United fan found in Bruges on the eve or day of the match without a ticket for the game would be arrested. Yes, that sounded pretty reasonable, we felt. After all, what more heinous crime could there be than to exercise one's right of freedom of movement as a European citizen and go for a little holiday to Belgium, spending one's hard-earned money and boosting the hard-pressed local economy but not buying a ticket for a football match? It sounded like we were going to be just about as welcome as the President of the European Parliament at a UKIP birthday party.

Hmmmm ... We wondered, however, whether for example German tourists not in possession of, say, a ticket for a fillum showing at a Bruges cinema would also be arrested. The irony of the situation was made all the more galling by the fact that the game was on the 8th of November – three days before Remembrance Sunday. Most of the visitors from Geordieland were wearing poppies, those poppies of course symbolising the fields of Flanders, the scene of the madness and carnage of the First World War's western front. So imagine the possible Blackadder-style court martial in a Bruges magistrate's court. 'You have been found guilty of coming here to Flanders, spending your money while wearing a poppy commemorating the sacrifice made by your great-grandfathers to liberate Belgium, but coming without a match ticket!'

Excusez-moi, Trigger, but didn't common sense just fly out of the window here somewhere, or jump off the famous Bruges market square belfry maybe? Fortunately, Martin Callanan, one of our North-East MEPs, also thought so and filed a formal complaint reminding the local authorities of people's right to move around Europe without let or hindrance. Mind, I can remember being hindered a few times over the years but I am not sure at all whether I have ever been let. Let's let it be, shall we? We actually bumped into Martin a few years back in a Brussels pub, Fat Boys (appropriately enough in my case), where we wanted to watch a Toon game. We were playing a Euro-qualifier in some Baltic State or other that we didn't have time to get to, and Fat Boys (in the square just in front of the European Parliament complex) has wall-to-wall tellies showing any number of sporting events simultaneously. I thought Martin's face looked vaguely familiar – he's quite often on the Sunday Politics show, for example – and he told us he was a Euro MP, a tory one in fact. I explained that as my Dad had grown up in Jarrow during the Great Depression I could hardly be expected to be a rabid thatcherite, and so we agreed to talk Toon, not politics. Martin is a season ticket holder at SJP and when we told him we were doing the Great North Run he very sensibly reminded us that there was a perfectly good Metro system that would get us from Newcastle to South Shields a lot quicker. Good point! And fair play to him indeed for intervening like that with the Belgian authorities on the Toon Army's behalf. Cheers, Martin Callanan MEP! (Note from the future courtesy of our built-in time machine: now ex-MEP but perhaps the future Lord Callanan of Low Fell.)

With all this pressure and carry-on on the ticket front, Club Bruges graciously made another 900 tickets available, easing the situation at least a wee bit. We don't want to be over-critical of our Belgian friends' organisational talents but we hadn't forgotten the chaos at Antwerp's decrepit ground back in 1994 when a whole section of Newcastle fans had to be moved to another part of the ground after the terracing under their feet collapsed. And let's not forget Heysel. The question of who was guilty of what, and the role played by a seemingly dilapidated wall, was never finally resolved to everyone's satisfaction. Well, Pete, I went a few times to the Heysel at the beginning of the eighties and it was a dump – for instance I recall having to clamber up a muddy slope inside the stadium to get to the terracing.

***

On a linguistic note – well, you must have known this was coming – our opponent's name is in itself intriguing: Club Brugge. Bruges is the French (and English) name for Brugge. The Germans call it Brügge by the way. Brug is the Flemish (a variant of Dutch) word for bridge, so one imagines the name reflects the large number of bridges. In a very real sense Bruges was a bridge between Flanders and other regions and countries because of its importance in the past as a cloth manufacturing centre whose roots go back to the thirteenth century. And with its wonderful and sometimes breath-taking cultural and architectural heritage it still builds a bridge to Flanders' and Europe's past. Because of the dominant role of France in that past, the Brits have tended to accept the French names of places which actually have local names that aren't that difficult to pronounce. For example, Munich for München, Ypres for Ieperen (though it is better known for the worst of all possible reasons as Wipers), Cologne for Köln, etc. Surely it would be nice where possible to always use the local name, and the trend is certainly going in that direction. Over the past hundred years we have adopted Koblenz instead of Coblence, Mainz instead of Mayence, Braunschweig instead of Brunswick. Unfortunately, more and more people, including some Geordies who should know better, have started saying NEWcastle instead of nyeCASS'l and also CARlisle instead of carLISLE. So let's stop that nonsense now, shall we?

***

So where were we? Ah yes, Flanders. It was only joined up with French-speaking Wallonia to form Belgium in 1830, and after the First World War they were joined by a slice of the German Reich (Eupen and Malmédy, a region that includes Sankt Vith of Battle of the Bulge fame). There is a strong separatist movement in Flanders.

The far-right *Vlaams Belang* (Flemish Interest) party is considered by the mainstream political parties to be beyond the pale, but the more moderate Flemish nationalists VLA are steadily gaining ground, and we may yet see a Flemish Republic being declared in the not too distant future, who knows? It's funny how the map of Europe is still constantly changing, isn't it? I was born in 1956 (7th February – and we won the Cup on 7th May 1955, work it out for yourself!), and even in my lifetime there have been plenty of changes. Germany's borders have gone on shifting. After already having got back, not long after the war, a sliver of land they had ceded to the Netherlands, they got the Saarland back on 1st January 1957. And after the fall of Communism, the German Democratic Republic (the former Soviet Zone of occupation) acceded to the Federal Republic of Germany on 3rd October 1990. The Soviet Union subsequently disintegrated, Yugoslavia likewise. The Baltics re-emerged, and the EU expanded eastward and south-eastward. Wow, actually! Who'd have thought it? And now the SNP's clever leader Alex Salmond has secured a referendum on independence. That concession by Cameron has indirectly lent fresh impetus to the Catalan, Basque and Flemish independence movements. Interesting times indeed!

We're not taking sides, but it seems clear that Cameron has scored a massive own goal and Salmond has won a huge battle in his campaign. The future of the UK could well be decided by the votes of sixteen and seventeen year olds, who at the time of the referendum being granted, were fourteen and fifteen years old. At that age, I for one was a very impressionable kid who would have taken very little persuasion to vote for, say, Northumbrian independence. I wouldn't have given that much thought to the economic and political implications. So if the SNP get their PR and general propaganda right, and make good use of Sean Connery *et al*, they could well do it. And that could persuade the Basque country, Catalonia and Flanders to follow suit. I could be wrong but I think all of them will gain independence, sooner or later. If you are reading this twenty or thirty years after the time of writing, you could be laughing right now at such nonsense or maybe acknowledging a degree of prescience. Another note from the future: well, as we now all know, it looks like Scotland is headed for the best of all possible worlds ...

So we were dealing with a club embodying not only national but also regional Flemish pride.

***

Barry had valiantly tried to persuade NUFC to send us tickets but that never really looked like happening.

'Yes, I wrote a nice e-mail politely pointing out that Pete, Brian and I had between us been so kind as to purchase six per cent of the entire Newcastle ticket allocation for the Atromitos game in Athens back in August (three out of forty-eight) which was equivalent to 150 of the 2,500 tickets for the away fans against Bruges ...'

So it was, you would think, not wholly unreasonable to ask for 0.06 per cent of the allocation for Bruges.

'Yes, and I was also in Madeira and travelled back for the home game against Bordeaux. I reasoned that the club would surely reward such loyalty. But I was once again reminded that pigs might fly. We were not beaten, however, as I had also arranged that mini season ticket I was telling you about earlier – for all three Bruges home games in this stage of the Europa League. We only intended to go to the Toon game, but it was worth the extra expense!'

It certainly was, Barry. Great idea! By coincidence I was working in Brussels on the Monday, Tuesday and Wednesday of the week of our match in Bruges, so I drove straight out of the Belgian capital after work on the Wednesday. It was rush-hour chaos and it took me all of two hours door to door. I was staying at the NH hotel located on the edge of the old quarter, just off the bus station in the 't Zand district, and a fifteen minute or so walk to the main square. Barry had driven up to Brugge as well to sample the atmosphere and the plan was to go to the stadium and maybe also catch a glimpse of the pre-match training. Even with the GPS system I managed to miss the 't Zand underground car park first time round, while Barry had parked on a little square near the hotel. I almost tried to park there too but we saw how exorbitant the rates were and we also saw that although it was now getting on for seven in the evening the parking warden was doing a roaring trade writing out tickets. Bruges is not a car-friendly place, not at all. It is a maze of old cobbled streets with some very narrow and sudden turns. And when you do get out onto a wider drag, there are bus lanes and cycle paths and pedestrian crossings galore. The setup seems to be designed in such a way as to ensure that you immediately get a guilty conscience if you are driving a car. But I finally managed to get parked up in the underground car park and we both made our way to the hotel, passing our friendly traffic warden en route who was merrily writing out his tickets, which are no doubt a useful source of revenue for the town. Maybe a German tourist with a parking ticket would be more welcome than a poppy-wearing Geordie without a match ticket, who knows?

I finally got checked into the NH hotel; and remarked to a baffled receptionist that I found it was jolly considerate of the National Health to provide lodgings for Toon pilgrims on their travels. The lobby was stowed out with Toon fans in optimistic mood. It felt like a home from home. It turned out that the hotel was a converted former monastery, which was welcome news as a bit of pre-match spirituality never did anyone any harm. I dumped my bags in what, for a monastery, appeared to be quite a luxurious cell, and we set off again to the little square where Barry's car was parked. We bumped into our traffic warden friend yet again. He gets about. By now we were on first-name terms.

'Well, Super Jan, super star, how many tickets have you written so far?'

'I have lost count, my friends. Be quick, you have only paid enough for another five minutes for your car, and if your time expires I will have to write another ticket immediately. Nothing personal, you understand ...'

Yeah.

Barry's GPS soon had us speeding on our way to the ground and a quarter of an hour or so later we were there.

***

Even without the GPS, I would probably have found the way myself as I had briefly been there before heading towards Pete's NHS hotel. I was hoping against hope that the ticket office would be open, selling some Bruges-end tickets at least, but no joy. The Don had already got a ticket and so had his fellow south-coast exile Rick. But we still needed more for Rick's son, Ross, and for Peter F. and his sister Pauline. Never easy, this ticket purchasing business.

We were out of luck on the training front, too. The facilities are impressive, mind. Arranged next to two sides of the fortress-like stadium are several training pitches, all floodlit and bright green on an otherwise dark but mild November evening. There were a number of youth matches taking place and there was a lot of coming and going around the ground. We got talking with an older gadgy who had the look of authority and officialdom about him. He was very friendly and explained there was no Toon training going on and that there had just been a press conference.

Bruges were under big pressure. They really needed to take all three points to have a realistic chance of reaching the knock-out stage. Bordeaux had beaten them four-nil in the opening group game but then they'd managed to beat Maritimo two-nil at home. We'd then beaten them one-nil in the hard-fought home fixture through a well-taken goal by Gabriel Obertan who was sent on a break-away by Shola at the beginning of the second half. But three points from three games were not going to get them very far if they didn't start winning some more matches soon. To top it all, they had just sacked the manager after losing their last domestic league game to our old Euro-opponent Zulte Waregem. And their previous manager, Chistoph Daum, hadn't lasted that long either. Daum's name had once been mentioned in connection with the Toon, we remembered. He had long been at that other Toon Euro-opponent Bayer Leverkusen; where he had been involved in a mini scandal – something about coke. Coca-Cola maybe? Well, Bayer make pills, so that could explain it. Come to think of it, you were once on Bayer Leverkusen's books, weren't you, Pete?

Yes, that's right, Barry. I had a summer job as a labourer at the chemical works, along with Chris and Mike C., back in the glorious summer of 1974, Auf Wiedersehen Pet style.

***

So our eve of match trip to the ground hadn't been a great success in terms of watching training or getting additional tickets, but at least we had got the lay of the land and had identified the gate we would need to get to less than twenty-four hours later. That would prove to be very useful intelligence for the purposes of our undercover operation behind enemy lines. More of which anon …

We made our way back to the town centre, reasoning that the Toon Army would naturally gravitate towards the main square, as we had done previously in towns and cities across the length and breadth of Europe. The cobbled alleyways were a challenge even for the GPS, but Barry courageously plunged ever deeper into one of Europe's most car-unfriendly cities. And luck was on our side. We managed to get parked up legally and for free only a few hundred metres, as it turned out, from the main square, the *Grote Markt*. That could be an alternative reason why we have a Groat Market, couldn't it? Although most people say it's named after some kind of grain.

As we bent our steps thither, we could hear the sounds of a boisterous Toon Army in fine voice. Emerging out of our lane and into the *Grote Markt*, we could not fail to be impressed by this floodlit Flemish masterpiece, with the *Stadhuis* (town hall) and the world-famous belfry immediately catching the eye. But equally pleasing were the two sides of the square lined by cosy-looking cafés at street level nestled under step-gabled brick houses and bathed in the soft yellowish light of the street lamps. Best of all, the whole scene was set off nicely by the clippedy-clippedy-clop of a horse and carriage – possibly the last of the day – gladdening the hearts of locals and tourists alike on this fair autumnal evening.

There were plenty of ours milling around the *Grote Markt* itself, but the main body of noise was coming from an alleyway just off the square, so there we headed. It led in turn to a mini-square in its own right, equally lined with its very own pubs and cafés. Was this heaven, or what?

***

It goes almost without saying that everyone was ultra-well-behaved in this heaving black and white crowd, and we soon joined in the singing and good-natured banter. We got talking to a couple who hailed, as it turned out, from Howdon, same as me. Did you know so and so? Yes, and did you know this, that and the other? But of course! It was great to hear the old names of characters of yesteryear. Some of them you really could not make up. Cuddy Hackworth, for example, or Boiler Korkly. They remembered that one particular family had kept a horse in their council house garden, or maybe in the house itself, together with the pigeons. The talk was of the Bewicke Pub, also known as the Last Chance Saloon. Stories had been told even into the seventies of a certain PoW returning shortly after the war who had pulled a German Luger pistol (a souvenir of *Stalag IVA*) when he'd been refused a drink at closing time. Such larks, such larks! Hang on a minute, wasn't that Uncle John J.? Didn't he also break into Kempes the grocers one night after leaving the Bewicke to steal some biscuits? The magistrate dismissed the case in the light of what the lad had been through. He had lived off tatie peelings in that *Stalag* located near Dresden. Well done, that magistrate.

I just loved those lanes of long-forgotten memories in the memory lanes of Bruges. So this paragraph is dedicated to the Queer Fella (in the proper sense of the word), Uncle John J. We'll write a novel about you one day!

***

We were feeling a bit peckish by now, so we went back into the *Grote Markt* again, only to find that most places were closing down – even though it was only ten o'clock or so. This didn't seem right for Belgium. But there was a nice place just off the other side of the square that was still open and clearly enjoying the patronage of the Toon Army. So we installed ourselves on the *verwarmd terras* and ordered omelettes and chips, and beer – non-alcoholic for Barry as he was driving. The friendly waiters were keeping people updated on the scores in various matches that were under way around Europe. There was much joy when everyone heard that Celtic were beating Barcelona and that both man u and chelski were losing. We were all genuinely saddened and disgusted when the final results were jammy wins for both of those London clubs, but everyone was over the moon when we got confirmation of Celtic's historic victory over Barça. Well done, you Hoops! At the same time we wondered if Rangers had managed to get a point off their close rivals Elgin City, but strangely that was not being televised in Belgium.

***

Chris and Sarah unfortunately couldn't make it to Bruges, as they were on holiday in Ecuador, and they were planning to go and see the penguins in the Galapagos Islands, Vonnegut-style. As a rule, penguins are black and white, however, so that's okay. Hopefully we would soon be meeting up with them in Bordeaux. With Chris and Sarah, that is, not the penguins. Though they would certainly also be welcome. The Cuths prediction league was by now well into its own season, and I was languishing in third-last place. I had briefly considered conceding the possibility of sunderland occasionally managing a draw, but then rejected that idea on principle. Chris was mid-table in mid-October, having fallen several places following a string of dodgy forecasts. While in Ecuador, however, he decided to ask the barmaid to make his forecasts for him and as a result he had stopped the rot. In a pre-match e-mail he said he was considering bringing Juanita back with him and we were now looking forward to maybe meeting her in Bordeaux too. Though whether Sarah would be quite so keen on the idea, we weren't sure.

***

It was getting late so we decided to call it a day. On the way back up a little lane lined with bars we came across some lads who had been visiting war graves in Flanders before coming on to Bruges itself. They had been to the famous Tyne Cot war cemetery. Yes, Tyne as in Tyne. It's just a little way out of Ypres, Wipers. I read somewhere that Geordies fighting in that area thought that some of the local cottages looked like cottages back home. The lads we were talking to showed us a photo they had taken of the cross that marks the spot where the Germans and Brits had played football during a famous Christmas truce. Is it true that the Brits were later put on a charge by their officers for fraternising with the enemy? We hope not, but no doubt it is true! At the foot of the cross were loads of footballs and scarves, laid by Toon fans, sunderland fans, Manchester United, Chelsea etc., and also Borussia Dortmund, Schalke 04, Bayern München etc. What would the media make of that? They just ignore such sentiments between football fans. They are only interested in negative headlines. I once read some pre-match report in a German paper ahead of Bayern playing some British team. At one point it said something like 'Police are expecting five thousand English hooligans´! Isn't it just great the way football supporters are branded in this prejudiced and toxic way?

Barry dropped me off at the hotel before heading back off home to Brussels. He would very sensibly be returning to Bruges the next day by train, not car. Time for a night cap in the hotel bar and then it's *bonne nuit* and *wel te rusten. Gute Nacht, Freunde!*

***

So match day had arrived at last, in the way that, well, only match days can. After early morning matins kneeling on the stone floor of the NHS monastery chapel and a frugal repast in the silence of the refectory, I decided to skip the scourging with the cat o' nine tails and instead made my way meditatively back towards the centre of town. Talking of cats, do you know there used to be a festival in Ypres called the *Kattenstoet*, where they flung cats off the top of the belfry? Stotting cats from up a great height. They still do it now, but with stuffed toy cats. They were a strange bunch back in mediaeval times.

It was now about half past eleven and I had missed out on the National Health breakfast, so I bought a local paper and sat down in a *brasserie* for a coffee and a *croque monsieur*. That's just a ham and cheese toastie, but it sounds much better in French, don't you think? There is also a *croque madame*, which is also a ham and cheese toastie, but served with two artfully arranged and anatomically accurate fried eggs up top. The Dutch, and Flemish too, have something similar but even better called an *uitsmijter*. We will meet, greet and eat a couple of them in the Cup Final chapter.

As I tucked into my own version of a continental breakfast, I read the pre-match reporting in *De Standaard*. The emphasis was on the pressure bearing down on Bruges to beat Newcastle to maintain any hope of making it into the knock-out stage of the competition. There was also confirmation of the police plan to contain the Toon Army in the central area and keep Bruges fans away. Also confirmation that plucky little Belgium would not be arresting the ticketless masses. So common sense was prevailing (thanks again, Martin Callanan MEP – see, Europe is useful for some things), but it was clear that those of us with tickets in the Bruges end would have to make a timely exit from *De Markt* that afternoon before the *Politie* clamped down with their ultimate *cordon sanitaire* (which is not a lavvy chain but a security cordon by the way), after which a breakout would be quite difficult. And we could be trapped in *italics* for ever.

Barry rang to say he had missed the train in Brussels and now wouldn't get to Bruges till mid-afternoon sometime. On a positive note, however, he had met the great and genial Biffa on the platform there trying to get the same train. That had to be a good omen! He also said he had read on the internet that Club Bruges would be putting an extra 2,000 tickets on sale for the Toon contingent. This appeared to be fantastic news as it meant there was now fresh hope of sourcing those missing tickets.

So there was a spring in my step as I left the *brasserie* and made again for *De Markt*. There were clusters of black and white to be seen doing the same thing, consulting maps, asking locals, scratching their heads. I quickly lost my own way and asked a local couple for directions. These they gave me and asked in turn was there a match taking place today. Er, yes. Clearly not a genuine football town. The noise of the singing rose to crescendo levels as I got nearer and there was black and white just about everywhere. This was surely the biggest occupation of Bruges since 1940-44 and I wouldn't be surprised if the number of Toon Army members present today outnumbered the war-time *Wehrmacht* several times over. The Toon Army's *Stadkommandatur* was certainly well established here in the centre.

Various regimental flags were proudly on display around the central square area, where a giant screen had meanwhile been set up. I particularly liked the black and white 'We are Wallsend' flag, which included the words 'Keep the Faith' and that venerable abbreviation 'SMB'. I was a lot less keen on the red and white England flags. Must remember to take our 'People's Republic of Geordieland' flag along when we go to Bordeaux.

On I wandered into the centre of the square and towards said big screen. That and some smaller screens were showing old Toon footage: there was twinkle-toes Peter Beardsley scoring a goal against somebody or other. Obviously. A nice touch, that. Another, much smaller screen displayed, against the background of the Newcastle United crest, the ominous words 'Do not believe the rumours about another 2,000 tickets going on sale.' So some twit had started the rumours on twit-uh and the waves had soon been awash with indignant messages from Toon Army members back home to the effect that if they had known, they would have come to Bruges too.

***

By the way, I am typing up these notes just as the Remembrance Sunday ceremony is getting under way on BBC 1. The date and time of course commemorate the very hour of the day when the guns fell silent at the end of the First World War. The Great War. Though there was nothing 'Great' about it. The War to end all Wars. I am looking right now at a photograph of one of my great-grandfathers, Ireland-born Jarrow resident Frank McCormack, in his British Army uniform of the time. The photo was taken when he was convalescing from wounds sustained in Flanders. Yes, we must remember those who were killed in two World Wars! No doubt about that! It is strange to reflect that in Germany on this same day, the 11th of November, at 11 minutes past 11, the carnival clubs of the Rhineland and elsewhere are celebrating *Hoppeditz Erwache*. This *Hoppeditz* character, who is being coaxed to wake up, is, as it were, the spirit of the carnival season who has been sleeping since Ash Wednesday. From 11.11 on the 11th day of the 11th month, preparations are made for the next carnival season. The carnival clubs of Cologne, Mainz and many other towns and cities will be having their *Prunksitzungen*, merry occasions indeed, on a par with Percy Main Social Club in its heyday! *Prunk* should mean prank not pomp, shouldn't it. So the first merriments and jollifications get going at the very time when Britain stands silent to honour the fallen of two World Wars. Strange. Very strange indeed.

***

Made my way to the mobile Bruges club shop right next to the big screen. And who should I bump into but the Other Clive and the Other Peter, making plans to make the most of it by visiting even more obscure grounds in true ground-hopper tradition. Mention was made of Friday night at Sint Niklaas, second (and now third) division no-hopers. They couldn't join us for drinks as they had to go and meet their wives for a chocolate and lace shopping session. Barry and I already had our half-and-half scarves, but I thought our deep cover might be further enhanced by something more Bruges-specific, so I bought a couple of blue Bruges scarves that included the crests of all the opponents in the Europa League group stage. We would look the part all right.

Got a call from the Don (whom we all respect most profoundly). He was in town and on his way. Let's meet next to the 'We are Wallsend' flag because it is so good, and black and white. Then Peter F. rang to say he and Pauline were on the coach bringing them to Bruges from Ostend airport. They were on a trip arranged ages ago by the Back Page. I had to break the news that the extra two thousand tickets rumour was, well, just that.

But the ticketless were not going to let a great day out be spoilt by such a minor technicality, and the bars and restaurants were again doing a roaring trade (after all, the Flemish flag is a red lion) in Jupiler, Stella and the hundreds of Belgian brews including the strongest *trappiste* beers, which at thirteen degrees pack quite a punch, especially if you set your limit at six pints of the stuff. Somebody I recognised from previous away days said they were charging eleven euros a pint on *De Grote Markt* itself, but in the mini-square of the evening before it was five euros. Made a mental note of that. The clippedy-clops were also thriving on the extra Toon business and the sound of the hooves on the cobbles of those historic streets rang true. And it wasn't just the Toon Army. No, the Toon Navy were in town, too. Well, it was actually a bunch of Russian *matelots* – their boat must have come in at Zeebrugge or Ostend maybe. In any event they were wearing a black uniform with a geet big flat white cap you could eat your Sunday dinner off. So they were very welcome. A good few of the Toon contingent were chatting with them and offering pints. Had the cold war gone wrong, we could have been hoyin' bombs at each other instead. Meeting up like this in places like Bruges is a much better idea, we reckon.

I got talking with a Geordie poliss (Edgar Wallace) who was wearing his normal uniform and whose presence was no doubt intended to remind people to be on their best behaviour. And he said that's exactly what they were on, the huge overwhelming majority of the visiting Geordies being nice, decent people. He and his colleagues had their eyes on the usual suspects in such circumstances, of course, but there had actually been just one incident with someone who got a little too horizontal the previous evening. As he said, where five thousand people gather for an outing there are bound to be a couple of eejits among them. I assured him there would be none in our little group, and right on cue the Don appeared. I immediately pledged my loyalty and expressed my deepest respects, and he said, 'Stop acting like a daft prat'. Only a true Don can come out with such words of wisdom. Genuine class! We went up the little alleyway to our now familiar mini-square, which Bruges town council was already thinking of re-naming *Toon-Army-Plein*. No sooner did we have a pint in our hands than we were joined in rapid succession, after three coordinating phone calls (what did we do before the age of the mobile?), by Rick and Ross (who was making the most of his last days of leisure before embarking on the world of work), Peter F. and Pauline, Alex, and Barry. Everything – or at least everyone – was falling nicely into place!

To say the place was heaving would be a gross understatement, but I'm afraid I cannot think of a more appropriate verb, so here goes: the place was heavin', though but. Lots of chanting and singing going on. To the tune of 'Harry Redknapp, you should be in jail' or 'Sloop John B' as it is sometimes known, we had 'We're drinking in Bruges, we're drinking in Bru – uges, sun'lnd supporters, we're drinking in Bruges'. And they weren't kidding – they really were drinking in Bruges!

I made a few fruitless phone calls to Jean Jackson and Paul English off the fans forum, but their phones were unreachable in all the cyber-traffic, and as it later turned out, low batteries.

Strangely, at no time did we hear anyone say 'What a boring place this is'. That's probably because Bruges is a fantastic, fabulous place. Fantabulous in fact. One particular highlight we had seen only just around the corner and over one of the many canal bridges was the *Collège d'Europe*. Students from all corners of the continent go there to study international politics and European affairs. The idea, I suppose, is to spread the word about European peace and unity and to try and forge a European identity among the youth of today and perhaps some leaders and decision-makers of tomorrow. It was also there that thatcher gave her famous eighties speech to the effect that she thought Europe was a load of crêpe, Suzette. Some say that was because of the mouthful she got as a result of her unsuccessful water-skiing trip along the Bruges canal when she was foiled by EU red tape in the form of a five kph speed limit and a waterlogged handbag. Not our favourite person, actually, to tell you the truth.

Back in our mini-square the singing was being led by a familiar-looking soul in a yellow jacket who was half hanging out of a window of the upstairs section of a pub looking square on to the mini-square. The crowd at one point were shouting, 'Jump! Jump!' It looked for a moment as if he would, but thankfully he didn't. The beer was flowin' like water all round and all of a sudden a good number of the lads decided to 'hoy beer if you love the Toon' and it began raining the stuff. We decided to beat a hasty retreat, but it was all good-natured and did not get out of hand. The local telly people were mingling among the partly shirt-sleeved throng (it really was a mild November day) and I saw some impressive interviews back at the hotel that evening. The Flemish commentator said they had unfortunately been unable to find an interpreter for Geordie!

*****

Some of the cafés had really exotic and impenetrable names. Our chosen watering hole, for example, was called 'The Belgian Beer Pub'. That had initially caused a great deal of confusion and apparently one group of lads had seen the name and moved on in search of a boozer as they were convinced it was a hardware store. Another place at the far end of the mini-square was called Ambiorix. It was immediately clear to everyone that this had to be a boozer as they recognised the name as that of a Celtic chieftain of the Eburones tribe who gave Caesar a hard time during his Belgian adventures in the Gallic wars of 55 to 50 BC. Like General Patton, none of the Toon Army top brass goes anywhere without his trusty copy of Caesar's *De bello gallico* commentaries.

In all the fun of the day that was in it, we had barely noticed the passage of time and were shocked to see it was already getting on for four. Ah well, one more pint and then we would make our break-out. Two lads standing next to our little group were thinking along the same lines. They only had one ticket between them; but showing great foresight they had made a colour photocopy thereof. It would not fool a barcode reader of course, but a quick flash should be enough to get through an initial police cordon. And you never know, maybe there would be such confusion at the ground that the two of them would both get in thanks to the bluff. Remember how the Don (may his name be always ... oh, never mind) got into our Marseilles semi-final after being relieved of his ticket by a pickpocket who ostensibly just wanted to exchange scarves? At any rate, I felt confident that if a bunch of Toon Army wallahs ever found themselves locked up in Colditz, there would be enough resourceful people among them for us all to make a home run. Good show, chaps. Carry on.

By now it was well after four and high time to make a move. So we did. Rick had a cunning plan. He had already sussed out a *bona fide* taxi firm earlier in the day. Why not ring them and get picked up at a café just outside the main central area? Great idea. So we tappy-lappied for about ten minutes and entered a suitable café, the Cambrinus, or maybe that was the name of the brewery, which of course was also suitably stowed out with the Toon Army. Rick rang the taxi man, and the message was he would pick us up in about forty minutes. That would be at half past five. Plenty of time for the seven o'clock kick-off, we reckoned. My round!

***

There was some great singing going on, including the proper version of the 'Blaydon Races', 'Bertie Mee said to Joe Harvey', 'We've got Terry, Terry, Terry, Terry Hibbit on the Wing, on the Wing' ... Great stuff, but time kept flying by. Rick called the taxi man, again. He would be there in ten minutes. It was now about a quarter to six. We got talking with a Toon fan from deepest and darkest Yorkshire. He had a ticket but not a clue how he was getting to the ground. Obviously someone who like us believed in forward planning. No problem, it's a seven-passenger taxi, you can come with us. That makes six of course.

Five to six, still no taxi. Barry reckoned that, if we decided to walk to the ground, we would have to set off no later than six to have a realistic chance of getting there in time for kick-off. Oops, someone had just got another round in. It's your call, lads, said Rick. Another phone call to the taxi man. Another ten minutes, said he. We had passed the point of no return, and the taxi was now our only option. We could all see the funny side of this and were mentally preparing to return to the *Grote Markt* to watch the match on the big screen. That would also be fine. Another call. He's definitely on his way! A Toon wallah with a ticket was watching our shenanigans and shaking his head. He very sportingly gave his ticket to Rick for free, reckoning our chances of getting there were not very good, and he was staying here with his marras anyway. That's the spirit. I read somewhere while helping with some homework that philosophers had recently concluded that there was no such thing as a selfless act. Have you nothing better to do? Who, us? Yes you, you boring philosophers, you. Well, you'll have to think again as your theory was shattered at the Cambrinus bar in Bruges this Thursday evening.

Twenty past six now and we're standing outside the café on the pavement in the darkening lane, hailing vans that look like they could be a taxi, and then in desperation hailing cars. After all, it had worked for the Don after the Panionios match – but of course he didn't have a ten-foot long flagpole to help this time. One black van stopped. But it wasn't our taxi. In fact it wasn't anybody's taxi!

'Will you take us to the match for thirty euros?'

'Really sorry, but actually I'm working. Got to deliver some things.'

'Okay, fair enough. Fifty euros?'

'Sorry!'

'A hundred?'

'Look, I'm really sorry. Best of luck, okay?'

We could now hear a group of Toon wallahs inside the café, gloating at the window, singing (to the tune of 'there's only one Bobby Robson'): "You'll get a taxi in the morning, a taxi in the morning ...' This was funny, so I briefly went back in and offered my ticket for sale, but only in jest. Anyway, no one took it up. Just then, Barry shouted 'taxi's here'. Out I rushed again, accompanied by a stirring rendition, to the tune of 'pogo if you love the Toon', of 'You're gonna need two seats'. I managed to turn and give a three-fingered salute, indicating that in fact two seats would probably not be enough. 'Ha, ha – up yours, we're going to the match after all!'

So we piled inside and the head count showed that all seven were present and correct. Hang on a second, there were only six of us a minute ago, including our Yorkshire friend – who was holding his black and white teddy-bear mascot. Looking around the taxi, I saw a court-jester-style black and white hat, complete with jingling bells. Where had that come from all of a sudden? Apparently, we had picked up another straggler. But what the heck, we had a spare seat so were happy to oblige. It was just short of half past six by now as we sped through the inner Bruges labyrinth. Our driver, Jan van de Speedo, was confident we would be fine but we felt we were cutting it very fine indeed. Fair play to Jan, mind – he weaved and he wove, threading through the lanes of the old quarter like a knife through butter. No doubt his ancestors had been Flemish weavers.

A few drops of rain – or maybe it was spilt beer – glistened in the streetlights' yellow hue to complete the early evening atmospherics, and soon we were out of the maze and onto the broader boulevards. Our spirits were gradually lifting, and with Poppy Day around the corner and in honour of Clive Dunn, who had died the day before at the age of ninety-two, we all joined in to sing 'Who do you think you are kidding, Mr Hitler?' Still in that nostalgic vein, we followed up with that old Colonel-Bogey-tuned favourite: 'Hitler has only got one ... (rhymes with wall), Göring has two but very small, Himmler has something sim'lar, but poor old Goebbels has no &@!!s at all'.

***

Oh dear, now we're in a traffic jam. And it's almost a quarter to seven. Jan left the shops and car showrooms of boulevard world and took us through a residential housing estate and then out into the open again. That must be it over there. But no, a false dawn. We reckoned the floodlit fortress had to be a prison or something of that sort. Rhymes with clucking bell. A final burst of speed down a main road, and there it was to our right. Everybody chipped in their money and out we piled and ran.

But of course we had been set down at the end for the Toon fans so Barry and I still had an obstacle or two to overcome. We decided to play dumb. Barry was soon a few yards ahead of me and he got past the police checkpoint with ease. But they looked at my ticket a bit more carefully. Maybe we had overdone the deep cover with the Bruges scarf. And maybe we were now out of our depth and the game was up. For a second I clung on to the hope that they would say just go ahead, but no. In any case our tickets would not have passed the barcode test at the Toon gate. So we were escorted to another gate, which was the one our tickets were for. And lo and behold: no barcode scanning. They just waved us through! Colour photocopies would probably have done! We were in and didn't even have to go to the seats with our ticket numbers, which were in the front row of the upper tier, directly above the Toon over-spill section. It was anything but full and we had a few seats empty on either side. So in the end I really did get the three seats I wanted for comfort!

***

The match was only a couple of minutes old, so we really hadn't done badly at all in the end. Newcastle for some reason were still playing in what were pretty much Borussia Dortmund's fluorescent yellow and black colours. Would the black and white stripes have caused a colour clash? We don't think so. It took us a while, what with all the non-regulars, but we worked out our team was made up of Krul, Coloccini, Williamson, Tavernier, Anita, Bigirimana, Marveaux, Tioté, Obertan, and for the first time starting together, the Ameobis. So this was hardly our first team, but maybe good enough to get us a result.

It was difficult being under cover, but we bravely managed to contain our enthusiasm when the Toon had the ball, and when we attacked we were able to applaud, pretending we were admiring the good defending. *'Goed verdedigd,'* we said in our Dutch-with-a-Geordie-accent Flemish. Two others of the Toon fraternity had run out of luck, however. It seemed that Bruges fans had rather unsportingly drawn the stewards' attention to the presence of spies in their midst and there was a lot of gesticulating going on. But when the stewards arrived it was a case of smiles all round, with the

Toon agents putting their hands up and saying it was a fair cop, and it looked like our brethren were merely being repatriated to the Toon section under the terms of the Geneva convention. Let's hope so. So we still had to be on our toes, but all the while sitting down of course. It was particularly difficult for different reasons when the goals went in. For their first, which came on the quarter hour, Trickovski ran on to a long through ball which was kicked straight down the pitch in our direction. Coloccini was in pursuit and appeared to drag him back, but the Bruges player shrugged him off, controlled the ball and side-footed it into the middle of the goal with Colo stranded and Krul wrong-footed. Right under our noses. Then just five minutes later, Tavernier dived to head out what might have been a good clearance except it went straight to a Bruges player, Jørgensen, standing about twenty-five yards out. With no one near him, he had time to stop the ball and studiously drill it without any great power straight along the ground and into the corner of our goal, evading Krul's fingertips. Everybody around us was jumping up and down, but still our cover held. When the Bruges fans were singing to the more international football tunes we were able to join in, singing our own verses and nobody seemed to notice in all the noise and excitement of a vibrant and hard-fought match.

Looking around the ground it was blindingly obvious that all the Toon fans in town could easily have been accommodated inside. Huge areas of seating were embarrassingly empty. Embarrassingly empty for Club Bruges, that is. In fact the next morning's *De Standaard* was to tell us that there had only been 19,000 in the ground, out of a capacity of 29,000 or so.

Now is that disgraceful or is that disgraceful? Yes it is. And it is also totally pathetic and, what is more, insulting. Is Club Bruges barking mad, and the local police and the local municipality as well? There would have been no need to go to the expense of setting up the big screen and providing all the extra security! Even on the afternoon of the match they could easily have sold tickets to our brothers and sisters in and around the *Grote Markt*.

Bruges were strong all right and probably deserved their two-nil lead. But they clearly were beginning to run out of steam and starting to think of a half-time rest when the Toon began rising to the occasion and we struck twice in two minutes up at the far end of the pitch. Our first with five minutes to go till half-time was also

Anita's first goal for the club with a beautifully-executed volley from the edge of the penalty area. It was a bit similar to Bruges' second goal as one of their defenders headed the ball out of their area straight to Anita who made no mistake with his shot to the keeper's right. And while we were recovering from trying to suppress our cheers and pretending to look disappointed with the Bruges defending, Shola and Sammy worked their Ameobi magic with junior dribbling through to the edge of the area before working a pass through to the on-rushing senior sibling to poke the ball into the left hand corner of the far-distant Bruges net. Should we jump up and shout? Wheyaye man! We couldn't resist, but we tried to pretend we were jumping up in exasperation. No one around us gave us a thought as they were all too busy shouting abuse at their team for letting go of a good lead.

With the score at two's apiece at the half-time whistle, we felt sure this was going to be like one of those man u games where the mancs go two nowt down and go on to win something like seven-two. Except in our case it would be a deserved seven-two victory of course. We were wrong. Of course.

Getting a half-time pint afforded an interesting insight into cultural differences in Belgium. Instead of queuing up to buy a drink, we first had to queue up to buy drinks tokens *(Drankbonnen)* and then had to queue again to exchange our tokens for beer.

After the shock of them going ahead, and the double hammer blow to the Bruges hopes, the black and blues fell apart and got very nervous and it was a surprise we didn't score a few more. Shola was having one of his inspired European nights and had a couple of good headers, and when substitute Cabaye came on in the final quarter of the match, he curled a free kick onto the crossbar. Our anticipated flood of second-half goals for the Toon failed to materialise despite a lot of pressure and a succession of corners and two-two it was to remain to the end. Though some sloppy, dodgy defending could have betrayed us a few times. But on the whole Bruges got very nervous and misplaced loads of passes. It was, as always, difficult to contain yourself when we went very close, or almost conceded another goal ourselves, but we survived and the natives were very friendly.

Funny that one of the Bruges favourite chants is 'Come on the Bridges' spoken in English, plus they have another one which is basically the same as 'Toon Toon Black 'n' White Army', so we sang along with that one. With about quarter of an hour to go, we threw our cover to the wind and started shouting for the Toon in broad Geordie. Our neighbours probably thought it was some obscure Frisian dialect, which may not be too far from the truth.

On the final whistle we were of course allowed out straight away with the Bruges fans while the Toon Army was kept in for twenty minutes of detention as usual. As we filed down to the exits the Bruges fans in our end were sportingly applauding the Toon Army immediately below. And this was reciprocated by the Geordies. I overheard one Flemish woman say to her husband '*Ze zijn echt sportiev, hé*?' ('They are very sporting, aren´t they?'). Right she was. And then the Bruges team actually came over and applauded the Toon fans too. Never, ever seen that before. Fantastic! *Echt sportiev!*

***

After stopping for sausage and chips, still within the stadium compound, we set off on our longish walk back into town, already going over plans for our next outing, to Bordeaux in early December. It had been a great couple of days in Bruges. And in fact I was staying in town till Saturday morning. As we got to the *'t Zand* district, Barry headed to the station for his train back to Brussels, and I made my way back to the *Grote Markt* and back up that alley to the pub opposite the Belgian Beer Pub. Peter F. and Pauline had repaired thither after watching the match on the big screen. The Don joined us twenty minutes later and so (after he had warned us not to talk any Godfather s#1te) we all joined in the general post-mortem, the upshot of which was that it was a good point for us. There was much talk of plans for travelling to France, and songs old and new were sung and sung again. One particular one took me back into the Leazes End in the early seventies. To the tune of the Black Velvet Band:

'They call us Newcastle United – they say we're the cream of the land,

And here's to Bobby Moncur, the Fairs Cup in his hands!

We're better than Glasgow rangers, we're better than Celtic too,

And if you don't support us, you must be a sunderland ...

Joe, Joe, Joe Harvey. Joe, Joe, Joe Harvey.'

We heard that Bob Moncur had actually been spotted in Bruges that afternoon. So again we sang the praises of the Fairs Cup team.

Then of Supermac, Terry Hibbit, Alan Shearer ... One fan bared his back, which featured an impressive tattoo of Supermac himself. Rick had told us about being awe-struck when he went into Supermac's pub in Worthing. And was served by the Great Man himself, his childhood Superhero. SUPERMAC! SUPERSTAR!

It was getting late, and time to head back to the NHS hotel for a good night's sleep. I briefly wondered if I would even have to pay anything, what with everything being free on the NHS. Even the mini-bar?

***

Next morning, the Toon Army still had a huge presence in town, with black and white milling around, frequenting the cafés, visiting museums and buying presents for loved ones – maybe the first Christmas presents among them.

I texted fellow Cuth, Toon and Celtic fan, Wilf, to say 'Greetings from Bruges. Not a bad couple of days. A well-deserved Europa League point for the Toon and a huge Champignons League victory for the Celts over Barcelona. By the way, who are Glasgow's third division club playing this weekend?' Wilf texted back that he wasn't sure but he thought it might be Pitlochrie Postmen, newly promoted from the Clackmannan Sunday League.

Happy Days!

***

So we had seen Bruges in all its glory and not been arrested after all for not having a ticket for the local cinema where they were showing, well, *In Bruges*. And yet by Saturday morning I had spent three nights in a cell – the NHS hotel is a former monastery, remember?

Now it was time to start thinking in earnest about Bordeaux. Actually, the travel and accommodation had already been finalised about a week before the Bruges game. All we needed now were the match tickets ... *plus ça change*, as they say in Monkseaton (so Biffa reckons).

Bruges v Bordeaux – 22nd November 2012

Couldn't find a B and B

Do you ever go to watch football games where one of the teams is not Newcastle? Even rarer, do you ever go to a football game when Newcastle are playing at the same time somewhere else? (Against Maritimo at home.) No! Well, I did, but it's just not the same, is it? I used the next one on my sausage-string of three Bruges Europa League home-leg match tickets that we'd bought as a mini-season-ticket, as that was the only way we had been able to get into the Bruges v Toon match.

It's an hour's drive from Brussels to Bruges if you stick to the speed limit of a hundred and twenty kph (about seventy-five mph) as religiously as all Belgians do, cough, splutter, *nom d'un pipe*, so I left home at about a quarter past seven on a bitterly cold November night. It might even have been Thanksgiving. We'd stuffed both of these turkeys at home very convincingly, and by the end of the night the European hopes of one or the other would be burnt to a cinder while the other would be *coq*-a-hoop. But which one? Did it matter to us? Not really.

The ring road around Brussels passes through Anderlecht, the arch-rivals of Club Brugge, old Fairs Cup opponents of Newcastle, and the scene of Alan Shearer's European début for the Toon in a pre-season friendly arranged as part of the earlier deal which had brought the greatest living Belgian, Philippe Albert (everyone knows his name), to Newcastle United. Anderlecht also has the best-looking cooling tower in the world at its Drogenbos power station. It is covered with thousands of bright computer-controlled coloured lights which they sequence to turn the tower into scenes such as Christmas trees with snow falling on them or tonight's theme of swirling and swelling blue waves on a stormy North Sea. Would this be the story of tonight's match – waves of blue-clad Bruggers attacking a Bordeaux rearguard?

We've probably told you before that the French and Flemish parts of Belgium don't much like each other. The only people the Walloons, the French Belgians, dislike more are the French French, and the only people the Flemish (Dutch-ish) speaking Belgians dislike more are the Dutch. But one thing they agree on is that neither of them likes Brussels. They have this in common with most of Europe at the moment, if you believe what you read in the papers from just about any European country and on the lips of a lot of politicians. This mutual dislike manifests itself in a childishly comical way in the road signs. In officially bilingual Brussels, the signs give the town names in their French and Flemish versions, but very often one of the names has been spray-painted out, leaving only the language of the spray artist readable. Raiding parties of linguistic zealots set out at dead of night into enemy territory to do their duty. The local police never seem to catch anyone red-handed with blue, green or white spray paint on their trigger fingers. And as I leave the *métropole* tonight and head into Flanders' fields and the town of Bruges, the French names miraculously disappear altogether and all that remain are the Flemish versions, this time courtesy not of the paint sprayers but of the Flemish government: in Flanders, Flemish is the only official language, so we'll have no French at all, *merci beaucoup*. Whoops, sorry, I mean *dank U wel*. Hence Gand/Gent for Ghent becomes Gent only and Bruges/Brugge becomes strictly Brugge. Even more childishly, some towns just drop off the map completely, as if someone doesn't want you ever to find your way to one of their enemy towns. For instance, you need to search high and low to find a road sign in Antwerp that admits the existence of a town called Bruxelles/Brussel/Brussels. Many was the time before the existence of GPS that I drove round and round the innards of Antwerp, vainly trying to find a way out that would lead me in the general direction of Brussels.

The road is packed from half-past seven to half-past eight, even though it's long past end-of-work time, with single-occupant cars heading home after a day's honest graft in the capital, sitting maddeningly in the middle and fast lanes with nearly no one in the slow lane. It's enough to make most English people feel really at home. There were so many people dawdling along in the middle lane instead of moving over that I spent the whole trip in a slow-moving queue in the fast lane. After an hour of this boredom, the GPS directed me off the motorway and within five minutes I was skirting around the south side of the stadium and multi-pitch training ground complex, looking for a car park in the salubrious suburbs of southern Bruges. I found a nice road-side spot in a row of cars, but when I got out I saw police stickers on two, but not all of them, saying that they shouldn't really be parked there, but not actually giving them a fine. Now that's what I call a good parking ticket. I mulled this over for oh, maybe two milliseconds, and thought I too would take a chance. It would give me something to wonder about on the way back to the car after the match – would it still be there, or would it have been towed off to some far-flung Flanders field full of forfeited Ford Fiestas? It's not as if I have never had to retrieve it before.

I was glad I had my Bruges Europa Tour 2012-13 scarf so kindly provided by Pete as it was parky out. I found that there was a well-drawn NUFC badge on the end of it, so I wrapped it around with that end most visible. Unlike for the Toon match where we hadn't needed to go through a barcode-reader turnstile, this time I had to, to gain ingress to the stadium grounds. Once you were inside the perimeter fence, you could basically go anywhere you felt like trying. In contrast to the corporate food and drinks outlets of Premiership stadia, the Bruges ground had the welcome sight and slightly sickly, savoury smell of stalls selling fast-food frites, fricadelles and frankfurters. I decided to forgo the frites till half time. On the other hand I could have done with a mug of steaming-hot Bovril to hold and warm my hands on, but that particular aspect of British civilisation has somehow never caught on with the continentals. You couldn't get any tea or coffee either – it really was freezing now and the last thing I wanted was frostbite off an ice-cold Jupiler. I made my way up to the top-level of Block 424, right behind the goal and had a look at seats fifteen and sixteen in row one. Such was the attraction of this match that I'd not found anyone who even wanted a free ticket, so I could sit on both seats.

The view was bad, impeded by the yellow safety barriers right in front of me. And beyond them was a big net screen and barriers to stop the ball sailing out of the ground and into suburbia. As it turned out, they could easily have done away with the net and barriers if they had known how few shots at goal there were going to be during the match. In the pre-match practice, however, the net came in very handy when all the first eleven and all the subs on the Bordeaux team took pot shots at goal. They had about two or three shots each, so it must have been around fifty attempts and they only scored twice. The rest were high, wide and unhandsome. It was a good taster for the match, as apart from their two successes they had a lot of chances which they fluffed. But at least they were better than the shower from Bruges.

The turn-out from Bordeaux was penned in over to my right and in very good voice, so to get some away-day atmosphere and because there were so many empty seats in my section, I shifted over to be beside the separating fence. The Bordeaux fans seemed a good bunch, and I was looking forward to going down their way for the Toon away leg.

I wasn't to know it at the time, but future January acquisition, Yoan Gouffran, was not in the team or even amongst the substitutes for Bordeaux, so he didn't make any impression. The match had hardly begun when Bordeaux came down to our end of the pitch and scored through Jussiê, their Brazilian striker, who got in first on a cross from the right. With five minutes to go of the first half, Jussiê took advantage of a lapse in concentration by one of the Bruges defenders and raced away one-on-one with the goalkeeper to slot away his second. He had looked nowhere near as impressive against us. It was looking pretty easy for Bordeaux, but then Bruges suddenly were attacking and Odjidja smacked a volley against the Bordeaux crossbar. And straight after it was half time, frites and mayonnaise time. If you've never had Belgian frites, you're missing something. A Toon chip, even a Seahouses one, can't hold a candle to a double-fried, crunchy, flavoursome, Belgian frite. Very few chips can hold a candle.

Bruges stirred themselves and were a bit more effective in the second half and they even had claims for a penalty, but this was waved away by the referee. They had to do something because otherwise they were going out of Europe, but Bordeaux contained them with ease and could themselves have scored a third goal. It came as a bit of a surprise when a couple of minutes before the end Bruges got a consolation goal through Lestienne, who took advantage of a poor back-pass by a Bordeaux defender to go on and score.

By the way, when I got back to where I'd parked the car, there it was, safe and sound and without even a polite police warning stuck under the wiper blade, so I was back home in good time.

In good time to find out that, back at the Toon, we'd somehow contrived only to draw one-one with Maritimo. Marveaux had opened the scoring for us mid-way through the first half after being fed through by Ben Arfa. The game seemed to change when injuries forced first Ben Arfa (even though he was replaced by Demba Ba) and then Cissé off, and Maritimo began to threaten our goal. Sammy Ameobi spurned a chance to put us two up and then Maritimo got their goal through faithful substitute Fidelis and that was that, we'd drawn against them again, even with a much stronger team than we'd put out over on the island of Madeira – Krul, Coloccini, Santon, Simpson, Taylor, Anita, Ben Arfa, Bigirimana, Marveaux, Cissé and Sammy Ameobi.

This meant that Bordeaux had leap-frogged us and were now heading Group D. We'd both qualified but it would be good if we could repeat our home leg victory over Bordeaux and be seeded for the knock-out Round of 32. The stage was set.

Bordeaux away – 6th December 2012

Blissful meanderings and a smelly nun

Setting off from Trier, it was a very cold and frosty morning. The five o'clock taxi to Luxembourg's central station cost an arm and a leg, but hey – shrouds and their lack of pockets and all that... And whether you spend your money on following Newcastle United around Europe or on lining the pockets of bankers, wherein ultimately doth the difference lie? Anyway, the first train out of Trier wasn't until 5.45 and was scheduled to get into Luxembourg at 6.31, leaving just nine minutes to scramble through that station to catch the 6.40 to Paris, and I wasn't going to take the risk of there being some delay occurring due to frozen points or whatever and causing me to miss that connection. The streets of Trier were virtually deserted and the *autobahn* to Luxembourg was not much busier, and so the taxi got me to the station in Luxembourg in more than good time. In fact I was ridiculously early, well in time even for the 6.11 TGV (*train à grande vitesse* = high-speed train), which would have given me a better time-cushion for my dash across Paris from the *Gare de l'Est* to *Montparnasse*, but my cheap-skate super-duper special offer ticket was valid for the 6.40 train and the 6.40 train only. It was a wee bit chilly as I paced up and down the platform to kill the time. Once safely on board and warm again, there was plenty time to doze and reflect on recent events. As the TGV slid majestically out of Luxembourg City and gradually picked up speed as it approached the French border, I recalled a recent text message.

The tide had turned, someone had claimed after that twelfth minute Demba Ba penalty had been awarded against Wigan, with their offending player Figueroa being sent off for fouling Cissé, who on his current form might well have shot wide anyway. And on the final whistle after our three-nil win, another highly apposite text message reminded us just how deftly we had ended an unplanned and unwanted run of four straight defeats in the Premiership against West Ham, Swansea, Southampton and Stoke. Our last victory had been a two-one win over WBA at the end of October. The message included the words: 'a sterling performance against the ten-man Northern Premier League high-flyers.' This huge victory probably meant that we would now go on to finish in the top four and win both the FA Cup and the Europa League. In fact we would probably never be beaten ever again (I see that the range of crisps sold by the buffet car of this sleek SNCF train includes 'extract of porcine wing' flavour). The tide had also turned in the Cuths Old Boys predictions league, by the way. My policy of always predicting a Toon victory and a mackem defeat was beginning to pay dividends. I had accurately predicted the mackems losing two-one at Norwich and correctly forecast that we would beat Wigan, though I got the actual score wrong. That meant I had gained three important points and moved up to third bottom.

***

These TGVs really are something. The scheduled journey time from Luxembourg to Paris, stopping only at Metz, where the train from Strasbourg is coupled to the Luxembourg one, is just two hours and eight minutes. As we left Metz, however, we were told by a Tannoy announcement that we would get into Paris about ten minutes late for some reason, so I had to think about whether to take the Metro or fork out on another taxi ride to be sure of getting to *Gare Montparnasse* in good time for the 10.20 to Bordeaux. If a more serious delay caused me to miss the connection, SNCF would of course let me on a later train as it would be their fault, but I wanted to see as much of Bordeaux as possible before the match, so I had to get the timing right in Paris.

Can that be the outskirts of Paris already? Yes it can, because the announcement says we will be arriving at the *Gare de l'Est* in a few minutes. It is 9.07. So yes, we are running a bit late and a taxi it will be. The outer *banlieue* is replete with medium-rise blocks of flats. So many shoeboxes stacked high and side by side. The bright but skittish winter sun was giving us a glistening suburban frostscape, softening reddish and yellow into coffee and croissants. The sleepers were now visible and no longer asleep on this December morning. As we slow right down in our approach to the station, the *fin de siècle* apartment blocks look a lot more attractive than some of the buildings near London's main line stations for example. Everyone in the carriage is getting ready to alight. Many of them are carrying just a briefcase, come to Paris for a day's business and returning to Luxembourg on an evening TGV no doubt. Small wonder that Luxair has seriously reduced its Luxembourg to Paris flights. Hard to compete with such fast trains. And you don't have to report at the station an hour before departure as you do at the airport. Unless of course, like me, you voluntarily get there ridiculously early. And of course you don't have to undergo those over-the-top security checks.

***

Out of the train and into the throng of the late rush hour. A rush of suits, briefcases and clickety-clack high heels dancing to the rhythm of sweet-smelling perfumes and singing life's long song.

The friendly African taxi driver pulled out into the busy Parisian streets and threaded our way to *Montparnasse* in about half an hour. There was a sign for *Saint Germain des Prés*. Sounds so good. Hadn't been in Paris for a while, and it's always a pleasure to take in even its more mundane sights. People having their coffee and croissants in the cafés, sitting at neat, burnished metal-top tables or standing at the bar, *le zinc*. Young women with pushchairs and baguettes, the newspaper kiosks advertising *Paris Match* and *Vogue*. We have just passed a *tabac*. Reminds me of my very first trip to France back in 1973 (there you go, time again). The ferry from Newhaven slid past the harbourside cafés and those French textbook pictures came alive in road and shop signs, and even in the smell of the *Gauloises* that hung in the air from the moment you set foot on French soil. The police wore their uniformed-Clouseau hats and stood, filled with their Gallic self-importance, on street corners. The cars were all French, some sleek and elegant, some tin-corrugated and battered, and some even a wee bit underworld-sinister with menacing big but half shut headlamp eyes. Yellow-tinged of course. Long-gone days. Now, the taxi I was in was a Merc and overall the cars in the streets were about the same mix you find in just about any western European city, France having finally given up its dogged struggle against the Asian auto-invaders. We have reached a degree of sameness in Europe, no doubt about it. But Paris is still Paris and France is still France.

***

The *Gare Montparnasse* was seeing off the tail end of the rush hour when I boarded the Bordeaux-bound TGV, whose final destination was in fact Arcachon on the Atlantic coast. More on the subject of French geography anon. We pulled out bang on time at 10.25 and were scheduled to arrive at *Bordeaux Saint Jean* at 13.32. A phenomenal journey time – France is a big country by European standards but these high-speed trains make the distances very manageable indeed. It was nice to have the prospect of three hours of stressless relaxation.

It was an interesting thought that the Toon Army would be converging on Bordeaux not only from Geordieland but from all over Britain and Europe. And it wouldn't be at all surprising if we met some fans who lived in France, maybe in Bordeaux itself. Just as we had met locally-based Toons in Slovakia, Greece, Belgium, Portugal and the Netherlands.

On the ticket front, we were well sorted. Chris had got two and, as Sarah unfortunately could not make this trip, he offered me his other ticket. Barry had ordered one and was going to pick it up from Steve Storey just as we had in Athens for the Atromitos match and in Funchal for Maritimo. The Don likewise had sorted out his ticket needs in advance, so that was one worry we would not be having on this trip, i.e. the uncertainty of actually getting to see the match. Barry's train would be getting into Bordeaux an hour or so after mine and Chris and the Don were taking the same flight from Gatwick, which meant they would be in town at around four. Barry, Chris and I were in the same hotel, the Best Western Bayonne Etche-Ona, and the Don's hotel was nearer the *Saint Jean* Station. As usual there had been a bit of confusion about the hotels. I had gone through a travel agency out of sheer laziness and had told Barry it was the Best Western. He found out there were two Best Westerns and in the event the other one was where the team was staying, the Best Western *Le Grand Hôtel de Bordeaux* just around the corner from ours but a lot grander. I belatedly told Chris that there were two, but he assured me he had also booked at the one with the funny name. Yes, *Bayonne Etche-Ona* certainly is a funny name, and as Chris said in an e-mail: try saying that after a couple of Kronenbourgs.

The last time I had taken a train from Luxembourg to get to a Toon match had been for that semi-final in Marseille(s). What a great trip that had been. But a very disappointing two-nil defeat of course, both goals coming from the boot of Drogba, as I recall. Tonight's match would be nowhere near such a tense affair, as both sides had already qualified for the knock-out stage of the competition. But coming first in the group had its advantages as it meant avoiding those teams that dropped down from the ever-mushrooming champignons league. So it was not a totally meaningless game. Or maybe it was. But who cares? Certainly not I. Our main hope was that we would also be going somewhere nice, and in particular safe, in the next round. We were not wildly keen, for example, on the idea of travelling to Russia or (the) Ukraine (luckily, a lot of even worse places had already been knocked out – Manchester City to name but one). Mönchengladbach or Genk would be far preferable. And after my stay there in the summer, I quite fancied the idea of going back to Bucharest.

Once clear of Paris, we were really picking up speed and clocking up the clicks. The Parisian suburbs had been replaced by rather flat countryside dotted with the odd small village. The TGV really is brilliant – just over three hours from Paris to Bordeaux. How long did it take before the high speed trains came on the scene, I wondered. Surely at least twice as long. It occurred to me that Paris was like London in terms of its main line terminus stations. The *Gare de l'Est* was Liverpool Street, the *Gare du Nord* was King's Cross and *Montparnasse* was Paddington. More or less, anyway.

***

We are more than half way to Bordeaux now and the passing countryside has gone from flat to a wee bit rolling and back to flat again. I am not sure what I was expecting because my geographical knowledge of this part of France is a bit vague to put it mildly. I think I was half expecting to catch a glimpse of the *Massif Central*, but clearly I was way out on that score. Even the layout in my mind of where towns and cities in England are located is pretty much dependent on whether or not Newcastle have played there. Hence I could probably pinpoint Hereford on an unmarked map. But Milton Keynes? Sorry, I haven't got a clue. My knowledge of France's political geography, on the other hand, is predicated on whether or not I have ever been there. And this was going to be my very first visit to Bordeaux. And here's a sad confession: I actually thought that it was on the coast. But no, this train's destination of Arcachon is on the coast, about thirty miles beyond Bordeaux. I knew of course that the origin of the city's name is *à bord de l'eau* but I thought that the *eau* in question was the Atlantic Ocean. In fact it is the Garonne river. Mind, in fairness, it is quite a wide river, and is even a bit salty as it is tidal up as far as Bordeaux and beyond.

I was beginning to feel the beginnings of inspiration thanks to a combination of the sunny December countryside and a pint of Kronenbourg, from the buffet car where a group of Toon Wallahs were making similar purchases in a bid to become acclimatised as soon as possible. So I decided, when back in my seat, to text Barry, Chris and the Don as follows:

'Wonderful TGV bang on time. ETA at funny-name hotel 14.00 hours. All set to dance in the West of France.'

The Don replied from Wetherspoons at Gatwick that he was taking some pre-flight medication. As he put it, 'Easyjet as carrier always a concern.' Then a text from Chris to say he had just checked in at Gatwick. So I was able to tell him, from a TGV speeding through France, that the Don was expecting him to come and pay his respects in the bar there.

And what's the news from Barry?

Well, Pete, did I tell you that I wrote to the Bordeaux club to see if we could have media accreditation on the basis of our two previous Toon books? Surprisingly, they haven't replied yet, and I suppose it's a bit late now.

What a wonderfully interconnected world we live in! And what fantastic railway infrastructure the French have put in place. We take our *chapeaux* off to them. France has always seemed a bit strange in some ways, but they certainly get the high-tech stuff absolutely right – from TGVs to nuclear power generation, to space-age facilities launching Ariane rockets.

But what is this? The TGV is slowing down just as we are passing through Poitiers, and has now stopped. This was not in the script and we are not in the station. Oh dear, a signal problem somewhere along the line, according to the announcement. Was my ETA over-optimistic?

And then this message from Barry: 'My TGV had a suspect package left on the platform at CDG, so fifteen minutes delay.' Plus: 'Nice lady beside me, probably a nun but smelly like a tramp so went to buffet car to take a breather. Literally a sprinkling of Toons on board too.' Tell us more, Barry!

Well, it had been blue skies all the way until a grey-dressed cloud loomed and fumed on the horizon. My reserved seat – you have to book a seat on TGVs, by the way – just so happened to be beside what I can only describe as a very stinky nun. She was unfortunately a devout follower of the order of nuns that forgoes soap as a penance not for themselves as they're well used to it, but for all those who sit beside them. And I was supposed to stand this for six hours? Hey, hey they're the monkeys, but I'm not a believer.

So I took a four hours, thirty minutes breather in the buffet car until Poitiers, where I managed to get a couple of nice empty seats at a safe distance.

And Pete, did you hear that the Toon team plane got caught up in the snow at Woolsington and they only got into Bordeaux pretty late last night and without a chance to test the pitch, and instead they'd trained in the snow at Benton. The rumour was that Alan Pardew would be putting out a pretty young team, as would Bordeaux too probably, knowing that this game was a formality as we had both already qualified.

***

Oh no, my TGV had once again come to a halt, and in the middle of nowhere to boot. Could that smelly nun have something to do with it? I was nun too sure. After all, I had heard they have very strange habits. But we are on the move again – a false alarm, thank goodness. I was able to text Barry that elements of the Toon Army had also been spotted on my TGV, and by a remarkable coincidence they had made their base in the buffet car, just as they had on his train. Ah, another announcement. The second unscheduled halt had also been because of signal problems, now resolved. Be that as it may, the points were set, and we were well on track to set in train a marshalling yard full of European victories.

We were now rapidly approaching *Bordeaux Saint Jean* station. The countryside had stopped its gently rolling nonsense and was back in dead flat mode. Any hope of catching a glimpse of the *Massif Central* on this trip had clearly disappeared for good. I really should have paid more attention when we did France in geography lessons.

Arrived at last in Bordeaux. I was quite knackered and decided to get a taxi to the hotel rather than mess about with the trams and buses. A costly mistake – twenty euros' worth. The taxi driver took me the scenic route along the river and into the old quarter. Clearly a seriously beautiful city whose imposing sandstone buildings exude almost Swiss-style wealth and prosperity. The wine-growing industry must be a very profitable one. We turned into the alleyway next to the very posh *Le Grand Hôtel de Bordeaux*, where he reckoned the Nottingham Forest team would be staying, though I think he meant NUFC. There was the funnily-named hotel. But when I got to the reception I learnt that there were in fact two funnily-named hotels with the same funny name, but fortunately the other funnily-named one was on the other side of the block, only about two hundred metres away. I checked in and promptly crashed out. I was cream-crackered. Back over to you, Barry.

***

My train was just pulling in. When you get off in *Bordeaux Gare Saint Jean*, it is not readily apparent which way you should be heading to get to the city centre as the station is in a pretty nondescript part of the town. But a friendly local put me right and advised me that I'd be far better off buying a 1.40 euro tram ticket rather than taking a taxi. He also needed to show me how to use the ticket machine, which seemed to be designed for use by locals only as it gave no explanation at all, and you have to have a ticket before you get on the tram as they don't sell them on board. It's a very nice trip along the banks of the River Garonne to the old part – the *Vieux Quartier* – of Bordeaux and the city-centre stop '*Quinconces*', which is in a wide square, the *Place des Quinconces*, populated by *platanes*, French plane-trees. The square featured Bordeaux's equivalent of the Haymarket's Dirty Angel to make us feel more at home. And still the sun was shining, its afternoon golden light raking diagonally through the ordered ranks of trees.

Just around the corner, for the first of three times this trip, I bumped into away-regular John who was one of the hundred and twenty or so on the club-organised day-trip and who would be back home by one o'clock tonight – a real referee's-whistle-stop tour. And speaking of tours, the Tourist Information office was right beside us and there, between dreamy phone calls, a very foxy lady assistant recommended a Bordeaux wine-tasting tour run from just opposite the tourist office by the CIVB, the *Centre d'Information des Vins de Bordeaux*, as a bonus to showing me where our hotel was, hidden down a little side street. Must try that wine-tasting next time.

Just around the corner, I chanced upon (now ex-) NUFC managing director, Derek Llambias, sitting at a pavement bar on the other side of the broad street from the team hotel, and chatting with a bunch of Toon fans. He certainly hasn't picked up any Geordie to smooth the rough edges off his barrow-boy speak, that's for sure, but he was very friendly and relaxed. Let's hope he took notice of the 'Don't sell Cabaye' song at the game later. A shake of the hand, an exchange of best wishes, and a photo opportunity – I am sure he will treasure the picture for ever.

Thanks to a bit of manoeuvring by the helpful receptionist, we all ended up in the same half of the twin-site hotel, which made things easier. I then rang to Pete's room. Meet at reception in ten minutes. And there we learned that *Etche-Ona* is Basque for 'good house', so we'd obviously chosen well. The Basque country actually sits on both sides of the Franco-Spanish border, starting not far south of Bordeaux.

We rang Chris's and then the Don's number, but there seemed to be some problem with the local network. We wandered a bit through the streets of the old quarter. Found a club shop and bought some scarves and woolly hats. Interestingly, a couple of the streets were called *cours*. For example, the team hotel was in the *Cours de l'Intendance*. Neither of us had come across this sort of street name in any of the French-speaking towns and cities we knew. Surely a local thing, maybe related to the Italian word *corso*, also a kind of road or street.

***

We thought why don't we give NUFC Head of Security, Steve Storey, a ring just in case he was still at their hotel? It might make it easier for him if we didn't disturb him later on when he was at the stadium and with a hundred other things to take care of. This suited Steve fine and we met up in the very plush reception, telling the *commissaires* who were guarding the hotel's revolving doors that we had an appointment with the Newcastle United officials. It's not often you can say that. Great to meet up with Steve again, and we told him we hoped to see him again in the next round – 'somewhere in Europe'; we could be no more specific than that, but hoped it would be in equally congenial surroundings. Steve told us that the team would soon be leaving for an early trip to the stadium, so we decided to hang around outside and await developments.

A small crowd of mainly Geordies had gathered in anticipation of the team's departure, so we joined them. In rapid succession Chris and the Don rang. Chris had checked in at the hotel and would be with us in a few moments and the Don was on a tram, centre-bound. We told him to look out for the stop called *Quinconce*s. Half way between here and there, on our left, was the Christmas market. Opposite the *Grand Hôtel de Bordeaux*, as mentioned, was the *Grand Théâtre*. The square in between, crossed by tram tracks, was well populated with Toons, locals and tourists. Barry wisely cautioned the Don that if he wanted to ask, for example, how many stops it was to *Quinconces,* he should at all events avoid pronouncing it *Quinze cons!* (Fifteen idiots, to put it politely.) Whoops, too late apparently, he already had – much to the bemusement and amusement of his fellow travellers. 'Well that's what it sounded like to me, *joli garçon,* he breezily told us when he joined our merry little group a few minutes later. We were now a two-deep crowd waiting outside the hotel, and the police were moving us back, so the team would surely be appearing shortly. Time was moving on, after all. It was now after four and it was a seven o'clock kick-off.

***

Various locals asked us what was going on. When we said we were waiting for our team, some asked '*rugby ou foot?*' This was not a football town, as we found out time and again. Imagine people in the centre of Newcastle not knowing that a football match was being played. Kind of unthinkable, really. But we saw very few people wearing what looked like their football club's colours. Isn't it funny the way the French adopt English words and then get them only half right. *Le foot* is a prime example. And I remember a French colleague once commenting about the fact that a female client we'd been dealing with had been wearing *baskets.* Well I know I don't pay that much attention to what people are wearing but I thought I would surely have noticed some baskets! Where was she wearing them? On her head? Or had she been wearing basket-shaped ear rings perhaps? But then the *centime* dropped and I remembered that by *baskets* the French are literally referring to basketball shoes, but in fact just mean any kind of trainers. Phew!

***

In one bizarre encounter, a nice petite lady of a certain age, on hearing that it was a football team we were waiting for, informed us that she preferred *le rugby* and that she herself once was an *aileuse* or winger. We asked if we could make up the numbers for their next match but that kind of got lost in translation. Then two very pretty Irish colleens asked us what was going on. We told them Tom Cruise was about to come out of the hotel. Okay, it was a bit of a porky – he had actually been there about four years earlier in a film which involved riding a bike, from what I recall – but it did prolong the conversation with two delightful characters whom we were to meet again the next evening.

The team coach pulled up and all the players appeared out of the revolving doors and just as quickly disappeared into the bus. The emphasis on youth was confirmed by the sight of evergreen young prospect, Shola, getting on board – he could be some player some day, given the right opportunity.

After cheering the coach on its way, we headed off down into the pedestrian streets again, in the general direction of Toon HQ which, according to the text message I had received from Paul English, had been set up in the HMS Victory Pub, down in *Place de la Victoire* at the far end from the team hotel. And was it throbbing. It was so stowed out, up to the gunwhales in fact, that no one could get in until someone else left – I am sure some people's feet were not even touching the floor, it was that packed, and the decibel level of the singing was tremendous. We tried our best but just couldn't find Paul, just like in Bruges. He certainly had a tale to tell about his travel to and from the game. The travel out had taken long enough – train to Edinburgh on Tuesday afternoon, Easyjet flight to Geneva on Wednesday morning and then a delayed Easyjet to Bordeaux, meaning that he didn't get into the city until well past midnight. But that was nothing compared to the nightmare return because of the snow affecting so many planes. Paul's was so late leaving Bordeaux that he missed his connecting flight out of Geneva and had to stay there on Friday night and then take a morning plane to Liverpool instead of to Edinburgh, where he and his three fellow-travellers ended up in a taxi all the way from Liverpool back home (which was actually cheaper than the extortionate prices charged for last-minute train tickets). What devotion to duty!

But Paul couldn't even tell us the half of this as it was impossible to see him anywhere in the thronging masses or hear a phone ringing or talk to anyone on a mobile even if they did pick it up, so we got our beers and stood outside in the triangular square between the Irish pub and the Victory, where even more songs were given an airing. One soloist, Keith, came up with a razor song that no one could join in with. The less said the better. But he also had some really good songs too and was in very fine voice. His friends made us an offer we could refuse, 'Here's some money, take him away with you!'

***

The Toon Army inside a net cage in the Renzo Barbera stadium, Palermo, Sicily.

Palermo 0 - NUFC 1 (Luque) with Tim Krul and Andy Carroll making their débuts.

Pav behind bars in Palermo.   Peter Lee.

Colo lifts the Algarve Cup.

The Estadio Algarve in the evening sunlight.

Algarve Toon Army.

Atromitos 1 - NUFC 1 (Ryan Taylor).

The Toon 48 at Atromitos.

After the Atromitos match.

Steve Storey with three happy Atromitos ticket-holders.

The Toon Army at Maritimo.

Maritimo 1 - NUFC 1 Just look at the home-made lettering on the scoreboard.

Mags from Worthing and everywhere congregate in Bruges main square.

Bruges 2 - NUFC 2 seen from the home supporters end.

In the little Bruges square that the Toon made their own.

Bruges: a carpet of plastic.

Bad news – no tickets left in Bruges.

Toon Australia.

Bordeaux at half time.

Bordeaux 2 - NUFC 0 The match itself was not the best thing about this trip.

Derek Llambias pre-match in Bordeaux.

Bordeaux best banner winner.

Bordeaux Toon Army.

Bordeaux post-match salute to the Toon end.

Stade Bordelais pre-match.

Clive courtesy of Toon Time Travel.

Down below in one of Kharkiv's many cellars.

It was now high time for us to be making tracks. We didn't want to get into the ground at the very last minute, or rather in the first minutes, as we had in Bruges. We headed back down the busy pedestrian shopping street to find the tramline to the *Stade Chaban Delmas*, named after a world-famous-in-France possibly socialist politician. The ticket machine was a bit like the ones in Brussels with a jog-shuttle circular knob to select what ticket you want, then you push and it asks you to put in a very reasonable sum of loose change. For a while we became unofficial and ill-informed Bordeaux tram guides as no one had a clue how to get the machine to let them buy a ticket. A single ticket costs the same price as an all-day ticket, but only on the condition that you never click it in the machine on the tram. No one else did, so on the way there we didn't know we were supposed to and on the way back it was so chocka that we couldn't reach the clicker machine.

In Bordeaux the trams don't have numbers but letters (I am not a number, I am a free letter). I think the one to the ground was a 'number' E, for 'Escaped Prisoner' maybe. The tram arrived and it was already fairly packed. We reckoned the next one would be too, so we literally squeezed on. It was very much a Toon-dominated tram, but there were a good few Bordeaux fans as well and there was much good-natured banter. Plus there were plenty of ordinary Christmas shoppers who had been blissfully unaware that there was a match on. They knew now, but I think I heard one ask *c'est pour le rugby?* We had been told in town that it wouldn't be a very big crowd as the game was being shown live on the telly. Yes, it's that kind of place. It was on that sardine-packed tram clanging its way through the late-December-afternoon but Christmas-illuminated streets that we first heard the Toon Army mournfully singing, to the slowed-down tune of 'Achy Breaky Heart' a song that went: 'Don't sell Cabaye, Yohan Cabaye. Just don't think you understand, if you sell Cabaye, Yohan Cabaye, you'll have a riot on your hands.' (We must be deaf as someone told us they were singing it in Bruges too.) Clearly there was something going on. We knew that Arsey Whinger's arsenal had its evil eyes on Demba Ba, but was Cabaye also in the shop window?

More got on at the next stop and the one after that. One local lass was getting a bit claustrophobic and everyone gallantly made way to let her alight. Half-way to the ground, the tram came to a stop because a fat man was blocking the door. As you might guess, he came in for some 'Who ate all the pies' abuse and 'Hoo man, hey man, make your mind up, get on or get off'. But he seemed genuinely wedged in. Luckily no one tried to give him a push to help him on his way out, as it turned out that he was a plain-clothes Bordeaux policeman. There were loads of Edgar Wallaces who apparently were looking for someone in particular (obviously that Escaped Prisoner who was for the time being still free) and held us up for about fifteen minutes until they decided that whoever they were looking for was not on his way to the match with us.

Finally, we arrived at what had to be the stop nearest the ground, as all the locals got out, and we all happily filed off in the direction of the stadium only a few hundred yards away. There were a couple of *bistros* in the very shadow of the ground, but they were completely stowed out, so we would be going into this match with only the merest modicum of sedation. Not what the doctor ordered, at all.

At the stadium, which like SJP is still nicely located within the streets of the town and not on some out-of-town building site, the police were directing us to a little street where the away fans' entrance was. Once through the turnstile we could buy those fifty-fifty scarves that we like to collect. They were selling for only five euros, which is half the usual price, and you got both halves. These were added to the Bordeaux scarves we had bought earlier in the club shop in town while waiting for Chris and the Don to arrive.

We then followed the crowd up the steps and into the *Stade Chaban-Delmas* itself. Some Bordeaux fans were also trying to get into the away section to get some more of the European atmosphere but the police spotted them and sent them off further round the ground. Our tickets told us we were in the *Virage Nord-Est,* so that was already a good omen, or so we reckoned. In the ground, it seemed like there was only one entrance to the stand, up a flight of stairs from ground level where there was only a simple little bar and some toilets, so everyone first made their way up there, all squashed in together and with no view any more. But then when you took a look around it was obvious that there were other away sections but we must have missed them so we went back down the stairs and tried again until we found ourselves another way in, bypassing the toilets. Bypassing was the thing to do as they were disgusting – after all this is France and that is their one blind spot – with only one door in and out so that the people pushing to get out were making others who were still busy over-balance into the urinals. Others were using the over-flowing wash basin, Basel style. Not good. *Et où est le papier?*

***

Once in the North-East Curve, we made our way up to the back of what turned out to be the pretty packed lower tier of seats (not that any of us would be sitting of course) looking diagonally at the corner flag with quite a decent view of the pitch. Looking around to get our bearings, we spotted the Other Clive and the Other Peter at the front of the upper tier but out of earshot to our right. Through universal sign language we got someone to nudge the Other Clive and we all gave each other the thumbs up. The ground was only about half-full and the rumoured twenty-thousand attendance looked like a big over-estimate. The home fans call themselves the Bordelais, I think, though it sounded more like the Bordelaises, but that couldn't be right as that would be the women's football team. They also were chanting the same GSB slow chant with a big cheer at the end that they had been doing at SJP. It sounded good.

Our team had a bit of an unusual look to it which made us think that maybe Alan Pardew didn't really mind all that much whether we were seeded or unseeded in the next round: Elliot, Williamson, Perch, Bigirimana, Marveaux, Shola, who was captain for the night, Sammy Ameobi, Ranger, Ferguson, Tavernier, and Abeid. At least the bench included Krul, Coloccini, Anita and Cissé. The Bordeaux side was also far from their strongest, and as a measure of how they were approaching the game they had only named five substitutes for the bench.

***

The match itself was crap. We lost two-nil. The singing was great, as were the various flags on display. One read 'F**k the Recession, we're on a session'. More of the Cabaye dirge. And then, to the same slow tune: 'Don't take me home, please don't take me home, just don't wanna go to work. Ah wanna stay here, drink aal ya beer, please don't, please don't take me home.' Some lads had a valiant bash at *la Marseillaise* with some Toon words we couldn't quite catch. And of course we had 'Let's dance in the South of France.' I had expected the West of France, but let's dance, not quibble. It really was all Bordeaux in the first half and it was only a great double-save by Elliot from a pair of close-range shots that stopped them from going ahead in the opening minutes. When they eventually scored it was only what they deserved with Diabaté rising high above our defence to head a cross from the left just inside the back post for their opener after half an hour.

At half time we went down to queue for some beer, but found they were selling Amstel 'Free'. The initial euphoria gave way to the realisation that it was not free beer at all. Rather, it was alcohol-free beer that was completely free of anything remotely resembling taste, as witness the three-quarters-full placky glasses that people had left standing on a ledge next to the counter. And they were charging five euros a glass. No way!

***

We decided to head for the next compound along towards behind the goal, where we had spotted lots of empty spaces, albeit lower down again, in fact almost at pitch level. On the way to the access gate to that section a young lad approached Barry and asked if we had written Toon Tales. It turned out that Andrew Thompson's dad had given him the book as a Christmas present when he was little and he had loved it. It inspired him to follow Newcastle in Europe if he ever got the chance. And here he was, following Newcastle in Europe. This was encouragement indeed. We took a group photo and promised to send Andrew a copy by e-mail but the picture came out blurred. Luckily we met Andrew again in Lisbon and explained the problem with the picture and managed to do a good one that time. So thanks, Andrew, and we hope you enjoy this book too, featuring your picture as promised.

Standing on the seats in the lower section we had a pretty good view of a pretty dismal second half. At least Shola had a bit of a go with a couple of shots. Running into the penalty area, he effortlessly controlled an aerial forward pass from Bigirimana and his left-foot shot would have brought the equaliser if it had not ricocheted off the Bordeaux keeper's shin and run wide to the right of the goal. The crowd was indeed disappointing, as we had been led to believe it would be, but as Bordeaux gained control (and they weren't offered much resistance) their supporters finally rose to the occasion and the two ends of the ground joined in some impressive end-to-end canon-like chanting and singing. It reached a crescendo with about a quarter of an hour to go when Diabaté raced onto a lofted clearance from deep inside the Bordeaux half, brushed aside a challenge from it looked like Williamson and walloped the ball past Elliot for his second of the match.

The ground itself was none too impressive. A wholly unnecessary moat or ditch, complete with barbed wire fence, separated the crowd from the running track that detracted still further from the general atmosphere. It looked like a whitewashed French municipal stadium from maybe the thirties, long on drawn out curves but short on cover for the fans. A bit of a throwback considering the excellence of SJP facilities nowadays. But there are those of us who remember the good old, bad old days of no cover at all in the Gallowgate and Popular, including in the bogs.

At full time we were kept unnecessarily in detention as usual, and to their credit the team and Alan Pardew came over and applauded their long-suffering following. Reminded us of the time when Barry Venison came over and really apologised for the team's lousy performance in a game at Selhurst Park in the Gullit days. Not sure now whether it was Palace or the Wombles and I think we lost something like two-nil. Never mind, throughout the second half the Toon Army incessantly chanted 'Ruud Gullit's Black and White Army'. So frenzied did their mantra become that at times it sounded like 'Through your teeth, Black and White Army'. Crikey, I saw Supermac make his league début at Selhurst Park when Palace beat us two-nowt. But that was forgotten a week later when he scored a hat-trick against Liverpool in his home début and was carried off semi-conscious and with a bloody nose. That's the kind of gladiators we want!

The next morning's local paper, the *'Sud Ouest'*, was to tell us that nine out of Bordeaux's starting eleven were home-grown graduates of their academy and that it was very far from their first-choice team. There was quite a humble quote from goal-scorer Cheick Diabaté in which he mentioned that he's been the target of whistles and abuse from their fans, but that he was getting his head down and doing his best – 'I know I'm no Messi,' he said, after his first chance in the team for two months. We also learnt that this was the first time after eight tries that Bordeaux had managed to beat an English team in European competition. Strange to say, it was also the first time since 2007 that they had not started a match with a Brazilian in their line-up. And on the money side, the paper told us that Bordeaux had made 2,800,000 euros out of winning the group with four wins and a draw, which meant that we must have made around 2,500,000 euros for coming second. All this was covered in a page and a half – it wasn't the multi-page minutiae we found in the Portuguese and Greek papers. They use those spare pages to drone on about *le rugby*.

We were being guarded by CRS riot police. The rank and file of them looked calm and almost friendly despite their impressive body armour and truncheons and shields held ready. They would not have looked at all out of place in the arena of the Coliseum in Ancient Rome, or even Whitley Bay's. But their captain or whatever he was had a mean and nasty look on his face and clearly would have preferred to see his boys in action, wading into the Toon Army. But we were not going to be provoked by his posturing. We follow the Toon around Europe to have fun and soak up the local colour, not to get beaten up. As we were milling about waiting to be released we bumped into the Other Clive, the Other Peter and Alan from Gateshead. We reminisced about past European trips and counted out the places where we had also bumped into each other. Everyone was pretty gloomy about tonight's match. And Alan from Gateshead said he thought he was at the crossroads. Oh no, we had a crisis of faith on our hands here. We all go through them from time to time of course. But this sounded particularly serious. The crossroads, eh? That's when you either go straight ahead, or turn left, or turn right, or even go back to where you came from, right? Fortunately, one or two of the lads standing near us were dressed as nuns (what, more of them?) and they immediately offered to pray for Alan from Gateshead over a pint or two. Well that was the crisis of faith sorted.

The Other Clive and the Other Peter were planning to go to a match between Stade Bordelais and Niort in the eighth round of the French Cup on Saturday evening. Did any of us fancy coming? Yeah, I quite fancied that, particularly as I had missed out on a Zulte Waregem game after the match in Bruges.

On the way out of the ground we stopped for a chat with Mick Edmondson of the Back Page, the finest sports bookshop you could ever want, who was busy marshalling his Back Page tour party onto their coaches to get them back to the airport for the trip home. It's quite a responsibility counting everybody out and counting everybody back, especially when 'party' has been the operative word on the tour, but he was doing it all with, as ever, a big smile on his face.

Out of the stadium at last, we made our way to the tram stop. It was so crowded that we decided to walk to the next stop, during which stroll we were passed by several trams and the one we finally boarded was only half full, so it was a very comfortable ride back to the centre.

A la recherche du fromage perdu

We were feeling quite peckish by now so we started to look for a restaurant. After some false dawns and very expensive menus on display at entrances, we happened upon *Le Garage* a few steps down from street level at *4, Place du Palais*, an unpretentious, almost Spartan place with equally unpretentious prices. Could have been Blyth.

On the menu they had one of the local specialities, five-star triple-A *andouillettes*, which are boiled sausages made out of something very like, and probably tasting very similar to, varicose whatsits. Nobody ordered them. Long ago, I made the mistake of ordering *andouillettes*, thinking it was some kind of bird, an *alouette* probably, and got a surprise when I was dished up a sweaty sausage. So instead, we all ordered the *potage du jour,* a nice warming vegetable soup that was very welcome after several hours outside on this quite cold December evening. For the main course, the Don, Barry and I ordered the *pavé d'agneau* with roast taties while Chris had *coq au vin*. Both the lamb in the *sauce bordelaise* and the chicken were excellent, as were the *Merlot* wine and the *Pelforth* beer (one of the few excellent French beers brewed outside the still suspiciously German-seeming Alsace region).

The restaurant was fine, and we recommend you go there, but there was just one WC for the whole place. So, man or woman, you had to wait your turn. This is one of the things we just cannot understand about France, and you often find this same problem in what are otherwise really nice bars or restaurants. As we have seen, the French excel at the high-tech, *haute couture, haute cuisine* and *TGV* end of things, but they sometimes let themselves down in such basic areas as proper and adequate toilets.

But let's dwell on the nice things instead. After the excellent main course, the menu offered a dessert of appetising-sounding cheeses, which would go great with the remaining wine. So we ordered a selection of cheesy comestibles, only to be told they had run out. *Le Garage*, it appeared, was a cheese-free zone tonight. What? *Pas de fromage?* But this is *la belle France*, you have over four hundred and fifty varieties of the stuff. General de Gaulle said so. You have got to be joking.

'Eet eez no joke, ah am afraid,' said Arnaud, our friendly and concerned waiter. *'But ah weel geeve you a teep. Go to ze place called L'Autre Petit Bois, ah used to work zere. Tell zem Arnaud sent you and you will 'ave your cheese.'*

Ah well, fair enough, we must go to 'the other little wood'. Arnaud took us half the way there through the rabbit warren of streets in the *Vieux Quartier*, past a beautifully floodlit *château* gate and pointed us in the right direction. How could we fail with a personal recommendation and letter of introduction from our excellent waiter?

After another couple of hundred yards we reached *L'Autre Petit Bois* and on being ushered in by the welcoming staff, we saw to our great surprise that there was indeed a tree growing inside this small and tastefully candlelit *bistrot*. Cramped, slightly shabby but in a spotlessly clean, stylish way, sagging armchairs, none matching. And oh, the clientèle. *Oh là là*, they really made the difference; the place seemed to be frequented mainly by very pretty young ladies. (If there was anyone else in the joint, we didn't notice them in any case.) Sat at one particular table were four of Bordeaux's finest visions of loveliness, all dolled up in an impeccably stylish way. Just perfect. It would take something truly spectacular to prise us away from here. What they thought about us cheese-crazed middle-aged gits suddenly appearing on the scene, goodness only knows. Be that as it may, on the scene we were, and very much *dans le marché pour le fromage de la belle France*. And it really did turn into a re-run of that Monty Python sketch.

'Sorry sir, we 'ave no cheese.'

'But Arnaud sent us. You know, wink wink, nudge nudge, Arnaud, the lad who used to work here.'

'Arnaud, eh?'

'Yes.'

A quick phone call.

'Sorry, but no cheese.'

Well we couldn't help it: we had to say things like 'not even some runny Camembert?' And yes, 'How about Argentinian beaver cheese?'

Over four hundred and fifty types of cheese were popular throughout France, but apparently not in these parts.

'Well okay, we'll just have some wine. What do you recommend? The *Médoc Château Noaillac* 2008? Sounds good to us.'

And what did they bring with the *vin rouge*? You've guessed it – a generous plate of cheeses and cold meats, standard accompaniment with any bottle of wine served on these premises.

At last, we had found *le fromage perdu*. Our *recherche* was over. Our spirits were uplifted. What was the score again? I think I heard someone say we won two-nil? Yes, we must have done. But our thirst for the local wine wasn't *perdu* and we had a couple of bottles more before we left this excellent establishment at around one thirty in the morning with a view to hitting the hay.

The Don asked if the last tram had already gone. Our charming waitress suggested he might like to wait for the first one instead. And possibly with that thought in mind, the Don persuaded us to enter a student pub we happened to find just as we were about to head for our hotels. We naturally put up a lot of resistance as *Mademoiselle Bordeaux* beckoned us once more into her welcoming bosom. The place was crowded and playing loud music, old and new, into the wee small hours. The kids seemed not to mind the presence of such aged visitors and quickly began practising their English on us. They were a hospitable bunch, slinging their scarves around your neck to grab your full attention to talk to you. They were happy they'd won and sorry we'd lost when we told them why we were in their town tonight and they were even happier that they had nearly no lectures to go to later that morning. The Don kindly got in a round of Pelforth, but not the Pilsener variety this time. It was a special *bière de noël* – Christmas beer, if you please. The Germans do something similar. They call theirs *Nikolausbock*, a strong dark beer produced by various breweries around the feast of Nikolaus, or *Saint Nicolas*. It goes without saying that he is very closely related to Santa Claus. So *bière de noël* it was that we took as a nightcap to round off this wonderful day. Pity about the game and the result, but as you know by now, they are only two of the many facets of the Toon Army diamond.

The bar staff saved us from the temptation of having a second by announcing that the bar was now closed. It was two o'clock. There was the usual sort of post-closing-time gathering on the pavement, and everyone wished the Toon well for the rest of the competition. And a delightful young lassy gave us a wonderful insider tip. 'You know, tomorrow evening you should go to a place called *le Monseigneur*. That's where *mon papa* and all the older people go.'

We pondered that as we headed for our hotels, and decided we should keep it for next time. A vague plan was forged to meet at the *Marché des Capucins* at ten thirty. I vaguely said I would quite like to lie in till about twelve.

***

The next morning arrived, as the mornings after the nights before have an irritating habit of doing, and I was awakened by a call on the mobile from a chirpy, cheerful and frustratingly wide-awake Don at about ten thirty. 'So where are you guys? I'm here at the *Marché des Capucins*. It's a really interesting place, it's the Bordeaux Grainger Market but without the Robinson's bookshop, yous should get yer arses over here.'

'Er, sorry Don. Still in bed, mate. You could, er, maybe try giving Chris or Barry a ring. I don't think I'll manage to get over there, mate. See you next time, in … well, somewhere in Europe.'

And with that I felt suitably contrite and went back to sleep for another hour or so.

***

It was a guilty moment for me too, Pete, when not so bright but early, I was woken by the phone call from the Don, who was the only one who had stuck to the rendezvous at the old market. In my mind it had been a faint hope, but the Don is made of stronger stuff and had stirred himself out into the autumn rain and was already sampling the recommended breakfast at the market. I really felt guilty about letting him down and having to admit that I was still in bed and just couldn't face getting up already to trudge through the rain. I'd have to save that for next time too.

***

It was just after midday when I got down to reception. There was Barry already, busy paying his bill. He had to catch a *TGV* back to Brussels leaving *Bordeaux Saint Jean* in the mid-afternoon, so still had time to have a bit wander around the toon with Chris and me. And there was Chris getting out of the lift now. As we had all three of us missed the hotel breakfast, we decided to set off in search of something to eat. Being creatures of habit, we decided to head back to the nice square where we had been the night before, the *Place du Parlement*, and after asking for directions from a friendly passer-by who asked us in turn if we had been here for a rugby game, we discovered that in fact it was only about five minutes' walk away, as opposed to the thirty minutes it had taken about ten hours earlier after I had convinced Chris and Barry that my internal radar and homing mechanism were virtually infallible (well it did get us back to the hotel, albeit by a circuitous route).

We got to the square and saw we had a wide choice of venues, not counting *L'Autre Petit Bois,* which was actually not yet open. 'The other little wood', I'm sure the Other Clive would really feel at home there. Barry liked the look of the Parisian-café-style woven wicker chairs on the terrace of a particularly posh-looking place called *Chez Edouard* and we all agreed that was a good enough reason to give it our custom, but first we thought it would be a good idea to check whether we really could have just a breakfast-type meal there – we weren't all that hungry after the feast the night before. We asked if we could have cheese and ham toasties, and the friendly waiter, who later told us he was from Senegal, like Demba Ba, said a *croque monsieur* would be no problem so that is what we all ordered, plus three *cafés au lait*. Looking again at our posh surroundings we nevertheless had our doubts about such a place serving such humble fare at lunchtime. And when our waiter disappeared across the square with the look of someone off to do the shopping, those doubts became greater.

***

While awaiting the waiter's return, we took in just how nice and laid-back a place we had the pleasure and privilege of visiting. The square had four sides (like most, but not all squares) of impressive sandstone buildings whose upper floors were apartments in most cases and offices in others. The square itself was entirely pedestrian and lined at ground level by half a dozen cafés and restaurants and a sprinkling of small shops. Nothing gaudy or cheap, all affluent and nice, and the atmosphere was rounded off perfectly by a fountain and elusive plane trees.

Here comes our friendly waiter carrying a carrier bag and a big smile for us. Ah, well.

Here we were sitting on the terrace in very mild temperatures for early December, though it was trying to rain and we could hear the tentative raindrops gently tap-tapping on the big green awning above our heads. Then minutes later our waiter appeared on the terrace again bearing three giant plates filled with fried potatoes, some salad and toasties which turned out to be of the turkey variety. He'd obviously seen us coming as what we ended up with bore little resemblance to a *croque* of the *monsieur* gender, more a Fawlty Towers-style *croque* surprise – without the ham, without the melted cheese and without the big slices of bread.

We felt at first that we had been tricked into buying more than we had actually wanted or ordered, but after a few mouthfuls we thought ah, what the hell. It was very tasty indeed, and as so often happens we regained an appetite very quickly thanks to the appetising food. And when the bill came it was actually quite reasonable and we were happy to leave a tip as well. As we were settling up, six Geordies sat down at the table next to us, so we warned them about what was likely to happen if they just wanted (and ordered) a light snack. But they assured us as one: 'Nah, w'a starvin', man'. Well that was okay, then. They had come to the right place. Barry still had time to kill before his train, and as we stood in the square pondering what we could do with that time, two other members of the Toon Army walked or rather staggered past us looking a bit puzzled by their surroundings and as if they were still trying to walk off the vapours of the night's debauch. We knew the feeling.

After a minute or so of discussing our situation, we decided we could do a lot worse than simply tappy-lappy the twenty yards or so that separated us from *L'Autre Petit Bois*. So that is where we went. Well, when in Bordeaux, we thought, it would be a great shame not to taste some more of the local wine. So we sat ourselves down in some very comfortable armchairs, this time at the back of the place, in an arched cellar type part of the establishment, probably not Roman but certainly very old none the less, and ordered, well, more *vin rouge*. And lo and behold the bottle of wine appeared and with it a generous plate of *fromage* and *charcuteries*. This was the life, all right. We were as snug as a bug in the proverbial rug. The Germans, bless 'em, talk about such very comfortable situations as being *wie Gott in Frankreich* – like God in France. So clearly they think that if God were looking for a nice place to chill out and enjoy the good life, he would choose France. We could definitely see why. As the rain drizzled gently outside, we were quite content to while away another hour or so quaffing wine and nibbling at the cheese and cold meats.

***

By now it was getting on for three thirty and it really was high time for Barry to make tracks for the station and his train home to Brussels. So we said more farewells and Chris and I decided to have a walk along the broad river Garonne for a couple of kilometres and then double back towards the city centre. That would clear the old head of cobwebs.

We had arranged to meet up with the Other Clive, the Other Peter, Eileen and Liz at the Connemara, the Irish Pub at *18 Cours d'Albret*. There it was again, that word *cours* for street or boulevard. It really must be cognate with the Italian word *corso*. We got there a wee bit earlier than the appointed hour. It was actually closer than we thought – only a ten minute or so walk along the *Cours de l'Intendance* and then across the *Place Gambetta* and then a few hundred yards along the *Cours d'Albret*. The Connemara is a very authentic Irish Pub, to be sure. The décor, the tables and chairs and the bar counter itself could have been equally at home in Dublin or Cork or possibly even Connemara, and indeed the furnishings may well have originated from one of those places. We asked the friendly barman whether there would be live music on, and he said there would, starting from about nine o'clock, and he said there was no problem with people who wanted to have their own impromptu singsongs – just as well, really. We took our pints of Kilkenny and moved through the pub towards the giant screen that was showing a rugby match between Connaught and coincidentally enough, not-so-distant Biarritz. So we sat down just next to that. As we were taking our seats we were pleasantly surprised by two charming young ladies saying 'Hello again, how yiz doin'?' It was the two Irish girls we had met outside the team hotel the night before. And two absolute charmers and hilarious entertainers they were. Dark-haired Olivia (from Bolivia) would be getting married in a vineyard near Bordeaux next summer and she and fair-haired wedding consultant Jane were here on a pre-wedding reconnaissance mission. Their mission had actually already been completed and had been a resounding success. They were absolutely sold on this part of France and who could blame them? We all agreed it was pretty close to what heaven must be like if it is all it is cracked up to be.

Ah, there come Clive, Peter, Eileen and Liz, and Alan from Gateshead. Great stuff. Handshakes all round. Get the pints in. I'm fine. How about you? Grand. We'll get some more chairs. That's it. We're settled. What kind of day have yiz had? For a brief moment we thought the musicians would be playing in a different room (it's a big pub). So we made to decamp, only to discover that in fact they were just practising in that other room, so we all filed back and brought our chairs back with us to near the big screen. Jane and Olivia were delighted as Connaught were winning comfortably and they were not slow to remind the more boisterous Toon Army members present in the quickly filling pub that their team was doing better than ours had, and no, nobody was going to turn the feckin' rugby off.

Another couple of pints and Clive and I could not wait for the official music to begin. It was already about half past nine. And we quickly found we had overlapping repertoires. Before long our end of the pub was joining in with a full length rendering of the Blaydon Races and in honour of our venue we got through a good number of old Irish favourites such as Peggy Gordon, The Hot Asphalt, and The Black Ribbon Band. Jane and Olivia (from Bolivia) were very good singers and joined in enthusiastically. The official musicians started up at the other end of this big saloon room, so we just kept singing our own stuff and lots of people nearby joined in. In the lulls between the singing, the talk somehow moved on to Monty Python's Life of Brian and Pontius Pilate's vewy good fwiend in Wome, Bigus Dickus. Jane and Olivia (from Bolivia) were both word-perfect and hilarious. They were also into Byker Grove and Geordie Shore, and had our end of the pub splitting their sides laughing when they came out with 'Haddaway n S#1te, wa Geordies, ye knaa warra mean. Wheyaye man.' Pure Geordie with only the slightest trace of a Galway brogue. A perfect combination. Chris suggested it was Wheyayirish! And that became the watchword of the night. One Toon Army wallah was a bit the worse for drink but was really quite harmless in his attempts to chat the two colleens up. Chris and I told him we were their uncles and that he had better behave. He cleverly quipped that we would have our work cut out with those two. But the girls needed no help in putting him in his place. Irish tongues that could lash a man to his knees at twenty yards. It was all friendly banter, and this Tommy Cooper lookalike with a Lee Marvin voice gamely had a go at singing 'I was born under a wandering star'. This once again brought the house down. And when he found himself in would-be Tarzan mode one last time, Jane skillfully told him to get lost just like that. Not like that, like that. Bottle, glass. Glass, bottle. Also of the party was an ice-skater Christopher Dean look-alike Toon fan from Leeds who gamely joined in the jollifications and the singing, along with his more taciturn and serious-looking marra.

***

So a great night was had by one and all. The Other Clive, the Other Peter and I agreed to meet back at the Connemara again the next afternoon (Saturday) at three o'clock ahead of our trip to the eighth round French Cup match between amateurs Stade Bordelais and second division outfit Niort. So our happy little gathering said its farewells outside the Irish Pub and when we were satisfied that the lassies were safely on their way back to their hotel, Chris and I set off to ours. Clive, Peter and their wives had to retreat all the way back to Stalingrad, a district of Bordeaux on the other side of *la Garonne*!

***

Another lie-in was in order after another late night, but Chris had said he would have to leave the hotel quite early to get to the airport in time for his flight to Gatwick. In the event, Chris was busy paying his bill at reception when I came out of the lift there at about eleven thirty. It turned out that he had misread the printout and in fact his flight was not until two o'clock so he had plenty of time for breakfast in town somewhere. We had both missed the hotel one again!

Once again we walked along the *Cours de l'Intendance*, seasoned Bordeaux-dwellers that we had now become, and decided to go into the *Grand Café*, at the far end of the *Cours*, just before you get to the *Place Gambetta*, in search of breakfast. Chris's bus would be leaving from *Place Gambetta*, so the *Grand Café's* location was perfect. Just in case you are finding this confusing, just think of us moving away from the river and deeper into the city centre.

This was a nice *bistro*-type place, with lots of brass, *art déco* furnishings, waiters in white shirts and black aprons, that sort of thing. Altogether a very French, very civilised sort of place. It was well after twelve by now, and our waiter was genuinely puzzled that we could still be in the market for breakfast: a number of his colleagues were already sitting down to their staff lunch in one corner of the restaurant. Our previous day's experience notwithstanding, we asked if they did *croque monsieurs* (or should that be *croques messieurs*?). But no, they did nothing like that. So we settled for ham and cheese *bruschettas* – that was nigh enough as far as we were concerned. And two large coffees, *s'il vous plaît*. After our not so petit *petit déjeuner* we walked to the airport-bus bus stop and said our farewells, and off Chris sped to the airport. And now thoughts turned to the next match.

Stade Bordelais v Niort, the French Cup – 8th December 2012

L'autre petit Bordeaux

I was left with a couple of hours to kill before the appointed time to meet up with the Other Clive and the Other Peter back at the Irish Pub. Actually we had originally planned to rendezvous at the *Place de la Victoire*, but then we could not for the life of us work out what that name could possibly refer to, as no particular French victory sprang immediately to mind. So we decided we would meet up at the Connemara after all. To put the pre-rendezvous time in, I bent my steps back towards the river and took in the sights and sounds of a big French city on a Saturday lunchtime. People were going about their Christmas shopping. At the far end of our *Cours* I was back at the team's abode, *le Grand Hôtel*. Trams were clanging and whirring as they crossed right through the pedestrian zone. No one seemed worried by their presence. I headed towards the *Quinconces* square with its major convergence of those same trams and more. To my left on the way there, on the other side of the street, was the Christmas market. Smells of candyfloss and sweetmeats wafted over. I passed a huge queue outside a restaurant. It must be a seriously good restaurant with a couple of Michelin stars, because those people would not be getting in for another hour or so. Reminded me of how a mate of mine from Leicester had been astounded when he first came to Newcastle and for the first time in his life saw people actually queuing to get into pubs. The other thing that had him utterly confused was the shouting of the Chronicle sellers. What on earth was it they were shouting?

Past the Tourist Information Office and over the *Quinconces*. Then beyond the Dirty Angel to my left and into an antiques/junk/second hand market just this side of the river. Just about everything and anything was on sale. Books, old motorbikes and scooters, army surplus stuff, you name it. Another short walk along the wide, wide river itself and then it was time to start heading back to the boozer.

On the way there, I couldn't help noticing what appeared to be a rather significant police presence for what seemed to be a very peaceful city centre crowd going about its Christmas shopping. Or was there a big rugby match on today as well as the smallish football game? And it wasn't just ordinary coppers. The CRS riot police were also out in force again (as they had been at our match) and again they were all kitted-out with body armour, riot shields and nasty-looking truncheons. I asked the barmaid in the Connemara and she could not account for the number of Edgar Wallaces in town. Looking around the pub in the main room area where the big screen was, quite a crowd of locals was building up for a big French game, I spotted Torvill and Dean sitting in the same seats as the evening before. Had they stayed all night, I asked. No, but automatic pilot had guided them safely back to this homely hostelry as soon as they had had breakfast. And they wished they'd had that here too, judging by what was being served to several customers by way of lunch: great looking and smelling fish and chips, steak and kidney pie, that sort of thing. Yum yum. I fancied a quiet read, however, and I sat down with my shandy (last night had been a long session) and started reading the sports section of the paper in the section of the pub looking out on to the street and separated from the big screen by one of those tasteful glass partitions that would not look too much out of place as a stained glass window in church. Looking out of the window I saw another two cops on the other side of the road stopping the occasional car and checking the driver's papers. What on earth was going on? Was there some sort of specific terrorist threat to Bordeaux? Hmm.

***

The sports section of *Sud-Ouest France* (an aptly named paper I felt – after all, this *was* the South-West of France) was telling me that the Cup match we were going to was a huge occasion for *Stade Bordelais*. The city's newly promoted Cinderella club were playing their first season in the *CFA (Championnat de France amateur de football),* the fourth tier of French football, where they were apparently still struggling to find their feet. In fact they were currently in fifteenth place and were therefore fourth bottom. This evening they were playing the full-time professionals of Niort, a second-division outfit based just far enough away from Bordeaux to make today's match fail to qualify as a local derby, if you see what I mean – a bit like us playing Leeds, say, except a lot further down the pyramid (maybe Blyth Spartans playing Hull City). Stade were apparently expecting what for them would be a bumper crowd and hence also a bumper payday and we were happy that we would be making our own modest contribution towards promoting the well-being of the local equivalent of Blyth Spartans, a small club with a Cup giant-killing tradition well worth emulating. On balance, they thoroughly deserved our support. I'll let you into a little secret:

112

sometimes I wonder why I ever go to see Newcastle. After all, they didn't come to see me when I was bad.

The Other Clive and Peter arrived bang on time at three and Clive was a lot better informed than I was. Maybe I should have started reading the paper not in the sports section but in the local news. Because, as Clive said, there were two *huge* marches scheduled to take place in the centre of Bordeaux today, one in favour of gay marriage, the other against. Hence the massive police presence. Tens of thousands of demonstrators of both persuasions were expected. The marches would effectively cut off the bus route that Clive had discovered to take us to the *Stade Bordelais*. It was a funny name for a football club, we agreed. After all, *Stade* means stadium. Fancy a club being called, for example, Stadium Durham, or even Durham Stadium. Of course, there is that French rugby club called *Stade de France*. At any rate our task of getting to the Stadium Bordeaux stadium was now going to be that little bit more difficult than we had originally thought. And Clive had also asked the staff at his hotel in Stalingrad what they thought the taxi fare would be. Around forty euros was the answer – taxis in Bordeaux, it has to be said, really are expensive. But in any case we would first have to cross the centre of town in a southerly direction before even thinking about finding a taxi. It would be no good getting in one here and then getting stuck in a traffic jam watching the taximeter clock up a record fare. Be all that as it may, it was only just after three, so we had time to discuss tactics over a pint (a proper one this time, not a shandy, before setting off).

***

Now Clive and Peter are truly dedicated Newcastle United supporters and they have followed the Toon across the length and breadth of England and indeed Europe over not just the years but the decades. They make a point of extending their stays on European trips in order to absorb some of the local colour by going to games to clubs further down the respective pyramids. Hence their attendance after the Bruges game at Sint Pieters and Zulte Waregem (though of course Zulte play in the same division as Club Brugge, so that was a bit of an exception – so maybe they make exceptions in the case of the Toon's former European opponents). Clive is planning to write a book about these Matches on the Margins, and we really hope he goes ahead with that project. Even before it is written, we hereby heartily recommend it to one and all.

The map of the town told us that the *Stade's*, well, *stade* was in Bordeaux's *Bruges* district. Now this was spooky, we thought. After one trip to Bruges, here we were off on another. And after the match, Clive and Peter would of course have to get back to Stalingrad. Now there is a good pub quiz question for you: if you can get from Bruges to Stalingrad in about an hour or so, using only public transport (no rockets, no lifts on the International Space Station allowed), where are you? Answer: Bordeaux!

We supped up and set off from Connemara for Bruges, some ten km away (another good quiz question – the centre of which French city do you have to cross to get from Connemara to Bruges)? Cross it on foot we did and within a few minutes we saw that the demonstrators and marchers had indeed come out in force. We supposed that the riot police, who had no doubt been drafted in from other parts, much as Essex police had been drafted in to County Durham during the Miners' Strike, had been to our match on Thursday evening in the hope of getting some useful practice at beating up innocent people ahead of their main event, following the tried and tested model of their thatcherite colleagues. Thankfully, as noted above, nobody gave them the least bit excuse. Not that such people usually need any sort of excuse, of course. We had seen similar uniformed types at the game in Majorca, as regular readers will recall.

We were allowed through the police barrier to mince our way across through the marchers (we were under deep cover after all) and on to the other side of *Place Gambetta*, where the streets were eerily quiet for a Saturday afternoon so close to Christmas. There was no sign of any bus, or taxi for that matter. After a ten-minute walk, with Clive bringing his map-reading skills to bear, we came to a bus stop for the number six and other routes, and quite a queue had built up there. A young couple told us that they had already been waiting for twenty minutes or so and were about to give up waiting and start walking. But it would take us a lot longer than that to walk to the *Stade*, so waiting was the name of our game.

We must have cut strange figures for our fellow would-be passengers who looked on bemused as we spoke our broad Geordie dressed in our mixture of Newcastle shirts and Bordeaux hats and scarves! Probably not all that usual a sight at the suburban-route bus stops of inner-city Bordeaux of a December Saturday afternoon.

We waited and waited and still no bus came. At this stage we were prepared to take a taxi, but there was no sign of one of those either. But a bus did finally appear on the city-centre horizon and as it got close we saw it was not a number six but a number twelve. We decided to take it if it would take us at least part of the way to the ground. It was also quite a full bus but we managed to squeeze in. Clive and Peter had sensibly bought a twenty-four hour city ticket and I still had the unused tram ticket I had been unable to stamp on the crowded tram that took us to our match on Thursday evening. Hurrah, it was also valid for the buses and this time I stamped it. The friendly driver told us we could take this bus as far as a stop called *Barrière du Médoc*, cross the road and get a number nine to the match. Fine, so we looked at the route map and started counting down the stops. Mind, we were getting some very funny looks from our fellow passengers by now. I overheard one elderly chap saying to his wife, 'There must be a rugby game on somewhere.' *Allez le Stade*, I heard Clive say. Look up, the next stop was ours. The bus turned right at a crossroads and stopped.

The image of the crossroads at which Alan from Gateshead stood came back to haunt us. What a position to be in. At the crossroads, like. Which way should you go? Straight ahead? Or turn right? Or left? Or go back the way you came. Scary choices.

As we got out, the driver kindly reminded us that we needed to cross to the other side and hop on *le neuf*. And just to be sure we had understood, he repeated himself in English. *You take the number eight*. Hmmmm …

So there we were standing at the number nine stop feeling our troubles were over, and the timetable told us there was a number nine due in about five minutes. And we were well and truly in suburbia now, a few miles from the disruptions in the city centre, so the bus was bound to be on time. It was just after five, so there was nothing to worry about. Fortunately, Clive is the kind of guy who does worry about getting to matches in good time and who likes to check and double-check the details of things as the match-day process moves along. He was therefore studying his map again and suddenly made an important announcement: 'Lads, that last bus driver wants to send us back to Bordeaux's ground, ye knaa, the one where we watched the Toon play.' Well spotted, that Clive. It was true, the number nine would take us back to the Europa League, not the *Coupe de France*. We've said it before and we'll say it again now: Bordeaux is *not* a football town. People simply do not have that match-day awareness that just about everybody on Tyneside has. Imagine an away supporter asking the way to St James's at lunchtime on a Saturday match day afternoon. He would have to be really unlucky to find someone, like my railway-enthusiast brother Mick, for example, who genuinely would not be aware that a match was being played – even though you might think those thousands of people dressed in black and white and heading in the general direction of Gallowgate might provide a tiny clue.

Clive quickly sussed that we needed to go back to that crossroads, turn right and look for another bussing opportunity, or hail a taxi if one passed. We could not be more than about four km from the ground. Before reaching the corner we passed a café and thought it might be a good idea to use the facilities there. We weren't in the market for a drink, however. The moustachioed *patron* leaning on the bar as he talked to three or four regulars sent a malevolent scowl in our direction. Could we use ...? *Si vous buvez quelque chose, oui. Si vous ne buvez pas, non.* Cheers, *mon ami. C'est l'hospitalité française*, we supposed. Never mind, we could probably last out. No choice, really, we would have to.

We turned the corner (literally, that is, not figuratively), and there was a bus stop just yards away. And hey, here comes, half empty, our elusive friend, the number six Bordeaux bus. All aboard. My ticket was still valid for another twenty-five minutes, so there was no need to pay any more. Our prospects were looking brighter. And after about ten minutes in slow but steadily-moving traffic we alighted at a bus stop just after a railway underpass and could see the welcoming *Stade stade* floodlights decorating the low- to medium-rise suburban evening-scape not a five-minute walk away behind what appeared to be a garden centre. *On y va.*

***

As we got closer to the ground, we could see it was pretty much in the standard French *stade municipal* mould. Stands, or *tribunes*, running the length of each touchline but no actual Leazes or Gallowgate type ends that we could see from the street outside, separated from the ground only by a six foot white concrete wall. We went through the turnstiles and emerged in an open area leading on to the *Tribune d'honneur* stand for which we had bought our tickets, ten euros a head. Blyth Spartans type prices – though when Barry and I went there a few Great North Runs ago (the Toon were away on the Saturday) it cost ten quid a head, so in fact it was a bit more expensive than here at the *Stade stade*).

It had been amusing at that Blyth game (they lost to Tamworth, by the way) to study the adverts around the ground. One read 'Why not visit the Miners' Arms after the game?' Now there was a nice solid advert that appealed to my innermost instincts. The advertising people had thought that one out, all right. No doubt about it. Yes, a visit to the Miners' Arms, only a few yards away from Croft Park, was a distinct possibility after the match. It would round off the Blyth Spartans experience nicely. Another, much bigger advert straddling the centre of the far stand, read simply 'Port of Blyth'. Again we felt this was a well-crafted, thoroughly thought-out piece of advertising genius. In fact we overheard one OAP spectator sitting next to us (we had paid an extra pound each to sit) saying to his mate. 'Ye knaa what, Jackie, noo that aah come to think aboot it aah might just ship those three thoosand tons of steel via the Port of Blyth after all, and not via the Tyne'. 'Good idea, Jimmy. D'ye fancy a pint in the Miners efter the game?' 'Aye gan on, why not? Wor Lass'll still be oot shoppin anyhoo.'

***

There was a stall selling scarves and hats so we did our duty and bought our *Stade Bordelais* gear. And joy of joys, they were black and white! Perfect! And we were told that the club had been founded, a good while back of course, by English residents of Bordeaux. Maybe they had in fact been Geordies! Must try to find out somehow. Lots of people, young and old, were milling about around the souvenir stall and the beer stall a few yards away. And there in the corner in a permanent concrete nook you could buy chips and *saucissons*. We made a bee-line for the beer stall, one of these round things you often find on the continent. But we were told you had to go to buy some vouchers, so we did, and got enough for three lots of chips as well. There was such a nice friendly, almost family atmosphere about the place. It made a refreshing change from the unrelenting commercial pressures so tangible at the big games. The couple running the scarves stall had been delighted to learn that three of the Toon Army had stopped over to come and support a local amateur club, and very soon we were enjoying our new-found celebrity status among the home supporters. Quite a few were surprised that what we were talking was actually a form of English. It was certainly not a form they had ever come across before and definitely nothing like the English they had learned at school.

***

Our tickets were for the home stand, so after we'd finished our beer and chips we walked the few yards to the whitewashed cantilever and curved-roof *Tribune d'honneur*, which by now was quite full. We decided not to sit but to go up the steps to the top and see if we could stand behind the last row of seats around the half-way line. We could, and we stood there along with a few locals. The gangway at the back of the stand was a good two feet above the last row so we had a perfect view. We looked around the ground. No Gallowgate or Leazes, as we had seen. The non-Leazes End was a railway embankment, and there was a suburban train trundling past, gladdening the by now quite cold December evening with its warm lights. Then it vanished from sight, gone with a clanking, rattling railway sound. The non-Gallowgate gave a clear view out on to the road our bus had continued along after dropping us off. Houses, shops and blocks of flats in the middle distance.

***

A hint of mist was in the air, but just a hint. It was nothing the floodlights couldn´t handle. Opposite us, running along the other touchline, was the stand housing the away support. But there weren't that many obvious Niort fans, so it seemed that most of the few hundred on that side were also home supporters. That stand was smaller than ours but essentially of the same *stade municipal* design. On the pitch you could also make out faded rugby markings, so it looked very much as though this ground was shared with a local rugby club. In Germany too, e.g. Trier, football grounds will often be municipally-owned, which may limit clubs' scope for redevelopment, but on the other hand it does mean that the grounds are genuinely woven into the fabric of the local community – not an elitist, members-only setup. School sports days are held there, as are the finals of local Cups etc. What a great idea.

***

There come the two teams out onto the pitch now, accompanied by twenty-two ten or eleven year old boys and girls. The young'uns are wearing black and white striped shirts, but disappointingly the senior *Stade* team are all in white. Even more disappointingly, *Niort* are wearing all-chelski blue, and one of their number bears a worrying resemblance to our old 'friend' Drogba.

(Unlike Newcastle's game, this was a great match. So let's dwell on it.)

After some initial signs of nervousness, the home side soon settled down and got into their stride, kicking towards the non-Leazes railway embankment end to our right, by the way. There goes another suburban train, this time in the other direction. They were holding their own defensively and the plan was obviously to contain the 'superior' opposition for as long as possible in the hope of subsequently carving out some chances on the counter-attack. Soon, however, *Stade* were actually beginning to dominate play, much to the surprise and frustration of the second-division visitors. *Howay Stade*, Clive was shouting, and the locals were joining in, though they weren't quite sure about *Howay* and it came out more like '*oway*. But then Clive went totally native and we all started shouting and singing with him: *Allez les Blancs, Allez les Blancs, Allez ...*

And would you believe it, *Stade* were the first to get a clear shot on goal – a twenty yarder from former Niort player Kevin Bacle in the eleventh minute. More vocal support from the Clive-led locals, some of whom seemed to be continuing in their new language of Geordie: '*oway the Stade*. And their boys went from strength to strength, their confidence growing with every minute that passed. Niort hardly featured at all in the last fifteen minutes of the first half, with only one half-serious shot on goal giving the home crowd anything to worry about. There was a genuine buzz of excitement at half-time as people were beginning to believe that the underdogs could pull it off. The realists among them were reminding friends that the full-time professionals were bound to have the edge in terms of fitness. But the crowd could do its bit to spur the amateurs on. We filed down to the beer and chip queues and soaked up this wonderful atmosphere of local patriotism melded with expectations of a long Cup run.

The Other Peter and I had got a half-time pint in, so the Other Clive went back to our spot in the stand while we stood at pitch level supping our beer for the first five or ten minutes of the second half. We were dead-level with the Niort goal at the non-Gallowgate End and that was where all the action was headed. The other Niort old boy Nicolas De Gea shot wide after deftly rounding the keeper in the forty-seventh minute, and then Dia hit the post with a vicious fifteen-yard shot on the turn in the forty-ninth. The crowd could sense that a Cup upset was definitely on the cards. By the time Dupuy fired wide on fifty-seven minutes, it was clear that Niort had no answer to *Stade's* all-out-attack tactics, for that was what we were now witnessing. On rejoining Clive at the back of the stand, we heard some locals saying they hoped the greater fitness of the *Ligue Deux* outfit would not become the deciding factor. Would the amateurs inevitably run out of steam?

But a couple of shrewd substitutions brought some fresh legs into play and the crowd's chanting, still led by Clive, ensured that the entire home side remained on the crest of a wave and firmly in charge of this game. The woodwork got in the way again in the sixty-first minute when Roland hit the far post with a low drive from the edge of the penalty area, but the team's sterling efforts were duly rewarded just two minutes later when a well-crafted move that had started with the goalie set Dupuy up for a well-struck fifteen-yard shot that ended up in the back of the non-Gallowgate net. The crowd went wild, and the *allez les Blancs* chanting became virtually continuous.

The tactics had clearly been well worked out and drilled, and the *Stade* team now kept the ball in the middle of the park whenever possible to avoid running around too much and risking a punishing Niort counter attack. Inevitably the home side began showing signs of tiredness, and in the last ten minutes the professionals pressed hard, going close on three occasions. But *Stade,* to their great credit, stood defiant despite being obviously dismayed on seeing that there would be three very tense minutes of added time. During those three minutes, Niort won two corners, the second of which led to a real chance. But the header went over and bounced off the embankment just as the ref was putting his whistle to his lips. It was all over, and there were scenes of great celebration and relief on the pitch and off it as the Niort players headed for their dressing room, heads bowed. Some fans ran onto the pitch, and it was all good-natured joyous stuff, and it was only at this point that I realised I hadn't seen even a single policeman in or around the ground – and the crowd must have been around the thousand mark or a bit higher. The club's own security people – no doubt all unpaid volunteers – were well able to marshal the high spirits of the home support. The CRS riot police's services would certainly not be needed here either.

It was a famous victory. Well done, *Stade*. They were now one of the last sixty-four clubs in this year's French cup. Another minor club, Calais, super-Calais went ballistic and reached the final at the turn of the Millennium and only just lost to Nantes through a last-gasp penalty, and we hoped *Stade Bordelais* would emulate that feat. We would be monitoring their progress with great interest and best wishes.

***

As we made our way from the stand to the exit, the couple on the scarf stall asked if we would be coming back for the next round. Clive said that if *Stade* were drawn against Lille away he would take the Eurostar to the match in that north-east French city, whose Flemish name is Rijssel by the way. The lady said, however, that if they did draw Lille or any team from a higher division (a very likely prospect!) they would still play the match at home. Then I remembered that the same arrangement applies in the German Cup, and memories flashed into my mind of then 'third-division' *Rot-Weiss Essen* beating *Schalke 04* two-nil in the second round proper of the German Cup in September 1992, with a pre-Arsenal Jens Lehmann gifting *Rot-Weiss* the second goal of a famous two-nil victory in the ninetieth minute. With Schalke throwing everything forward in a bid to equalise, their Essen-born(!) keeper strayed well out of his box, almost to the half-way line. He tried to thump a clearance by the home side right back into their penalty area but fluffed his kick and inadvertently laid the ball straight in the path of Jörg Lipinski, who hoofed it forward and raced towards the Schalke goal line as Lehmann gave up the chase all of forty yards out. Lipinski decided to savour the moment and kept the ball on the line unchallenged for fully five seconds before tapping it in, to the delight of the delirious home crowd. Check it out on http://www.youtube.com/watch?v=CrM4ivLWPAM and see for yourself! A season later *Rot-Weiss* made it to the final in Berlin, only to lose three-one to *Werder Bremen*.

And so we left the *Stade stade* saying we wished this friendly amateur club a long and money-spinning cup run. As it turned out, the gallant *Bordelais* went out at home to Lens, which is very close to Lille, in the Round of 32 and, funnily enough, the Cup was eventually won by Bordeaux.

***

Well the journey back to the city centre was a lot easier than the outbound one, as we hopped on a bus virtually immediately and were back in the centre about twenty-five minutes later. Before Clive and Peter headed off back to Stalingrad we had time for a farewell pint. And we looked forward to meeting up again soon 'somewhere in Europe'.

The driver of my taxi to the station the next morning was a Bordeaux supporter who also followed his team around Europe. He showed me a phone picture of Bordeaux supporters at Olympiakos. He said he had feared for his life. Yes, that brought back vivid memories, all right.

My *TGV* to Paris set off on time, but soon we were at a standstill because of a goods train that had broken down somewhere further down the line. As a result we were two and half hours late getting into Paris, but an announcement said that people with reservations for onward trains need not worry as they would be found seats on later ones. I took the Metro from *Montparnasse* to *Gare de l'Est,* where an announcement said trains east were being held up by snow. To cut a long story short I finally got home at about eleven o'clock that night, so it wasn't too bad really, especially considering a lot of people like Paul had far greater difficulties making their journeys home.

***

What a fantastic place Bordeaux had turned out to be. Compared to maybe fifteen years ago when it was already pretty good, it has been renovated and a big part of the centre has been pedestrianised. The *Vieux Quartier* of Bordeaux is like a clean version of the old part of Barcelona, the *Barrio Gotico*, and you can't get a much higher recommendation than that. Try the narrow pedestrian streets and little squares and corners around the *Place du Parlement* and *rue Saint Remi,* where on all sides you are surrounded by sturdily-built old stone buildings with their big, heavy doors, most of them seemingly giving access to bars, cafés, *brasseries* and restaurants. You could easily spend a month wandering the alleyways and hidden squares and never have a dull moment.

So a great trip was over. We wouldn't say no to being drawn against Bordeaux some other time, even during this year's competition. Mission accomplished in style, at least by the fans, and now looking forward to somewhere equally nice in February. The draw for the next two rounds would be on the twentieth of

December. What with finishing second behind Bordeaux in Group D, we would be in the unseeded half of the draw. Of the prospective seeded opponents in the Round of 32, we were hoping for somewhere like Genk, Hanover, Lyon or Lisbon. Not Siberia or some Gulag, please – we could equally end up in deepest Russia at Rubin Kazan, or in (the) Ukraine at either Dnipropetrovsk or Kharkiv. Or in Istanbul facing Fenerbahçe.

Such is the excitement of following the Toon around Europe.

***

With the 'winter break' now upon us, it is once again time to settle into that comfy armchair in front of the fire, contentedly open a bottle of *Châteauneuf du Pape* and reminisce about European adventures past. So courtesy of our trusty time machine let us now drift and spin, pleasantly sozzled, through the swirling mists of time to revisit one of our most memorable trips ever, where we were introduced to the skills of a couple of youngsters when they made their first team débuts in the city of …

Palermo – 2nd November 2006

They made us an offer we couldn't refuse

I am writing this with strangely mixed feelings: we've just brought a great result back from Palermo, but Sheffield United have now scored a goal at the Leazes End which has taken us down to equal bottom of the Premiership. In Palermo, I was hoping we'd avoid a humiliation, and so would have been quite satisfied with one-nil. To Palermo. A draw was beyond my wildest dreams, just as a home loss to the bottom club less than two days later was beyond my worst nightmares. That's part of the problem – there were only about forty-three hours between the two games, most of which were taken up by celebrating, sleeping and travelling. What a sudden change.

First things first – back safe 'n' sound from Sicily. And it was a great trip – not least because of the result. I headed out from Brussels at Wednesday lunchtime, and was lucky to get on the plane as Alitalia had over-booked. It looked ominous when they asked 'Do you have a Frequent Flyer card?' I replied, 'Is SN Brussels Airlines any good?' and she shook her head regretfully and picked up the phone to the air-side gate. After ten nerve-wracking minutes spent with a few others in the same position, we were let on and they even upgraded us to Business Class all the way. The check-in girl explained that if it hadn't been for my having a connecting Alitalia flight to Palermo, I'd have been left behind. A narrow escape which would have thrown all our carefully laid plans into confusion.

On the flight to Rome, we were served one of the best airline meals I've ever had, including grilled Italian vegetables and *Nero d'Avola* red wine. This looked like a good omen to me: Sicilian wine on a Rome flight. So I stuck with it throughout the trip apart from a couple of bottles of Italian lager, *Nastro Azzurro*, meaning Blue Riband. They were good choccy biscuits, weren't they? What ever happened to them, I wonder? And we read somewhere that Italians place a blue riband on the front door to tell everyone there is a newly born baby in the house. And maybe the Dad wets the bairn's head with a pint of *Nastro Azzurro!*

Another good omen at Palermo airport: one of the washbasins at the toilets in the arrivals area was actually called New Castle. I like good omens.

I met up with Pete, who'd flown in via Milan from Ireland where he'd been to 'run' (note from Pete: more like walk) the Dublin Marathon and to where he was returning to complete his 'Irish' holiday before going back home to Germany. Now does that sound Irish, or what? To do some sightseeing around the countryside and to get us to and from the excellent Genoardo Park Hotel, where we constituted half of the guests in a hotel hidden in a rather remote little village five minutes from Monreale, we'd pre-booked a Fiat Grande Punto from Sixt at the airport. With it getting close to the beginning of the evening, we thought why not go and have a look at the *Stadio Renzo Barbera 'La Favorita'* and maybe try to see if the team was training there before we headed to the hotel? I'd taken my GPS with me, so we set the controls for the heart of sunny Palermo, and after an hour in a prodigious Sicilian traffic jam, we arrived at the ground at dusk.

We parked on the other side of the wide, busy road from the main entrance. A big, shiny red coach turned out through the iron gates just as we were waiting to cross the road and we thought 'Aargh, we've just missed them,' but in any case we decided to take a look inside the stadium precincts. There were a few Sicilians hanging around, getting back into their cars, when we spotted a little man in a white shirt and light grey overall trousers holding onto a big Alsatian walking towards the big metal doors of the stadium itself. Pete brought his dodgy, make-it-up-as-you-go-along Italian to bear and explained that we were '*tifosi* of Newcastle United and could we please have a look inside the stadium even if the team had left?' To our surprise, he put his finger to his lips as if to indicate 'Don't tell anyone,' opened the door for us and said in Italian 'Newcastle are training in private – no press, no TV.' It must have been the press going off in the coach.

And all of a sudden, there we were, just us and the little guard and a couple of other stadium workers in the big, curving, empty stadium with the team training a matter of feet in front of us. It was a fantastic feeling, being that lucky. Pete´s makey-on Italian had swung it for us. A perspex barrier, occasionally broken by yellow-painted, metal mesh gates separated us from the team. The whole squad was out on the pitch, and even though they were ineligible to play, Rossi and Pav were there too. We walked down to the *Curva Nord* end, the Ultras' end, where the forwards were having long-range shooting practice. We had our big young keeper in goal, with shots flying in from Luque, Milner, Sibierski, Rossi, N'Zogbia and Solano and some young ones we'd never seen before. Luque hit in a Robert-style thunderbolt from miles out and let out a roaring 'Yessss'. Whatever we've seen of him, he is popular with the rest of the team, and he certainly was laughing and enjoying the training. So there's hope yet. The big goalkeeper came over towards us to collect up the loose balls and Pete, in Dutch, shouted across 'Tim, how're you doing?' He came over closer with a questioning look on his face and said in a Geordie accent with a smile, 'Aa'm not Tim!' So much for our knowledge of the reserves! We didn't have a clue who he was until we got the papers the day after the game and found out that the name of the last-minute substitute was Andy 'Aa'm not Tim' Carroll. Don't ask us what he was doing in goal. Glenn Roeder even took a penalty against him and showed everyone how it should be done.

At the end of the training, we walked back up to the *Curva Sud* end, where we would be standing on the following night and spotted Pav near the yellow mesh gate. We welcomed him back to the Toon and hoped he was going to get a game some time, though of course he told us he wasn't eligible for the UEFA Cup. Still, would be good to see him back in goal for at least part of a game. We took a photo with him and he signed our match ticket receipt. We managed to have a quick word with Glenn Roeder too and wished him well and said we thought we were going to be all right this season. Which we were in the end, even though we couldn´t have imagined the sort of results that were coming our way over the next few days. The last to leave the pitch were Lee Clark, and Terry Mac who was picking up the last ball-bag. They both stayed behind to have a bit *craic*, wondering how we'd got there so early and how we'd managed to get into the ground. Again, we got some great photos and a couple of autographs. They seemed genuinely grateful for our good wishes and our confidence that they'd do all right, as Glenn Roeder had been. We thanked the security guard and slipped him a fiver and then headed back to the car. Shades of the Italian Job: '*Molto bene*, dad'.

While I was fiddling about with the GPS, we spotted the blue flashing lights of a police car turning sideways across the lanes, and we realised the team coach was about to leave. Forget the GPS, we thought, we'll follow the team instead. So we latched onto the back of the coach, and the blue flashing police car took it and our car on a high-speed ride, slicing through the chaotic traffic out to the docks area and a hotel that looked like an old castle, the Villa Igiea Hilton. Lee Clark should have felt at home because it was surrounded by the kind of pecking shipyard cranes you used to see in his native Wallsend. We thought maybe we might pass by the next day before the game, but now the priority was to find our hotel. The GPS took us there in half an hour, right through the traffic-lawless streets of central Palermo and the astonishing antics of the Sicilian drivers. Hesitate an instant and you're lost. The only way is just to press on and say three Hail Marys – it's obviously what the locals do. The GPS takes away all the worries about which turn to take, so you can concentrate solely on the dodgem-car race. It certainly is something you need to experience. I've got the tee shirt now – 'I drove through Palermo and survived'. No wonder the hire car had a big dent and a black scrape running all the way down the right-hand side, even before we got it. Luckily we got back to the airport at the end of the trip without having added any more.

Because of all the stories and graphic photos of trouble with West Ham fans (of whom more anon in the Schalke Cup chapter), and after talking to my Sicilian friend Mario (from Catania, not Palermo), we had booked ourselves a hotel up in the hills above Palermo in Monreale, which turned out to be a very friendly little town. The cathedral there was built by the Normans, and according to our unofficial guide, Marie, who attached herself to us after we asked her to take a photo of us in our Toon tops, the monastery cloisters apparently boast the most suggestive, digestive, sculpted friezes in Christendom, but we gave them a miss. Our shirts attracted a lot of attention, all very friendly. We felt safe and brave enough to give them an airing in Monreale, but we would never have shown them in Palermo after all we'd heard. We learnt in Monreale that part of the problem was that the West Ham fans hadn't been at all welcoming to the Palermo travelling fans during their first leg visit to cockneyland, and the word had got back to Sicily with the travelling fans on their return. So the Hammers fans had at least partly brought it upon themselves, though of course there can be no excuse for any of the behaviour of the Palermo locals.

After our trip around Monreale on Thursday morning, we went back to the airport to pick up Sarah and Chris and then headed further along to the west to the ancient mountain-top town of Erice full of little stone houses and churches almost a thousand years old. Like all of Sicily, it has been ruled by successive invaders, including the Phoenicians and the Normans, all leaving their different traces to this day. The trip up was so full of hairpin bends that the display on the GPS looked more like a pink X-ray of your intestines than a road map, and it was literally a bit stomach-churning. But it was all worthwhile when you saw the view of the bay from the top of the sheer cliffs – it was like looking down from a cruising plane, it was so high up. On the way back there was a major storm, and we were glad that it blew over as standing out in that with no cover for three hours would have been no fun at all.

Our trips to Monreale and Erice kept us nicely occupied through the day until it was time to head back to *La Favorita* Stadium. We decided to take a taxi down to the ground, and this turned out to be a good idea when we saw the traffic – cars heading in all directions. The taxi driver assured us that, in a taxi, you were allowed to drive contra-flow down bus lanes on one-way streets, and through people's back gardens if necessary. Who were we to argue? The funny thing was, it seemed like quite a few cars and hundreds of scooters were convinced that they had an equal right to drive the opposite way up the same lane. In our own car, we would never have made it to the ground through that traffic.

The taxi dropped us, for an extortionate forty Euro fare, right in the middle of the Palermo fans on the opposite side to the away fans' entrance and in sight of the main stand where we'd been the night before. Luckily, we had our Toon tops well covered. There were loads of stalls selling souvenirs and drinks and hot dogs, and we got ourselves some Palermo-Toon half pink, half white scarves (note from Pete: mine is still proudly on display in the garden shed, together with souvenirs from other European adventures). There were *carabinieri* everywhere and they started to put up a perimeter fence about a hundred yards around the stadium. I saw what was happening and slipped through quickly, but everyone else got caught. I was called back and we were held off to one side and told by the very friendly police that they'd gather a few more of us together and then escort us into the ground. The whole atmosphere was very relaxed and friendly and we got the police to take some photos for us, and some of the Palermo fans came over to stage a photo for their website. There was no feeling of any menace at all, and I really don't think we'd have had any trouble, but who were we to turn down a friendly escort? Two more Toon fans, a couple from the smoke, turned up presently and after a wait of about ten minutes with no one else appearing the *carabinieri* walked us down into the same entrance we'd used on Wednesday evening. More photos with the police and friendly chat with the locals and then the confusion started. The ticket collectors tore off the stubs of our tickets and we were told we were going to be taken through the main entrance and then walked around the field and over to our corner, a bit like what had happened in Marseille. Then instead they decided to take us around the outside of the stadium nearly a full circle to the away entrance. We passed through multiple barriers and were handed over from one set of *carabinieri* and club official escorts to another and finally ended up going through a wire cage tunnel to the away fans' entrance. And as I was half expecting, the inevitable happened as none of our original escorts were left with us and when we showed our stub-less tickets, they wouldn't let us through the turnstiles. We spent ages explaining the situation in broken Italian to a sharp-suited, walkie-talkie wielding, baldy Vialli 'Luca-like', who called through to the other side of the ground asking if they had the ticket stub numbers corresponding to our tickets. As if they'd ever be able to find them in a pile of thousands! Eventually they gave up and let us in.

By the way, I spent the whole trip assuring everyone who'd listen that *carabinieri* means 'charcoal-burners' and was something to do with freedom-fighter Garibaldi of dead-flies biscuits fame. I now know that I was half-right as the charcoal-burners were a secret society whose members did indeed help Garibaldi in his fight to unite Italy, but they were the *carbonari*, not the *carabinieri*. Why all this talk of Garibaldi? Well, we all know that Garibaldi had strong links with the North-East, stronger than he ever had with Palermo, having stayed in Tynemouth during part of his exile from Italy, and there is even a Garibaldi monument in Blaydon. And as far as the *carbonari* are concerned, besides helping Garibaldi to squash the flies to make his exceedingly delicious biscuits, they went on to invent a new form of *spaghetti* laced with bacon and cream.

Once inside, we were surprised to find only about seventy or so Toon fans inside a perspex and mesh cage with a net draped over the top. So despite being held for so long, we were nowhere near the last in. More of the Toon Army arrived in groups of five or six at a time, including quite a few who were brought in around the edge of the pitch, as the stadium staff had originally said they were going to do with us. I would have liked to come that way too. In the end the Toon Army swelled to 167 people – someone standing beside us counted them and also told us that the club had only sold 172 tickets. I suppose it explains why we succeeded so easily to get our tickets. Apart from the *Deportivo La Coruña* away game, was that the lowest ever number of travelling Geordie fans (at the time) in Europe since Kevin Keegan got us back? There were certainly more of us even in Dubnica for instance, and that was much harder to reach. The poor current form and all the bad news about the West Ham fans' experiences must have done the damage. (A voice from the future reminds us that this was written before our Atromitos and Anzhi trips.)

Any remaining doubts about what the net above our heads was for were soon dispelled when there was a blinding pink flash and a loud bang directly above our heads and the smouldering remains of a flare fluttered down through the net. Despite all the mesh, barriers and netting, we had a pretty decent view. You saw it on the television, maybe better than we could see, and it's a pity that we could only see Milner's cross and Luque's header for the goal in the far distance. It was so unexpected after all the heart-stopping clearances off the line that it took the Toon Army what seemed like a couple of seconds before we registered that we really had scored. It was like slow motion. Then our corner erupted into noise and leapt up and down while the rest of the ground went totally silent. And actually their fans didn't make much noise at all at any time during the match. For 167 people, a hundred times fewer than the half-empty home support, I thought we more than matched them. Lots of old songs from the Joe Harvey period, as well as all the usual ones. We tried shouting 'Pink Fairies' in response to the constant tumbling and diving of the rosanero pink-black players, but that didn't catch on. During the lock-in at the end, the longest-lasting chant, to the tune of 'Go West', was 'One-nil, even Luque scored,' which I thought was a bit unfair.

Of course there were quite a few tense moments when we wouldn't have been surprised if Palermo had scored – right in front of us near the beginning of the first half when our defenders made a series of last-second clearances off the line, and in the second half just after the double substitution. The number seventeen, di Michele, received a huge cheer from the *Curva Nord Ultras* when he came on. We were hoping he wasn't going to have as big an impact on the game as on the noise level. But Tim Krul dived and stretched to save a header going to his left and then beat away a shot from di Michele from the rebound. From our corner, it had looked certain that the initial shot would go in, but Krul's arm seemed to stretch improbably far to fend it away with his fingertips. Then he made another point-blank save where he spread himself in front of the approaching Palermo player and managed to keep out the shot with his right shin. You could see all this on the television. But what you couldn't see was the Palermo goalkeeper coming out of his area and long and demonstratively applauding Krul's double save. Fair play to him! When I noticed this, I thought, he's thinking it's not their night, they're not going to score.

As well as Krul, I thought Nicky Butt and James Milner had good games. Nicky Butt was always at the centre of things, tackling sturdily and breaking up Palermo moves, while Milner's determination nearly brought him a goal in the opening minutes and his cross for the goal was inch-perfect for Luque to head it home. At another point, Luque showed wonderful ball control to stop a long, hard cross-field ball dead under his foot. He's definitely got something, but often seems to need a fraction of a second more than the opposition are prepared to give him.

In the second half, apart from one miracle where we strung more than twenty passes together, albeit including a hari-kiri back-pass to Krul, we couldn't hold on to the ball when we occasionally got it back from Palermo. But somehow we got through, and the time ran out earlier than I expected (discuss!) – I didn't even see the board for extra time, if there was one. In those last few minutes, Andy Carroll came on and became our youngest ever player in European matches. The team came over in twos and threes to acknowledge our cheers, and Tim Krul got a special welcome, of course. The team came back out to warm down while we were in detention, which helped the time to pass, and after maybe half an hour or so, we were led back out through the wire mesh tunnel and onto three waiting buses. We were escorted by police vans and Land Rovers and bikes, all with flashing blue lights, which took us through a park to the outskirts of the town. We were then brought back into town down a main road with armoured cars and squads of police at every junction. There must have been about five police for every one of us, and apart from them, there was no sign of anyone else out on the streets. We eventually arrived at the impressive *Teatro Massimo* in *Piazza Verdi*, where we were let out. We made our way straight across to the taxi rank and jumped into the first taxi that appeared and were high-spirited away out of town. We were taking no chances that there might be any reprisals. By the time we got back, the hotel was closing for the night, so we got some drinks out of our mini-bars and took them down to the bar ourselves. This really was a luxury hotel – all tiled and marbled swimming-pool extravagance set against a backdrop of moonlit Mafia mountains. The kind of place where maybe the families used crisp, clean and freshly ironed notes to pay for their weddings and other important gatherings. Such were our late-night Godfather-inspired thoughts. And yet the hotel was so very reasonably priced. In fact, they had made us an offer we just couldn't refuse.

***

To, er, kill some time the next morning before my plane left, I drove down to the small town of Trevisino, filled the hire car up with petrol, got myself a Sicilian haircut, and bought three papers to read in the café – the local *Giornale di Sicilia*, which is obviously their Journal, and the two national sports papers, the *Gazzetta dello Sport* and the *Corriere dello Sport*. I settled down on a bright, crisp sunny morning on a seaside terrace and noted that the main headlines, apart from those saying that Palermo should have won, were two separate stories about Mafia trials – an obvious cliché, but still an everyday reality apparently – and the intriguing news that they were going to ban cars more than five years old from Palermo city centre. New cars might be more fuel-efficient, but wouldn't this just encourage more consumption and probably more environmental damage in the end?

At the airport, four identically dark-blue suited men came up to me and they asked if I could take their photo out on the terrace of the departure lounge. As I took the camera, I noticed that one had a UEFA lapel badge and I asked if they were the match officials, and they were. That's why there were four of them, of course. It turned out that they were all from the Czech Republic. They asked if I'd ever been to the Czech Republic and I replied that the closest I'd got so far was to Dubnica in the Slovak half of the old Czechoslovakia. One of the linesmen started singing for a joke 'We hate sunderland and we hate sunderland' when he heard I was from Newcastle. I thought that was pretty good of him to have such local knowledge. I asked the referee, Mr Jara, if he knew that we had just got back Pav as a reserve keeper, and he said that he knew him well and had actually been talking to him after the match. I thought he'd done a good job in keeping control over the game, and he said it had been a difficult game to referee, what with all the play-acting. I got a picture taken with them too. That's the first time I've ever talked to a referee – shouted at, yes, but talked to, no! They were on the same plane bound for Milan as me, and John Barnes was on it too. A good end to the trip.

***

And now let's hop aboard our time machine again, because it's high time to fast-forward to a cold Newcastle in February 2013 …

NUFC at home to Metalist Kharkiv – 14th February 2013

Heavy metal, as it turned out

'I wrote to the club to see if we could have media accreditation – but then I thought: pigs might fly. Media accreditation? More chance of creature meditation, or come to think of it, levitation.'

My heart had been set on a nice temperate draw in some feel-good Mediterranean resort. And what did we get from those blazered UEFA functionaries who spend their time juggling their balls in a bag? The Ukraine in the depths of winter, that's what! And, as so often before, I am now sitting in a Brussels Airlines plane. But far from being headed to the Eastern Front, I'm actually bound for the Promised Land – in the company of a monk, judging by the clip of the gadgy sitting next to me. Yes, one time it's a nun on a train, now it's a monk on a plane. A raggy robe the colour of old loft insulation, a pair of scuffed hiking boots of the same muddy colour, spindly legs, and a tonsured baldy heed. Things have certainly changed for monks since the days of Saint Cuthbert. Though I know that Pete and his fellow Cuths Old Boys do their best to follow in their Patron's footsteps, both sartorially and otherwise.

It's the Metalist Kharkiv home tie on Thursday and I have to be in the wilds of Scotland on Wednesday at Linn Products of Sondek LP12 fame, so it all fits together very nicely. It only takes one clever man, this time it was Gilad Tiefenbrun, to come up with an immaculate design which captures the spirit and the desires of the moment, in this case the late seventies hi-fi boom, and he has himself a world-famous business enterprise which is now in its fifth decade.

I've just missed by half a day the belatedly announced match that the Metals played as their first game after their winter break to acclimatise themselves to temperatures above zero. They drew one-one against the Bay at Hillheads, renamed Metalheads for the occasion. Howay the Bay! Winners of the FA Vase three years in a row and now unbeaten this season v European competition. If the Seahorses can do it, then surely the Magpies can too. Otherwise we'll never hear the last of it. I wonder if our lads will be heading across next Sunday to play the locals down on the Crimean seaside equivalent of Whitley Bay? Not much chance of miles and miles of golden sand down there – the Black Sea's probably white at this time of year and full of icebergs.

For their match doon the coast, Metalist kindly agreed to spectators being allowed in for what originally was going to be a behind-closed-doors practice game, but they unexpectedly asked to have the kick-off brought forward by two hours so quite a few people got there too late, not least the Look North cameras! About seven hundred fans were nevertheless there, wearing blue and white, with black and white banned along with cameras. Not only are the Bay unbeaten in Europe after their one-one draw, but they have also scored a European goal, through Lee Paul Scroggins, which is more than the linesmen at SJP would be allowing us.

***

We've split the duties on this one – I'm going to the home leg and Pete to the away. In case you're wondering, I've got a very good excuse as my wife's going into hospital at the Belgian equivalent of Dr Steadman's Colorado Knee Institute, having a spot of keyhole kneehole surgery done. The surgeon's done lots of famous sporting knees, mostly Belgian, Dutch and German ones, so she'll be in good hands. When she was having the tests done, she asked the doctor whether after the operation she'd be able to play football to a high standard like some of his other patients and he replied 'Of course!' which was amazingly confident of him as up till then she'd never played before. The old ones are the good ones, eh? Knee bother? Nee bother.

The Metalist Kharkiv fans seemed an enthusiastic bunch. Apparently the club owner, some rich Ukrainian billionaire – have you ever met a poor billionaire? – had paid the travel costs for five hundred fans. A free trip! I wonder how many came just for the trip and a taste of freedom and didn't actually turn up at the ground? And how many would lose their return tickets and claim asylum like those Soviet gymnasts used to do? From the size of the away section, to be honest I think they all came for the match and they were all so enthusiastic about their team that they would surely be returning to their homeland to watch the second leg. They were in great voice, pogoing up and down, arms around each others' shoulders. Of course we could have no idea at all about what they were singing, but it was good to hear some completely different tunes, which made a change when many European fans seem to share the same chants and songs amongst them. For instance, why on earth do Celtic fans sing 'You'll never walk alone' like Liverpool fans? I ask because, as I mentioned earlier, I was up in Scotland a couple of days before and in the Busby Hotel (no relation) near East Kilbride, they had Celtic's champignons league match v Juventus on the screens in the bar, and they were singing as if they were sitting on the banks of the Mersey not the Clyde. Celtic undeservedly lost three-nil by the way, and were the victims of a terrible referee who allowed continual fouling in the penalty area by the Juventus defenders which, had it been sanctioned, would have given Celtic a six-three win.

Anyway, the Metals' songs sounded pretty original to me, although who knows, they might have copped them from Dnipropetrovsk or who knows which other clubs are good at making up Ukrainian football songs. They even took all their blue and yellow tops off during the second half to copy the Toon fans either side of their corner of the East Stand up by the Leazes End. They actually had quite a lot to cheer about as their team played very well and on the whole, apart from a few Ukrainian schoolboy howlers, retained possession much better than we did.

***

The ground looked pretty strange with Level Seven deserted all around. Maybe there were just over thirty thousand there – the Gallowgate End was pretty well full and there was a great atmosphere coming out of its strong singing section. Out onto the pitch came Krul, Coloccini, Santon, Yanga-Mbiwa, Taylor, Cabaye, Sissoko, Gutierrez, Tioté, Obertan, and Cissé to face a team which turned out to be mostly South Americans. Since the Group games we'd lost Demba Ba but we'd gained French reinforcements represented here only by Yanga-Mbiwa and Moussa Sissoko, as Yoan Gouffran, ex of Group opponents Bordeaux, was Cup-tied and, because of some tricky UEFA rules restricting the number of incoming players who could be registered to three, Mathieu Debuchy from Lille was not registered even though he had played in the champignons league, not the Europa League. Young Massadio Haidara was chosen instead as the third new registration, and he was sitting on the bench for this one.

The place erupted when we 'scored' twice and the celebrations went on long and hard before we eventually realised with disbelief that the linesman/assistant had somehow decided neither goal was good enough for him. Mid-way through the first half Obertan lofted a through ball down the left to Sissoko who broke away before crossing to Cissé who side-footed the ball carefully into the net before celebrating long and hard in front of the Leazes End. Poor Cissé. He's having a hard enough time getting goals this year, is wor Papiss. He'd already had a one-on-one earlier in the first half when he really should have scored, but he'd shot straight at the keeper. Our new signing Moussa Sissoko really made his presence felt throughout the match. With about twenty minutes to go, Cissé burst thrugh the Metalist defence to latch onto a right-wing cross from Yanga-Mbiwa and steer it in off the inside of the left post, but again the linesman judged he was offside. Shortly after, Sissoko had a hard and low long-range shot saved, and right at the end their goalkeeper came to the rescue again with a save from a point-blank Cissé header. The ball just wouldn't go in. At the other end too, Metalist had quite a few chances, all repelled by Tim Krul on top form. The whistle blew and it was a nil-nil draw but that didn't tell the story of a game packed with lots of incident, and goals. On this form, we had to have some hope that we could go to Kharkiv and come away with a result.

The referee and his assistants must look back on this game and hang their heads in shame for some of their decisions. We certainly should have had one if not both of the goals that Cissé scored, but they decided that both were offside. OK, we all know he's spent most of the season standing offside, but in this game he scored fair and square. Norwegian I think they were, the officials, and maybe they were getting their own back for us beating *Lillestrøm* and *Vålerenga*.

I freeze-framed the Look North highlights of our first 'goal' when I got home and Sissoko was about a yard onside of a Kharkiv defender over on the other side of the pitch when Obertan passed the ball to him, and Sissoko was ahead of Cissé when he passed the ball to him, so obviously Papiss could not have been offside either and in any case there was a Kharkiv defender and their goalkeeper between him and the goal. I am sure if that goal had been allowed then the floodgates would have well and truly opened. The second 'goal' was onside too, but Cissé appeared on the scene so fast that you could understand a bit more how the linesman had got it wrong.

One of their substitutes wore the number 86, and another was number 50, and I am pretty sure if you added up all the numbers on their backs, there's never been such a high total on the SJP pitch ever (that has the makings of a great pub quiz question). Strength in numbers. Maybe that's why we couldn't get a goal. They even had a number 99, but he didn't get onto the pitch. Some problem with the chocolate flake stuck in his hair being against UEFA regulations. The 86 was a bit of a joker, a little tubby, who did the most imaginative belly-flop in the penalty area when Jonas came within breathing distance of him, and then implored the referee to give him a penalty. Based on his previous decisions, no one would have been surprised if he'd given him the nod, but for once the referee was on our side.

We had seats in the Platinum Club, not far from where we had sat for Bordeaux, Access 12, L2F, Row B, Seats 100-102. Seeing it was Valentine's Day, brother Ian had invited out sister-in-law Lesley for a romantic evening of Ukrainian folk music from a choir of five hundred in the company of thirty thousand other Geordies. I read in The Journal that Alan Pardew had asked the fans to 'bring the missus along' and quite a few had obliged. I am sure the missuses were charmed to hear their husbands serenading Coloccini in the opening few minutes and inviting him to sample their wares. Strange, because it seemed to be sung with even more gusto tonight than ever before, maybe also because it was Valentine's Day?

There were loads of little lads in the ground too, some with their dads and some in little gangs of five or six on their own. It was great to see. The club's policy of making the tickets very affordable is a really excellent idea as it gives these lads – and a fair few lasses – a night to remember. It was just a pity that the referee and his assistants spoilt the party by not giving us anything to celebrate and sabotaging what might have been a Saint Valentine's Day massacre.

***

Platinum Club bog-sign mystery solved at last

At half-time we made the obligatory trip to the bogs. The Platinum Club queue is even longer than the normal ones. I again noticed a sign on the wall with some big writing at the top saying 'Avoid the queue' and lots of small writing that I couldn't read from the back of the queue. I was wondering what it might say, because it would have been good to avoid the queue when you were borstin'. As I got closer I could see it was saying 'Book your place ...' something or other, and I was wondering whether it might say, '... in the Mags Lavvy Club, a fiver for priority seating.' I wouldn't put it past them. But it turned out to be '... and pay for your half-time drinks in advance.'

***

Something else you really noticed was the number of foreigners on the pitch for both teams. Our only Geordie was Steven Taylor, and their only Ukrainian was their goalkeeper. They had even more Argentinians than us, plus some Brazilians, while of course we had all our French-speakers. You could see all the berets, strings of onions, and tricolours in the crowd. I don't know what all the Latin Americans in the Metal ranks make of the Ukrainian weather, but I hope they're still not acclimatised when it comes to next week's return leg in the frozen wastes that I imagine the Ukraine to be. On the other hand, it's not as if Cissé's Senegal and Tioté's Ivory Coast will have much weather in common with the Ukraine either. That's not to say it wasn't pretty well freezing in the stands tonight – when you were exposed to the wind from the North, you could feel the blood icing up in your fingertips.

For some strange reason I'd bumped into a few known faces on this trip. Paul, the big man off the weather on Look North was wandering with a colleague along the lane outside the Forum Cinema in Hexham, looking for some early-morning sunshine. Then as I was leaving Hexham across the Bridge over the Tyne, I saw someone who looked like Harry 'The Far Corner' and 'Tall Man in a Low Land' Pearson, carrying a green plastic bag and probably thinking up some interesting anecdote. And then, as I crossed the threshold of the Central Station on my way back home via London, who should be walking out through the portico but whatsisname the man who does impressions, including a very good Geordie. No, not Paul Whitehouse, he's the best. No, I mean the other one who looks a bit like Rory Bremner. I've got him – John Culmstock – no, that's the village in Devon where my globe-trotting friend Koorosh is based – well something like that. He was with a lady who was chaperoning him through, so probably he'd just arrived off a London or Edinburgh train and was being taken to some local theatre or event. If I had the time, I'd probably find him listed in The Crack magazine or the newcastle.gov.uk What's On website. (It took me a year, but he's called Culshaw.)

***

It had been great to be home of course but, worryingly, I had the uneasy feeling that it was a case of mission unaccomplished. And the Toon would certainly have to be on their mettle if they were to grasp the nettle and fettle the Metals in the Ukraine. Otherwise, an iron curtain would descend on our European season! Somebody call a scrap merchant.

No! Not Freddy ...

Time to pause and reflect

The next chapter covers our trip to Ukraine in February 2013. It was a great trip and we have left the wording of the chapter exactly as it stood when our notes were written up at the time. That wording reflects our happy, care-free few days in Kharkiv. Though even then there was talk and signs of disagreement between Russian speakers in the east of the country, including Kharkiv, and Ukrainian speakers elsewhere, nobody could have imagined at the time the bloodshed that was to follow, or the tragedy of flight MH 17. As we now all know, that tragedy claimed almost three hundred lives, including those of two of the most loyal members of the Toon Army. John Alder and Liam Sweeney RIP. When reading our account of the Metalist away trip, please remember we are trying to preserve the memory of a happier time for the Toon Army in a place that will always be remembered for very different and very tragic reasons.

Metalist Kharkiv away, a diary entry from 20th February 2013

All gain in (the) Ukraine

'I didn't bother writing to the club.'

Here we go, we're off to (the) Ukraine.

Isn't it funny how the definite article has somehow gone out of favour over the years? In the distant days of my youth it was always *the* Ukraine, but nowadays it seems to be plain old non-articled Ukraine. Clearly it wasn't exactly an article of faith. Maybe definite articles don't travel that well, and (the) Ukraine is a fair old way away, unlike the just-next-door Netherlands. Then there was the Argentine, of course, remember that? Now it's just Argentina. Again, the article seems to have got a bit lost when making the long journey across the Atlantic, maybe via (the) Falklands. Thankfully, though, some things never change and it will presumably always be the Felling.

I have a strange theory about why it was called 'the' Ukraine in the first place. It is, I reckon, because the Ukrainian language doesn't have a word for 'the'. Now I have never learned Ukrainian, but I do know that it is wedged not just geographically but also linguistically between Poland and Russia, neither of whose languages have a word for 'the'. And no word for 'a' or 'an' either. Maybe the Romans started it because they didn't bother with 'a' or 'the' either! Imagine getting through your day without saying either 'the' or 'a'. Must save a load of wear and tear on the tongue, and you would probably be less thirsty by opening time. Actually, I'm not too sure about that, as Slavs apparently are not renowned for their lack of thirst.

So in Russian, or Ukrainian, or Polish, 'the cat sat on the mat and ate a mouse' comes out literally as 'cat sat on mat and ate mouse' (could be Yorkshire-speak, I suppose). And these languages are so inflected that they can switch word order around virtually at will, so you could even have 'on mat ate mouse cat who sat' or 'ate cat who sat on mat mouse'. So there is a bit of an ambiguity problem. No wonder Churchill couldn't get any sense out of Stalin – was it 'Russia sit on Nazi Germany for you' or 'Russia sit on you for Germany'? Of course, context is everything. If two consenting adults know they are talking about a particular cat on a particular mat that ate a particular mouse, well there is nothing to worry about (unless you are the mouse of course).

However, if dad comes in from a hard day's work in the salt mine and announces to little Johnny, 'I just saw cat run over by car on road,' there will be an awful moment of uncertainty in little Johnny's (or little Vladimir Ilyich's) mind as to whether 'cat' means our cat, the neighbour's cat that pisses in our cabbage patch or some stray moggy. So one has to be very careful.

So I reckon that a while back some Ukrainian had learned English and had to learn how to use the definite and indefinite article, and when in doubt always threw in a 'the' or an 'a' just to be on the safe side. And when one day he told someone where he came from he added a 'the' to his native country for good measure. And somehow the idea caught on, only to eventually fall out of favour. Just as well he didn't get it wrong and say 'I come from a Ukraine,' otherwise we'd have been talking about 'a Ukraine' for years and years.

***

Anyway, articled or not, we were off to (the) Ukraine. To the North-East of the country, appropriately enough, and to a town called Kharkov, or Kharkiv, take your pick. Yes, two official names. The thing is, the city is in (the) Ukraine but most of the people in the east of that country apparently speak Russian while those in the west speak Ukrainian. And there are all sorts of dialects in between. And the closer you get to the Polish border, the closer Ukrainian evidently gets to Polish. Support for joining the European Union is strong in the west, while in the east a lot of people want closer ties with Russia. It turns out Kharkov is just thirty km away from the Russian border. It is roughly as far east as Moscow, which was the furthest east I had ever been, and lies on the fiftieth parallel, so about level with Brussels. It's on trips like these you realise that, taken as a whole, Europe is not a particularly small place. 'The continent of Europe is so wide, *mein Herr*. Not only up and down but side to side, *mein Herr,*' as someone once sang.

***

And so we were headed east. Some decades earlier, of course, that would have meant crossing the Iron Curtain, applying for visas, putting up with mindless bureaucracy and all that sort of thing (more of which in the next chapter). Nowadays, however, it could not be easier to travel to (the) Ukraine. No visa necessary, just book your travel and accommodation and you're sorted. Oh, and get some of the local money before you go, if at all possible. I went to a bank in Luxembourg and asked if I could buy some Ukrainian currency (I wasn't sure how to pronounce Hryvnia, which is the local money, as I learned from the Internet) and the guy behind the counter thought they still used roubles! When told they didn't, he rang his head office, who didn't know whether they could get Hryvnias or not, but would get back to me. Obviously a very popular tourist destination, I thought. That was three weeks before the trip, and on the day before travelling I had still heard nothing, so I popped in on the off-chance and to my surprise they had two hundred and fifty euros worth of Hryvnia (we later heard the locals calling it something like Grievnya, so let's just call them Jimmy Greaves, or Greavsies, for simplicity's sake). So I was sorted. Sarah had been on a trip to Lviv/Lwów/Lemberg (whoops, don't mention the Austro-Hungarian Empire) a couple of years ago and had been unable to obtain any Greavsies before going, so this time hadn't even tried. It should be easy enough to change in (the) Ukraine, she and Chris had thought ...

***

No sooner had the draw for this round been made, with the possible pairings for the next round being determined at the same time, than it was generally accepted that it was the worst of all possible draws. After all, we could have been going to Rome again (fantastic) to play Lazio, Lisbon (ditto) to play Benfica, Athens (ditto) to play Olympiakos, Lyon (pretty good and easy to get to), or Genk (easy to get to). Because they were unseeded like us, we would certainly not be going to just-up-the-road-from-Trier-and-just-around-the-corner-from-Brussels Mönchengladbach, which Terry Collier of the Likely Lads once famously described as the West Hartlepool of West Germany.

No, we were off to the north-east of the Ukraine, and in the by now unlikely event of us beating Kharkiv/Kharkov, our opponents in the next round would be either Hannover 96 or Anzhi Makachkala – a club about which it has been said: Who? Well, the Anjies are at home on the western shore of the Caspian Sea, in the

Republic of Dagestan. Where? Yes, that's exactly what we wondered when we first found out.

At least if we were drawn against Hannover 96 (where booking hotel rooms would be, er, difficult because of the world's biggest industrial fair going on at the same time), we would have the option of staying in Berlin and taking a really fast train to Hanover.

Then again, it could be a trip to Anzhi Makachkala in Dagestan. Wish I'd paid more attention in geography lessons. Thankfully, we didn't have to search too long on the map, because the match wouldn't be taking place anywhere near there. The venue would be … Moscow. That is because Makachkala is in a neck of the woods not usually associated with the words 'stable' and 'peaceful'. In fact, the more you read about those parts, the less you want to go there. A patchwork of nationalities and tribal loyalties, spiced with a rich cocktail of religious bigotry and mindless thugs. And no, we're not talking about the Old Firm here.

Thankfully, UEFA had told Anzhi Makachkala well, okay, you can be in our competition but you cannot expect anyone to come to a place as horrible as your home town so you will have to play all your home games in Moscow. Okay, the Anzhis said. There is serious oligarchic wealth involved there somewhere, so money was no object. To be fair, the seriously rich owner of Metalist Kharkiv had flown five hundred of their fans over to the Toon, as Barry told us in the last chapter. Some unkind souls reckoned that if their owner could afford to do that then he could probably also afford to bribe the match officials. But we all fully accept that the words 'FIFA or UEFA officials' and 'corruption and bribery' will never, ever be read in the same sentence, so that certainly could not account for those two goals we had disallowed.

**

Such are the rambling thoughts going through my aged and decrepit mind as I scribble down these notes in the Campanile hotel just a few hundred yards away from Luxembourg airport. So close, I swear you can smell the kerosene. Never mind 'wake up and smell the coffee,' get a whiff of that. Mind, I have to say they do a nice omelette and chips here, and I know from previous experience that the draft Bofferding beer and the house red are also good. But this time we are a week into Lent, so clearly it had to be Clausthaler non-alcoholic for me, much to Chris's disbelief when he rang me as I was quaffing my second bottle thereof.

'You'll never stay the distance. Ye'll be back on the booze well before Easter, ye knaa ye will, bonny lad.'

O ye of little faith.

Chris just wanted to check we definitely were on the same flight from Vienna, and we were. He and Sarah were getting up at the crack of dawn for their flight from Heathrow. Mine left Luxembourg at 7.05. But as I was sleeping virtually on the runway I could have a nice lie-in till 5.15 and get parked up in the airport underground car park in good time to check in at six. Chris gave me clear instructions to delay the departure of the 10.10 Austrian Airways flight from Vienna in case Sarah and he were rushing through Vienna airport while their names were being embarrassingly called out on the PA system.

***

That instruction having been made clear, we took the opportunity to go through the arrangements for what was, after all, going to be yet another deep-cover operation. Okay, this time we wouldn't be in the away end – assuming the ticket collection arrangement went smoothly. Barry had ordered a ticket for me using his season ticket credentials and I was going to pick it up from our friend Steve Storey in Kharkov. But we were not travelling with an organised group. We were *off-piste*, as it were. Though we hoped that at some stage we would in fact be off *on* the *piste*.

In the initial flurry of e-mails, (the) Don (may I take this opportunity to once again express my deepest respect and undying loyalty) was first off the mark on the hotel front. He had found a nice-looking boutique hotel, name of Mirax, nicely located a mere twenty-minute walk from the Metalist stadium, and right next to the unfortunately-named *Ploshcha Povstanni* (Uprising Square) Metro station from where it was only two stops to the city centre. Sound, thought I. My trip was being arranged through a travel agent – what with me being tied up with a million work things, plus the fact that I basically couldn't be arsed – and they sent a shortlist of hotels, including Mirax, so I gave the green light and I would be there too. Then Chris booked himself and Sarah also into the same place. The Don then went and booked a hotel right next to the airport for him and the Steve! We never seem to get our hotel arrangements one hundred per cent synchronised, do we? But never mind. In the past, the Don has even stayed at hotels in cities other than the one we were playing in. For the Basel game (6th November 2003, we won three-two with goals from Robert, Bramble and Shola), for example, he stayed at a hotel in Zurich. So I suppose we had to be relieved that this time he wasn't staying in somewhere like Novosibirsk.

At all events, we were now all set, and about to converge on Kharkov. Deep cover needed ...

***

Chris and I had done a short introductory Russian language course at the Cuths back in the 1970s during our A-Level years. Our Russian teacher was our German teacher, the wonderful Mr Bill Charlton, affectionately known as Charlie. What a great bloke! Charlie had learned Russian during his national service in Germany and on the afternoon of our first lesson he drew a long vertical line in chalk on the blackboard (some of you may remember what chalk and blackboards were, though if you can you probably can't remember what you had for supper last night or where you have left your keys). This white line, said Charlie, represents the entirety of the Russian language, all that can possibly be known. He then drew a parallel but very short line which, he said, represented the amount of Russian *he* knew. I think it was about one hundredth the length of the first line. Then he looked as though he were about to begin a third line, starting from the bottom, but the result this time was no more than a small and barely perceptible dot. Chris and I and our fellow would-be students of Pushkin – Tim and Mike – leaned forward at our desks, craning our necks in anticipation, and could just about discern the mysterious chalky speck. 'And this, proclaimed our *Magister,* is how much Russian you will know at the end of this introductory course.' Wow, as much as that, we thought. Seldom had we been so motivated.

***

The Don had informed us that his Brighton marra Steve had done O-Level Russian in the early seventies. So it just got better and better. Here was the veritable gold standard! What more could we possibly need? But then I remembered that I myself had O-Level Maths and O-Level Physics to my name, both of which achievements I have always attributed to an administrative error somewhere in the workings of the examination board concerned. Either that, or the examiners in question had a psychopathic grudge against humanity and thought that by giving someone as innumerate and unscientific as me such 'qualifications' they might set in train an uncontrollable sequence of events that would eventually lead to nuclear disaster and the end of life on this planet. Or possibly to a financial melt-down such as the one we have experienced in recent years. Hmm …, I wonder how many of the responsible bankers, brokers, hedge-fund wonks and other such worthies did their maths O-Levels with the same examination board at the same time …

Chris and I went through plan 'R'. This was the scenario we had devised in the event of us needing to pass undetected through a mass of potentially hostile and Russian-speaking Metalist fans. If we found ourselves in such a tight spot, Chris would say:

'*Пётр в саду?*' (Is Piotr in the garden?)

I say: '*Нет, он в доме.*' (No, he is in the house.)

The Don nods and says: '*да, да*'. (Yes, yes.)

Sarah says: '*Луна на небе*'. (The moon is in the sky.)

I say: '*да, и река сияет.*' (Yes, and the river is glistening.)

Then Steve says: '*Советский Союз производит больший объем тракторов, чем любая другая страна в мире.*' (The Soviet Union produces a greater volume of tractors than any other country in the world).

What could possibly be a more natural conversation? Piece of cake (or whatever that is in Russian). *Кусочек торта*?

(Reading the above, can you see that the Russian word for tractor is *traktor* – not so difficult after all, eh? Once you know the funny letters.)

***

All the arrangements were thus in place. I had even e-mailed the Mirax from work that day and asked them to arrange the transfer from the airport for Sarah, Chris and me. It would cost a hundred and fifty Greavesies, which was around fifteen euros, so well worth it. When you hop in an ordinary taxi in such a new and unpredictable place there is always a risk of being ripped off immediately upon arrival, so we are prepared to pay that little bit extra for peace of mind and security. Once we get our bearings and have gauged the price of things we start to venture forth, use public transport and so on.

The Don and the Steve would be flying out from Gatwick a bit later and landing in Kharkiv around ten, so we would not be meeting up till matchday morning when they would come to our hotel around eleven. At some point I would ring Steve Storey and hopefully collect my ticket. Otherwise I would have to chance my luck buying a ticket locally, or try to bribe my way through the turnstile.

***

Metalist had had a winter break, so their players were not really match fit – or were they? Before the Toon game they had played that friendly against Whitley Bay at Hillheads, of course. Perhaps they had heard that the Toon had gone oot to (the) Bay in the Northumberland Senior Cup. If they had, then they had heard wrong, as it was Bedlington who knocked the Toon out three-two in the quarter-final in January. Just testing! The Seahorses' one-one draw with the Ukrainians was clearly pretty good preparation for the SJP game in the event.

I had checked the weather forecast for the next few days in Kharkiv, and temperatures were expected to drop to around minus eight or nine, so we could count ourselves lucky really as the twentieth of February could easily have seen temperatures as low as minus twenty according to long-term trends. I had even made a point of watching the BBC Breakfast programme weather forecast. In my opinion, Carol the weather lady is the best qualified meteorologist in the world. I tried to concentrate on what she was saying, but somehow I became distracted by two warm fronts.

***

Still in Luxembourg the evening before flying, I asked at reception for a wake-up call at five o'clock, and back in my room I set the mobile phone alarm for five past. Belt and braces as always. Then I tried to locate the phone in the room. I was tired and, honest, I just could not find one anywhere. The telly was a flat-screen hooked onto a whiter-than-white wood-chip-wallpapered wall. It looked like such a high-tech TV that I reckoned it must also feature the wake-up call facility. Still, it was a bit worrying thinking there was no fixed-line phone.

Phone worries aside, I could go to bed safe in the knowledge that we had thought of everything, as usual. Time to get some sleep and dream of European glory. As I was drifting off, I thought maybe I should have asked my travel agent (Herr Prim is a Stuttgart supporter and was also following our progress through Europe with interest) to make arrangements for the next round in my absence, in the event of us getting through – as I wouldn't be back in Germany till Saturday and was then off to Belgium on a work trip for three days ... Yes, it could be tight, especially if it were Moscow, but then Hanover would be easy, ... zzzz , no need to worry zzz, we won't be going through anyway, zzzzzzzzzzzz. It wasn't a sound sleep. I dreamt that the wake-up call failed to come through as there was no hotel-room phone to ring ...

***

The hotel-room phone rang promptly at five with the confidence of the Northern Goldsmiths' Big Ben chime-alike, so I leaped out of bed wondering where I was and, more to the point at that moment, where the phone was. The walls of the room were all white, all right – definitely had been decorated recently ... maybe there'd been a particularly bloody murder ... I fumbled around the place like a lunatic, immediately banging my knee against the wardrobe, which I was sure had been somewhere else the previous evening. *Ring, ring*, it went – *ring, ring*. Where was the wretched *ringing-thing*? But eventually I found the white phone, as white as a whitewashed whitener against a whiter-than-white wall. Everything quite white. S#1te. But on the bright white side, I was now white awake.

***

With the act of getting out of bed out of the way, the way was paved for the day to begin. We were headed east, just like Napoléon's *Grande Armée*. And we were now *le Toon*. French tricolours and onion sellers had become an everyday sight on Tyneside, and our friend Spug – himself an avid onion seller – was coming to look more and more like Louis de Funès with every passing day. So the Toon Army had become *la Grande Armée du Toon*. We should not forget, however, that the original Napoléonic army became somewhat unstuck (having been stuck a bit in the autumn mud) and had to withdraw sheepishly and sleeplessly from Moscow, which the Russians had basically abandoned and left to them. So we would have to learn our history lessons. Truth to tell, Napoléon's troops weren't sheepish enough, because if their supplies had been a bit more sheepish they might have had enough to eat. But they didn't. In fact, in the bitterly cold Russian winter that accompanied their slow and painful retreat they were reduced to calving out steaks from their officers' still living horses as they struggled along. It was so cold that the horses didn't even notice.

Well not at first anyway. You thought that 'calved' was a typo, there, didn't you? Not a bit of it. The French squaddies apparently kidded themselves that they were eating beef – hence it was 'calved', get it? This fits nicely with the current scandal about horsemeat being sold off as beef and pork just about everywhere in Europe. Doesn't bother me, mind, you can't beat a nice horse goulash. And remember: shamburgers is an anagram of 'Shergars' bum'. Hamburgers isn't.

***

As you walk from Luxembourg airport's underground car park to the terminal proper you pass a great big partition wall with a life-size railway station scene painted on it. Hidden behind is an underground railway station, though as yet it has not got an underground railway. Alas it will still be a few years yet before that scene becomes reality. You'll remember Newcastle airport had a similar problem for quite some time.

There was snow on the ground in Luxembourg (but they kept the runway clear), and it was quite cold walking the few yards from the apron bus to the steps into the aircraft. But after take-off I soon warmed up and began half-dozing until I was abruptly woken by the sound of the undercarriage clunk-clicking into position and I looked out of the window into a winter wonderland set in the promising reddishness of the Austrian dawn. The hills in the distance looked alive with the sound of music and the fields between them and the ever-closer ground below were a thick patchwork of snowy white snow.

***

Out of the plane into the bus, out of the bus into the terminal. And if Luxembourg airport had been antiseptic, Vienna Schwechat was in the operating-theatre-clean league. Spotless. Ten out of ten. Switched the mobile on and there was no message from Chris. Surely the fog of the previous day, which had led to dozens of flights out of Heathrow being cancelled, had lifted and everything was going to plan.

As I had got off a Schengen flight, there was no incoming passport control to go through and I could march straight through the airport towards our jump-off point for (the) Ukraine. But that was outside the Schengen zone, so there was one security check and passport control to go through. Hang on, this was Vienna, right? So where was the Third Man? And more to the point, who was the Third Man? Had to be Barry, I supposed, as I was already there and Chris would soon be joining me.

Having reached the gate, I went up to the desk and asked the lassie if any London flights were delayed. She checked on her computer and everything was running to schedule (computer said no). But she said my friends would not have a lot of time to spare. At least that is what I think she said. Because even after living in Germany for about thirty-four years, I still find Austrian German a bit of a challenge. And also very quaint. Chris on the other hand had lived for a while in Austria, so this would be like a homecoming. Albeit a short-lived one. The clock was ticking down, and soon passengers were told that boarding could begin. I just sat around and let the queue form. It included quite a few independent-minded members of the Toon Army, veritable free spirits, and there were some familiar faces among them. It's always nice to hear the odd 'Y'aalreet there?' and 'Wheyaye man. Champion,' on these occasions. A Toon Army home from home.

The queue was rapidly dwindling, however, as the door behind the lassie's desk swallowed up more and more passengers. There were only about half a dozen between me and the door when I turned around to see Sarah and Chris hurriedly headed my way.

We immediately slipped into Cyrillic mode.

Chris: *'Галау бонни лад.'*

Me: *'гуз ит ганнен?*

Chris: *'канни ман, анд ясел?'*

Me: *'Ай, канни н аал.'*

Chris: *'Дие синк уа ганна уин?'*

Me: *'Уайай ман!'*

And from thereon in, we spoke only in the Cyrillic alphabet, so if you don't mind, just mentally transliterate into Cyrillic everything you read from now until the end of this chapter. *Спасибо!*

(I am particularly proud of that Cyrillic transliteration of 'Wheyayeman' which you have just read – *'Уайай ман'*. I reckon it's a world first. Never been done before. And remember, you read it here!)

The three of us were the last to show their tickets. And for some reason the lassie asked me to wait a second. She then gave me a new ticket. We thought this was strange, but ten minutes later as we were looking for our seats on the plane we discovered that Chris and Sarah were in two seats on one side of the aisle and I had the aisle seat opposite. A nice touch by Austrian Airlines, we thought. Clearly in honour of Chris's triumphant return to the home of *Edelweiss.*

The flight took around two and a half hours and we had plenty of time to catch up and eagerly anticipate what the next couple of days would bring – in what for Chris and me was a completely new country. Sarah, remember, had already been to Lviv/Lwów/Lemberg. Still true to my Lenten alcohollessness (if James Joyce and the Jormans can do it, so can we – string words together, not disregard Lent, we mean), I had two cans of Austrian non-alcoholic lager. Well, I suppose it wasn't bad. Chris, however, looked increasingly sceptical and reminded me that not only would there be a special Papal dispensation for Saint Paddy's Day weekend, but the fact that the German Pope was stepping down meant there would also be a special double Papal dispensation for any Toon Army outings during Lent. He was beginning to sound quite convincing. As we came into land in Kharkiv Sarah took some great photos of some Communist-era blocks of flats. It was a very smooth landing and as we taxied to our final parking position we thought we saw a church to our left, adjacent to the apron. It was certainly a very ornate and white building with what looked like a cross between a stepped gable and a spire. Almost a squat, compressed version of Warsaw's Palace of Culture.

We all piled out of the plane and into the bus, out of the bus and into the terminal building. Passport control was at first sight very reminiscent of such places in Communist times. And having personally crossed through the Berlin wall several times, both by car at Checkpoint Charlie and by *S-Bahn* surburban train at Friedrichstrasse, I remember the set-up very well. The unsmiling faces of officialdom in eastern European uniforms, complete with Kalashnikovs, served only to reinforce the feeling that we had slipped through a gap in the space-time continuum and into a scene from John le Carré, complete with the smell of two-stroke. But the passport control people, when we got that far, were not unwelcoming at all and they wished us a pleasant stay in their country. And hey, don't forget that where we come from Socialism is definitely NOT a dirty word! Quite the opposite in fact.

So we went with the flow into the arrivals greeting zone, and sure enough there was a *Chelovek* – the ideal new Soviet man – holding up a piece of the people's cardboard with my name on it. We homed in on him and soon he was leading us out of the airport and into a four-by-four. Looking around us, our first impressions were of low-rise provincial austerity and we quickly spotted a good few cars that had long since gone way out of fashion in Western Europe. Ladas in particular stood to the fore. That said, there were plenty of the usual marques as well. As we drove out of the airport car park we saw that the terminal we had left was basically one big gleaming glass and concrete block that had clearly been built specially for Euro 2012 and what we had taken to be a church was in fact the original old Soviet-style terminal building. Actually, the older one was the prettier of the two.

***

We were soon speeding along an urban dual carriageway towards our hotel. The driver was constantly having to swerve to avoid pot-holes, and the rusty, clanking single-car trams running along the central reservation were regularly dipping and bobbing almost boat-like on their undulating tracks. The closer to town we got, the higher-rise things became, with plenty of those old-style blocks of flats. At ground-floor level, shops protruded bungalow-like from the blocks into wide pedestrian spaces next to the road. We puzzled over some of the shop names as we gradually but surely deciphered the Cyrillic script. Several times we transliterated KONFISKAT, which from all appearances had to mean some kind of pawn shop. There were plenty of supermarkets and filling stations. Everywhere people were milling about, weighed down by carrier bags. The middle-aged ones looked not particularly healthy but not particularly badly dressed either. Everyone, though, looked utterly miserable. Didn't see anyone smiling. And did the looks on some faces suggest that Communism hadn't been that bad after all? And had we known …

The young ones were dressed just like their peers in Western Europe. A great many girls and women were absolute stunners. Very tidy tackle, as the parlance has it. As we subsequently swept down a wide but single-carriageway boulevard, we caught sight, between blocks of flats, of the Metalist stadium itself. And even at a distance it looked very modern and very impressive. A mural on one of the blocks near the stadium read '*Willkommen*'. Clearly Germany had played here.

There must have been a lot of heartache and soul-searching when taking the decision to write the word *Willkommen* in this city, because by all accounts Kharkov was the scene of some very bitter fighting indeed during the War. But more of that later.

At the end of that boulevard we saw the *Ploshcha Povstannia* Metro station, which the hotel website had mentioned as being very close by, and sure enough we turned left and were soon pulling over onto the other side of the road to park outside what was to be home for the next few days.

***

The Mirax Boutique hotel would turn out to be, well, a boutique hotel with only about eleven rooms, and unless we were very much mistaken they were themed on Marilyn Monroe. The buildings in the immediate vicinity were quite old and hunched-up, some of them looking as if they had been left over from what at one time had been a village some distance outside town. Others, however, were Communist-style workers' dormitories on the heroic scale of the Byker Wall, but nowhere near as nice! One such specimen was directly opposite, about two hundred yards away on the other side of our very wide and very pot-holed street. Centre-stage from this perspective was another snow-dusted central reservation down which the battered old trams were still surfing invisible but gentle waves. The building housing the hotel, on the other hand, was a modern five-storey apartment block. To the right of the hotel entrance as we approached it from the taxi we noted a ground-floor twenty-four-hour Spar supermarket which was to come in handy over the course of the next few days. Even the few steps from the taxi to that entrance were a wibbly-wobbly way over a wide, cracked and uneven – and very old – pavement.

Once inside, however, all was modernity. After a very friendly welcome from Elena, the tightly elegant and very leggy receptionist, we went to our rooms to unpack and freshen up. Ten minutes later and we were asking wor Elena some basic questions such as how much would, say, a pizza cost in Kharkiv? The local price she quoted worked out at about eight euros, which didn't sound too bad. So how much should we expect to have to pay for a large beer, pet? This time it worked out at about ten euros. You sure? Yes, have a nice day. Big smile, very charming. Hmmm …

Chris and Sarah needed to change some sterling and Elena had told us there were two *bureaux de change* within about a hundred yards of the hotel, so off we set. It was about four in the afternoon by now and the late-afternoon winter sunshine gave the street scene a hopeful feel that was further enhanced by the snow and the crispy cold. Leaving the hotel, we turned right to head in the direction of the Metro station and were immediately confronted with Ukrainian reality when, two buildings along, we almost fell down the steps leading into the probably now disused cellar of an old two-storey house coloured a very faded red. The steps were literally in a hole in the pavement – no fencing around it, nothing. No warning sign, *nada*. Anyone strolling along paying no attention, chatting on the mobile for example, and walking too far to the right on the pavement could have broken their neck quite easily. We saw this sort of thing time and again.

We came to the first *bureau de change* and the sign said they changed only from dollars, euros and roubles, not pounds. We asked the miserable-faced security guard if this was really true, and he confirmed that it was. 'Nyet pounds,' he said. Moving on, we passed a cardboard cut-out of Russell Crowe in his *Maximus* role and then came to the second place. 'Nyet pounds,' again. *Royaume Uni: nul points*.

On we moved again, and at the corner of the street we turned right onto the boulevard we had come down in the taxi (where we had already glimpsed the stadium) and after twenty metres or so crossed at the tram-stop traffic lights to the Metro station on the other side. The metal and glass doors at the entrance were a lot heavier than expected and as we left the sunny and cold air of the surface we were hit by the draught and the special whiff of the Kharkiv Metro. Helpfully, the Cyrillic (and definitely Ukrainian) signage within the Metro system came with English (or at any rate Latin-alphabet) subtitles. It was a bit weird, this official-language business. For example, place names and suchlike were in Ukrainian, whose alphabet, unlike the Russian one, contains the Latin letter *i*. For example, the word for 'exit' in the Metro system was *Buxið* (*Vichid* with a guttural *ch* as in the Scottish word Lo*ch*), but in the restaurants, where Russian was used, it was *Выхоð* (with an '*oð*' on the end). Very similar, yet different.

We got to the ticket machines and of course did not have the right money, or for that matter any clue how the system worked.

Fortunately the *babushka* in a blue uniform sitting behind an important-looking desk seemed to be delighted to have found someone who needed her help. In fact I think she was happy to have found something, anything to do. Very kindly, she more or less took us by the hand, changed a twenty Greavsie note and showed us how to manage the ticket machine. Each ticket cost just two Greavsies, or twenty euro-cent, i.e. virtually nothing. My iffy Russian meant I could just about get her message and she seemed to be telling us that one ticket would take us anywhere within the system. We had our three tickets and we were in business.

Then she showed us how to feed our tickets into the barrier. It swallowed the tickets and we walked through into the system proper. I say barrier but actually it was just a row of ticket-swallowing machines. There was no physical barrier, so, at this station at least, the system seemed to be very much honesty-based. Though no doubt our *babushka* was keeping an eagle eye on everyone. We descended a very wide set of steps to a huge single central platform in what in effect was an enormous concrete cavern. No doubt the Metro had originally been designed to double as a system of air-raid shelters in the event of war. And those heavy doors at the entrance had no doubt been designed to withstand a certain level of blast.

Trains were departing in both directions, but there was no need to worry as Sarah had read that there was one every couple of minutes. There were plenty of people using the Metro system considering it was just after four o'clock on a Wednesday afternoon, but then again I suppose the afternoon rush hour had begun. And Kharkiv does have a population of getting on for one and a half million, after all (about three times the population of a country called Luxembourg)! But apart from us, there was nobody laughing or passing any kind of comment. Why did everyone look so miserable? It occurred to us that things must have looked pretty much the same here during the Cold War – a time when Soviet propaganda had hammered home the message that there was always a threat of American aggression. And a town with a major metal production facility was always going to be a target, just as it had been during the Second World War. Thank goodness that we in the free West had never been told any propaganda lies about the Soviet Union. And it is so reassuring to know that we were the goodie-goodies!

Our train soon arrived and we got on board. It was surely at least forty or fifty years old and no doubt had done hundreds of thousands of kilometres serving the people. It was creaky and rolled about a bit, but was very atmospheric, and quite full. We were the star attraction, speaking our strange language and generally laughing and carrying on and showing an interest in just about everything. Everyone else continued, well, to look thoroughly miserable. But at the same time, many of the women were absolutely, stunningly beautiful, though in a miserable sort of way. The carriage was literally plastered with adverts of all sorts, including on the windows! Capitalism had come to such countries quite literally with a vengeance, making many people winners but many more of them losers, some of them big time. We were to see plenty of examples of both categories.

Ours was the second stop (the distances between stations being quite considerable), and the train slowed down with screeching and screaming noises and a clunky thud as it came to a halt and spilled some of its contents out onto the platform of *Ploshchad Svobody* (Freedom Square – as in free to obey Russia, or else). This station was, if anything, even more cavernous than the one in which we had started our journey. And on the 'landing' at the top of the escalator there was a space reserved for about twenty chess players! There they were, playing speed chess in a public space as the madding rush-hour crowd rushed past them on both sides. A few people, however, took some time out from the rush and stood behind the glass panel behind the chess players for a few minutes to take in their more-exciting-even-than-dominoes games.

We moved on from our behind-the-glass vantage point and pushed open the heavy swing doors: we were coming out onto Europe's biggest (!) square and were greeted by no less a personage than Lenin himself. A huge statue looking out over the square and the cityscape at large. This was a seriously big square. When I was little, I used to think that Northumberland Square in North Shields was big, but hey, this was the business – truly huge! Walking away from Lenin, who was no doubt looking down on us benevolently, we had the tower-like Kharkiv Palace hotel (the team hotel, as we later found out) on our left, and then also on our left a long row of medium-rise administrative buildings, banks and suchlike. At the other end of the square, in the distance, the façades also had the look of old office buildings, with an onion-domed Russian

Orthodox church as a neighbour, and on our right was a South-Shields-market-square-style market, behind which lay the entrance to Shevchenko Park. A bit further along on the right was an un-Irish Pub, with more of the park behind it.

***

But Chris and Sarah still needed some Greavsies, so we decided to check out the *Crédit Agricole* which we spotted on the left-hand side of the square, about half way along, a good five-minute walk from the Metro station. There were half a dozen customers inside, watched over by a Lurch-like Happy-Harry security guard who looked as miserable as sin, and menacing with it, and whose face would surely crack if he ever smiled (no chance of that). The place was silent, and we wondered how the customers communicated. We established that this bank was prepared to change pounds, but first Chris had to let them photocopy his passport. Then the lassie behind the security glass refused to accept some notes because they weren't clean enough. Maybe they dealt in laundered money only, we thought. With notes both dirty and clean being passed back and forth, she managed to cause some confusion, and in the end she gave Chris (mostly dirty) Greavsie notes worth seventy quid, though Chris was sure he had given her eighty. Quite a conjuring trick. But hey, such is life, and Lurch was looking even more menacing than he had a couple of minutes earlier. Time for a drink in the un-Irish Pub, and let's put it all down to experience!

Although Freedom Square is a square (and no doubt they used to hold huge great military parades on it, and maybe they still do), there is quite a bit of traffic on it and you have to be careful crossing. So we were. And we safely reached 'Patrick Pub' (*sic*), whose sign also said 'Drink. Drive. Friends.' Hmmm … We went into what surely qualifies as the most un-Irish Irish Pub we have ever been in. It was more like a Russian-style Indian restaurant. The layout of tables was most un-publike. But never mind, we sat and ordered some drinks. Chris and Sarah had local lager and I ordered alcohol-free beer. What I got was non-alcoholic German wheat beer. Not nice. Soon there came in a friendly Geordie woman and her son. She was not into football, she said, and had only come because her son was under-age and could not otherwise have travelled. Under-age or not, he had brought back as a souvenir of his trip to Madeira a very impressive tattoo on his chest. It was the

NUFC crest. And yes, as you've guessed, we were impressed by the crest on the chest.

Our intrepid travellers had apparently been told at Newcastle Airport that the charter they were booked on had been cancelled because the company had gone bust. But then they had been interviewed for Look North, which made everything all right again, and they got on another plane instead. For the second time, she told us that she was not interested in football and that they had had a canny drink on the plane. And it was nice to bump into some Geordies, and cheers, spilling only a little of her lager onto our table. And were we here for the match, then? No, we had come here on our holidays because we were sick of Majorca and all those Germans. Then another female Geordie voice from somewhere piped up: 'Ee, ah never thought anybody would come here for their holidays!' Never mind, pet.

We supped up and thought we might explore a bit. First we went into Shevchenko Park, which features a very impressive, in fact huge, statue of Shevkenko, the Ukrainian national poet and (we think) part-time footballer and politician. Shevchenko, it has to be said, appears to be a not uncommon name in these parts. We bore left and came out of the park onto *Ulitsa Sumska* (Sumska Street), where we turned right and saw the prospect of a long and busy street to walk down. It seemed to be a main shopping drag, with lots of recognisable big-name shops and some less recognisable ones. To the left we saw a little park with a fountain that was being illuminated in different colours – it was quite dark by now. And on our right we passed a municipal theatre. It was made of sixties concrete, Communist-style, very white gone grey, and very square – T. Dan Smith would have been proud of it.

We got talking about the Cyrillic alphabet, and the fact there is no equivalent of the letter 'h'. Russians and others have problems pronouncing the associated sound, often replacing it with a 'g'. In fact if someone in a Russian-language war film has to say *Heil Hitler*, what he actually says is *Geil Gitler*. This is particular funny from a German perspective as *geil* means randy. Except that nowadays people say *geil* all the time, but meaning nothing more than great, as in really good. In the same way the youngsters say 'wicked' in Britain. In other words it has virtually lost its original meaning. Discuss. (Well, Pete, who'd have thought it – Geil Gitler, Randy Git-ler. Have I ever mentioned that there is or was a vicar around Hexham way really called Randy Vickers? We went to his Christmas Carols once, and I kept the parish pamphlet with his name on as a reminder.)

No sooner had we established this than we passed a shop called 'Shopagolic'. That was written out in the Latin letters and was clearly meant to be 'Shopaholic'. So the point was proven. Nice one. We continued walking down this pleasant and interesting street, noting possible eating venues as we passed them, until we came to a crossroads of the kind Alan from Gateshead would immediately recognise, and we found ourselves standing outside the History Museum (*Istorichesk Muzei*) Metro station. It was in fact a cross between a busy crossroads and a square, beyond which we could see an Orthodox Cathedral and Monastery which we decided we would like to visit at some stage, and to the right there opened up a broad vista down towards the river. It was a nice, quite lively spot, and we reckoned this would definitely be a good place to come back to, but for now we were hungry and decided to retrace our steps along Sumska Street to check out one of the eateries we had earlier earmarked. We hit upon *Zdrownie Boolie*, or something like that. It was a beer-cellar type place down two flights of stairs and featuring what appeared to be a labyrinth of large rooms. We sat down in one of them and had great fun communicating with a friendly waitress whose English was even dodgier than my Russian. We wanted sausages with chips, but apparently you were not allowed to have sausages on the same plate as chips, so we ordered them on separate plates. We were allowed to have ginormous beers, however, so Chris and I had a litre each, Sarah a more modest pint.

Oops, I had forgotten it was Lent. Well, it would have been impolite to drink the non-alcoholic stuff, so I didn't complain. The beer and the nosh were steady, and there was football on various tellies, including a giant screen. As we were leaving we bumped into two Geordie lads. They told us some of the locals had invited them to have a fight after the match tomorrow night. Our compatriots had politely declined, and nor were we all that keen on the idea ourselves. The two lads tagged along with us as we walked back along Sumska Street and back to the un-Irish Irish Pub. By now the place was absolutely heaving, and it was mainly the Toon Army. We had a great old singsong and while Sarah, Chris and I were singing the praises of Supermac, one young lad came up and told us it was great to hear the songs his Da (or was it his Granda?)

had taught him! We had a couple of vodkas, as we were in (the) Ukraine, and I blame the vodka for the very strange dream I had that night … more of that anon.

It was getting late and we decided to call it a day and make our way back to the hotel. We made the Metro trip in reverse and as we were coming out of our home Metro station we saw a couple of very scrawny cats looking for food and sympathy. It was just a few minutes' walk from *Ploshcha Povstannia* to the hotel, and then it was time for beddie-byes, so night night. Zzzzz … zzzzz.

What a strange vodka-induced dream it was. *Two black-and-white kittens were trying to charm their way into our house and an easy life. Wor Lass was all for it but I put my foot down with a firm hand. I gently threw them out of the bedroom window with the aim of giving them a gentle landing in the garden. While they were still in mid-air, however, down swooped a pelican and grabbed one of the kittens before the wee thing could hit the ground running. I was treated to a close-up of the pelican having its feline supper.* Like I say, blame the vodka.

(Hey, Pete, I tried your dream out on daughter Emilie, who is about to start studying psychology, and her comment was, 'Ooh, that's mean!')

***

My room was on the side of the building away from the road, and the next morning I realised it was the east side when the very bright rays of the sun said it was time to get up. I opened the window to the cold and to the view of some pretty dilapidated old-style tenement buildings and courtyards. A tolerable view for a couple of interesting days but no doubt quite depressing if it had to be endured for very much longer than that. There was a slightly sulphurous tang to the air, which I put down to a combination of road traffic and industrial facilities not too far away. And probably pelicans as well.

***

Breakfast was on the fifth floor, and we met up as arranged just before ten in what turned out to be more or less a roof-top restaurant with quite a panoramic view. The hotel in Athens had had a roof-top restaurant and bar with a fabulous panoramic view of the city. This wasn't quite in the same league but it was very nice and very interesting nonetheless. Once again we had a view of the

Metalist stadium in the middle distance and the waitress agreed it was only a twenty-five minute walk away. We saw lots of four, five or six-storey blocks of flats, and, very interestingly, loads of old-fashioned television aerials. So it was once again a bit of a journey through the past. The story of my dream was not greeted with a great deal of enthusiasm but it did attract the attention of a couple sitting two tables away, the only other breakfasters on this Thursday, match-day, morning. Ah, you're English?

Well, Geordies actually.

Turned out that Dave was from Wales but a Spurs supporter because of that club's Welsh connections in his Dad's day. Dave was staying at the Mirax with his Ukrainian girlfriend and was a frequent visitor to Kharkiv. He knew a great deal about the place and its history. Metalist, as we had kind of guessed, took its name from the local iron and steel industry. Before the war Kharkiv had been one of the Soviet Union's main battle-tank production sites and the country's highly successful WWII tank, the T-34, had been built here. After Hitler had declared war on the Soviet Union, the city was clearly a major target for the *Wehrmacht*, but before the Germans got here the Soviets dismantled as many of the region's industrial facilities as they could and re-assembled them behind the Urals. That is an easy sentence to write, but can you imagine the superhuman effort involved in doing such a thing. People must have been working around the clock. Convoys of steam trains must have been chugging to and fro in a race against time and against hope. Fair play to the Soviet Union! Relocating so much of its military manufacturing capability like that went a long way towards thwarting the Germans' efforts. Nevertheless, the *Wehrmacht* did capture Kharkiv, lost it and then re-captured it. They briefly named what is now Freedom Square *Platz der Leibstandarte*. So Freedom Square is a pretty good name for the place! And yet, as we saw earlier, one of the murals on a block of flats near the stadium reads '*Willkommen*'. That speaks volumes for the good people of Kharkiv! Over breakfast we also talked of course about the disgusting recent treatment of Spurs fans by right-wing lunatics in Lyon. It is just too bad. No football fan wants this sort of s#1t to happen. Dave wished the Toon the best of luck and we wished Spurs the same.

The three of us hung around reception waiting for the Don and the Steve to arrive. While we were waiting, the receptionist kindly asked in Russian how we were. I answered, using a phrase a

Russian-German colleague had taught me years ago. It means 'every day a day nearer death'. Elena the beautiful receptionist burst out laughing. A nice sense of humour, the Russians and the Ukrainians!

Bang on eleven, as arranged, the Steve and the Don came up the stairs into the reception area. Steve is a Brighton fan, but of course was more than welcome to join in the Toon Army fun and games. And his O-Level Russian made him a vital asset for our deep-cover operations.

Taking care not to fall into the open cellar stairwell on the pavement next to the hotel, we made our way back to our local Metro station with the self-confident air of long-term local residents who knew they could hold a meaningless conversation in Russian for all of thirty seconds. In the ticket machine area we bumped into a black-and-white shirt and helped him get his ticket. This time there were a few polisses standing at the top of the stairs leading down to the platform. Our *babushka* must have called in reinforcements to look out for fare dodgers. Once in the train, and very much at the centre of everybody's attention thanks to our language, laughter and now a black-and-white shirt, we asked our new friend how his trip out had been. He had come via Moscow. Wow, an interesting route! Not really, he lives in Stavanger, Norway. Turns out he is Norwegian. But speaks great Geordie. Howay the Scandinavian Mags!

Back at Freedom Square station, we walked through a few cavernous passages to change Metro lines, taking care not to bang our heads on the stalactites and stalacmites. The lines have different colours (what a good idea!) and we switched from blue to green. We then took that Metro for one stop to the History Museum station, to which we had walked the day before. When we came out of the Metro paid area we came into an old-style shopping precinct still within the station building. There were loads of little kiosk-style shops, cheek by jowl, selling just about everything you could think of, but a great many of them selling some very tasty-looking sausages and cold meats. This reminded me very much of a similar but larger-scale market in Warsaw Central Station. It is good to see that some of the nice things from the old days are still there despite the appearance of the glitzy shopping malls and big-name stores. This type of thing helps places retain their local character in the same way as the Grainger Market, for example. We emerged into the cold sunshine and made our way along Sumska Street again, passing the 'Shopagolic' shop. By now we were feeling quite at home. We spotted another cellar-type bar, and this time the name was *Toggle Kafyarnia*. It seemed to be a cross between a cellar bar and a café, and we reckoned there should be something for everyone. So down the stairs and into the cellar, and that will be four local beers and a coffee, please, Pet. The local beer turned out to be bottled Stella Artois, but let's not quibble. It was steady. I rang the ever-friendly Steve Storey, who said he was at the team hotel, the Kharkiv Palace on Freedom Square, and we arranged to be there at two o'clock to collect my ticket. Perfect, we had time for another pint.

When we'd supped up, we left the Toggle Café to head back along Sumska, through the park and across the Square. Lenin had by now seen the error of his ways and had become a Newcastle supporter, and a few fans had draped a black-and-white 'Keep the Faith' flag on the base of the statue. We went into the Kharkiv Palace, a huge ultra-modern tower building. Inside there was an enormous atrium with a bar and seating from where you could stare up to the various floors and a huge great chandelier dangling down over about twenty storeys. We thought about ordering a drink but wondered about the prices. I rang Steve and he appeared a few minutes later, just one Storey. He told us we'd brought a strong squad with us, so our manager was clearly taking things seriously. Good news.

We wandered out into the square again and had a walk around the market, hoping to find a sausage stand or something similar, but instead finding clothes and pots and pans. We were a bit peckish so headed back to the un-Irish Pub, only to be told they were not serving beer, as it was match-day. You don't get more un-Irish than that! Unable to work out the underlying logic of this state of affairs, we said no thank you and went instead to an Italian place only a few hundred yards away called *Buon Appetito*. Again it was in a cellar and very cosy. There really did seem to be a lot of emphasis on eating and drinking below street-level in this city! Here, it was deep enough for us to hear the rumbling of the Metro only just beneath us, something you also used to be able to experience in a Chinese just next to the Monument in the Toon (it's not a Chinese any more, sad to say). We had a super pizza lunch with starters and drinks, and I don't think we paid more than the equivalent of about twelve pounds a head. Great value. But then we remembered that Dave the Spurs supporter had told us that a Ukrainian poliss earns the equivalent of only about two hundred or two hundred and fifty pounds a month, so all of these prices are relative.

Time was getting on and the match was going to start at the somewhat strange time of 19.05 (television dictates), so we decided to make our way back to base, using our trusted Metro transport. Steve and (the) Don decided to wait for us in the little bar called *Maximus* just next to the hotel (the one with the Russell Crowe cardboard cut-out outside) while the three of us went to freshen up. We then joined them in *Maximus* for a final pre-match drink. *Maximus* was yet another cellar job and we emerged at the bottom of the stairs into a cosy little bar which by rights should have been called *Minimus*, as it was no bigger than a largish living room. The barmaid had no English at all but she was delightful, and once again communicating was big fun. Somehow we all made ourselves understood and were so taken by the place that we thought it would be nice to come here after the match as well. However, the beautiful Karina would be shutting up shop at ten. Ah well, never mind.

***

So off we set at last for the match. The Other Clive was unable to come on this trip but he had asked me to get him three programmes if possible, so I would have to keep a look-out for a programme seller. We marched briskly through the crisp early-evening air, breathing out plumes of white mist as we crunched our way through pavement banks of frosted snow, and very soon had a clear view of the stadium floodlights with their intense yellowy-white glow somehow offering warmth despite the cold – always a particularly exciting sight on a European football night. As we got closer to the ground there were more and more fans milling around. We went through one security check but found we needed to be at another end, so left the security zone again at a different point, and had to explain exactly why we wanted out. Then we spotted a scarf seller, but no programmes. I couldn't get a half-and-half scarf but bought a Metalist one. Unfortunately, it had only Latin lettering, no Cyrillic, so that was a bit disappointing. But maybe there would be other opportunities.

In addition to the floodlights, there was some quite clever multi-colour (though mainly blue and yellow) lighting around the outside of the oval arena. And the effect in the cold winter air was very atmospheric. We passed what looked like a really old-fashioned, almost Prussian-helmet-shaped ticket office that had been left standing anachronistically out in the open on the stadium perimeter. And there were a couple of sausage stands sending tempting smells in our direction. Several *babushkas* were selling what looked like sunflower seeds – apparently as popular at outdoor events in eastern and southern Europe as peanuts (tanner a bag) used to be at St James's Park.

On we went, ploughing a furrow through throngs of home supporters. Chris said something in Russian about Piotr being in the river and I replied that the moon was in the garden. The Soviet Union is glistening, remarked Steve.

We showed our tickets to a poliss, who pointed to an entrance a few hundred yards away, and sure enough we were soon hearing more familiar Geordie tones and cadences, as quite a few of the Toon Army were grouped around a beer stand just outside the entrance to the stadium. The Don kindly got a round in, and we knew that would be our last till we were let out after the match. We stood there happily in the neon-lit winter cold, looking forward to the match and gazing out into the wide-open suburban spaces surrounding the stadium. Dimly lit and very full old trams trundled past every couple of minutes, and Communist-style blocks of flats stretched away into the distance, as far as the eye could see. There was that classic sense of pre-match tension and anticipation that only a mid-week game in Europe can provide. All the more exciting for being so far from home and in such a very different and truly exotic country.

***

We were supping our pints when an authoritative Geordie voice said 'It might be a good idea to sup up and get in the ground now, lads, because a load of their supporters are going to be using the same entrance.' It was a Newcastle poliss (not in uniform) who was saying this. He and his colleague had made the trip to help ensure everything went smoothly. They told us they would be getting in to see the match themselves and were not expecting any trouble, as they had not seen any known trouble-makers. That was good news, we said, and we told them to enjoy the match, which after all they were getting to see for free. Can't be bad.

So up we supped and in we went through the turnstiles. The searches were a bit over the top and the local polisses looked a bit intimidating. The really surprising thing was that local supporters were coming through the same gates, going up the same access stairs and using the same toilets. Only at the top of the stairs were the two sets of supporters segregated into their respective sections. The Don had managed to swap some Toon regalia and some money for a half-and-half scarf before we had come through the turnstile. Now, half-way up the access stairs, a Metalist fan, accompanied by his two charming daughters, was asking for my woollen Toon hat in exchange for a Metalist cap with ear warmers. I was a bit dubious at first, but then managed to say, in still very dubious Russian, 'Long live (the) friendship between Metalist and (the) Toonskaya Armiya' (for the record: *Да здравствует дружба между Металлистом и Тунской Армии.*) And henceforth I was the proud owner of a Metalist cap with ear warmers.

So there was a kind of segregation, and there were security people in amongst us, plus a row of polisses on the other side of the fence next to which I was standing. There were plenty of familiar faces around us, including a few we had seen on the plane. With an N and an E and a wubble you C … there was plenty of singing and we had to clap our hands and stamp our feet to keep out the cold. We were to the side of one of the goals with a pretty good view in prospect. The Metalist seats to our right were rapidly filling up. Our section was raised a little so we were looking down into a section of their fans. Some passing along the access just below us were exchanging scarves etc. with Toon fans, and it was generally a friendly atmosphere. We saw one fan helping his marra up the steps to take their seats just to my right, at the slightly lower level. At first we thought the chap being helped must be disabled in some way, but we quickly realised that in fact he was seriously pissed, and it soon became apparent that his helpful friend was also drunk. Beer was being sold to their fans by vendors carrying trays full of the stuff and the very pissed fan bought a plastic glass of beer which he immediately spilled through his drunken clumsiness onto the back of the bloke in front of him, who wasn't very pleased. The polisses to our right did nothing. The very drunk bloke then staggered down the steps on his own and a few minutes later staggered back to his seat, fresh plastic glass of beer in hand.

Along the access path leading away from his section to our right came another completely pissed fan with beer in hand. He was getting a bit frisky with a particularly nice looking blonde lady steward, and a poliss came along and told him to mind his manners, but that was all. He was clearly well and truly scuttled. All very strange! These people would have been unceremoniously removed at any match in Western Europe but here this sort of behaviour seemed to be perfectly acceptable.

Meanwhile, in the Toon section, the singing was non-stop and was getting louder and louder. No singing as yet from the home support, however. Some of our fans were beckoning to the beer vendors to sell them some liquid comfort, but they were obviously under strict instructions not to sell us any, and none was forthcoming.

We were in the black and white again and despite the cold only a couple of our lads were wearing tights and gloves. Some were even in short sleeves, which must have sent shivers down the spines of the well-wrapped-up-in-yellow Metalist players. The team tonight was Krul, Coloccini, Simpson, Yanga-Mbiwa, Haidara, Cabaye, Sissoko, Anita, Marveaux, Cissé, and Ameobi. Two forwards for a change. The general consensus was that we were not going to go through, but when the match finally got underway we were definitely the better team and created several decent chances throughout the first half. In fact Cissé twice had the ball in the net but the linesman harshly raised his flag both times. (Sounds familiar, Pete, just like the home leg!) And Shola got in a bobbling deflected shot from outside the penalty area which just crept past the right post. Metalist were attacking the goal we were right next to, but they never really looked at all like breaking through. At half time, there was hope in our hearts. And sure enough, on about sixty-nine minutes one of their defenders, Papa Gueye, made a totally useless back-pass and the keeper, Olexandr Goryainov, brought down Sissoko. Penalty! Shola made no mistake, blasting the ball to the goalkeeper's right as he dived the wrong way. The support from the Toon Army rose to a crescendo with a tremendous roar of 'You're sh1t but your birds are fit!'

Thereafter Metalist pressed hard and Tim Krul became the undoubted man of the match with a string of brilliant saves, two of them in very rapid succession from Jonathan Cristaldo and Willian. Very strange that our two opponents Metalist and Anzhi both had a player called Willian the Brazilian.

***

When the final whistle went, the team came to salute us, and hero Tim rightly got our rousing cheers. The only downside was that he damaged his ankle during the match and was out for the coming game against Southampton (we won four-two after going a goal down within three minutes; and as it turned out, Tim Krul wouldn't be back in action until the away leg at Benfica.)

We would be meeting either Anzhi in Moscow or Hannover 96 in, well, Hanover. We were kept in detention of course, and some of the home fans were making obscene gestures that would get people arrested just about anywhere else. Here, it seemed okay as far as the local polisses were concerned. Most of their fans applauded however, and we applauded them back. After about half an hour the police decided we could be let out and by now it was very, very cold. The next problem was that the local police thought all of the Toon fans had to be bussed to the airport to be flown immediately home. There was a huge number of polisses, at least two for every Newcastle supporter by the look of things. It took a lot of smooth-talking diplomacy to talk our way through the not-so-thin blue line and not end up on a bus for the airport.

***

And so the five of us were back behind enemy lines under deep cover. For the first few hundred yards there were still plenty of polisses about, which was good as we were passing any number of Metalist fans. We thought about getting the Metro into town and from there another Metro back out to the Mirax, but the Metro station at the ground was still heaving with their supporters, so we decided to walk back instead. Before long, we were in not so well-lit streets with groups of Metalist fans to be seen here and there, so we kept a low profile, only occasionally asking each other whether Piotr was still in the moon and whether Soviet tractor production was still glistening. And we mouthed the occasional *da, da, da*. But after a good half an hour's walk, through the now bitter cold, we were back at the Mirax building. The hotel doesn't have a bar as such, but it has a pleasant enough reception area, so we bought a few beers, some crisps and some nuts at the Spar supermarket and had a little party in the reception area, which was fine by our very pretty night receptionist, Olga. While chatting there, Sarah found out that Hannover 96 had lost, and so the next European away game would be in Moscow. On that note, we presently said our good nights, and the Steve and the Don got a taxi back to their hotel. We would be meeting up at the History Museum Metro the next day at noon.

***

We spent another very enjoyable day in Kharkiv, taking a walk down by the river, visiting the Orthodox cathedral and monastery and strolling through a pleasant park where local artists were displaying and selling their paintings. I particularly liked a local winter street scene featuring one of the trams we had seen, and the price was quite reasonable, but I was travelling light by my standards so didn't buy it in the end. For old times' sake, we revisited the Toggle Café, where to our regular waitress's surprise Chris had two neat vodkas. And, sentimental fools that we are, we had a final lunch in the Boolie cellar bar that we had come to regard as our local. We discovered that its labyrinthine cellar also featured a self-service restaurant area, which was very convenient given the challenges we still faced on the communication front. When asking if it was self-service, I think I said in 'Russian' the equivalent of saying in English:

'Eat, self-slubberidge, yes?'

And indeed it was self-slubberidge, so hey!

We then went back to the ground to visit the club shop, where I bought a Metalist scarf with Cyrillic writing and a couple of club newspapers, including one for the Other Clive. There we bumped into a couple of Toon fans, Neil and Paul, and went for a drink with them in the club bar. The telly was showing highlights of the game, and oh how we fretted that Shola might miss the penalty! Thankfully he didn't. That reminded me of a time when I was having a lunchtime pint in the Centurion and on the telly was that famous five-nil victory over Man U when Philippe Albert, everyone knows his name, scored that fantastic goal. The people in the bar behaved exactly as they would at a live game and cheered every goal with a 'get in'!

We piled into two taxis and went back to the Mirax area with a view to re-visiting the *Maximus* bar. But when we got downstairs there was a wedding reception going on. There were no signs on display to the effect that there was a private party going on – nothing. Very strange! We made a discreet exit and took the Metro back into town. There we went to our regular Kharkiv Italian, and although they were already keen to close despite it being just ten o'clock or so on a Friday evening they offered to make two huge off-menu pizzas for us all to share. So we had our pizza and beers and said our farewells to our two new Toon friends and to the Steve and the Don, who had to get up at five for an early flight. Sarah, Chris and I crossed the Square one final time and did our 'Goodbye, Lenin' bit. Before we went through the heavy Metro-station doors we took one last look at central Kharkiv, its floodlit Orthodox churches, the Ladas speeding across the snow-covered square, the neon cold of the night that was in it, and decided we had had a good trip.

Back at the Mirax we supped our beers from Spar in reception and were curious about some comings-and-goings across the reception area and towards the room at the end of the corridor. In the door of that room there appeared a guy whose naked torso was covered in tattoos. A very leggy and immaculately turned out young lady left the room and a similar one entered while yet another sat opposite us in reception. Another bloke took some drinks to the room, handed them in but did not enter. Another lady arrived and entered the room. Chris and Sarah were staying in the room next door to that one. I eagerly awaited their report in the morning.

***

Another cold sunny morning and it was the day of our departure. We ordered a taxi for twelve, which would get us to the airport in very good time for our 14.25 flight to Vienna. Then we went back to our panoramic-view breakfast room, where the delightful and delightfully named Svetlana, little flower, served us our bacon and eggs. Chris and Sarah reported that they had not been disturbed by Mr Tattoo and friends, which surely speaks volumes for the quality of the hotel room walls. Dave and their lass were also at breakfast, and when we told them the tale of the previous evening's gannins-on, they told us that the description we were giving fitted that of a world-famous-in-(the)-Ukraine singer whose name escaped them but who had been giving concerts very nearby. Mystery solved.

After breakfast we packed and then met up at reception at about five to twelve. Dave was also there and told us he was on the same flight to Vienna, but had already booked a separate taxi, so we would meet up again at the airport. Our respective taxis came punctually at noon, and ours took us along a slightly different route from the one we had come two days earlier. This new route took us down yet more pot-holed and tenement-lined boulevards with trams surfing their way through the snow on undulating tracks. Then some even more pot-holed back streets with older single-storey, very faded-glory buildings. There were clapped-out Ladas parked at the side of the road or in the middle of unkempt gardens where chickens were strutting briskly around and keeping out of the way of emaciated cats and dogs looking for a chance to kill something in order to stave off hunger for a while.

Interestingly, we passed a huge industrial complex marked *Metallbaza*, *baza* literally meaning base but here surely meaning something like facility or works. Run-down factory buildings extended for as far as we could see, and we wondered if this was where they used to make those famous tanks. The battle of Kursk, in Southern Russia, took place not far from here. Apparently it was the largest series of armoured clashes and also the bloodiest single day of aerial warfare in the history of modern carnage. The victory gained by the Red Army handed the strategic initiative back to the Soviets for the remainder of the War. No doubt a lot of the tanks involved had been produced in Kharkiv. Quite a thought. We got to the airport in super good time and as we entered the car park we once again admired the old church-like terminal building before entering the glitzy new one to check in.

***

But what was this? No sign of our flight on the board! There had been seriously heavy snowfall in Vienna. In the end we had to hang around in Kharkov airport for a few hours before we could finally check in for our flight, which we were told would now be leaving at four thirty. That messed up a lot of people's connections, including that of Chris and Sarah. The parallel queues at our check-in desk were moving painfully slowly as staff tried to sort out everybody's onward connections as they checked in. Chris and Sarah were told they would not be flying on from Vienna that day and they were offered another night in Kharkiv. Vienna hotels were already full up, they were told. They sensibly decided that they would nevertheless fly to Vienna where Chris would be able to smooth-talk Austrian Airlines staff in their own language and tell them they would have to sort something out.

In the parallel queue for the same flight some entertainment was developing as an evidently very drunk Russian started complaining rather loudly, using some dramatic gesticulating techniques at the same time. Silly man. Patience was what was really needed. It wasn't long before the *Militsiya* appeared and took him off to a quieter corner. But they did not remove him from sight, which we found a bit weird. He even managed to get as far as the queue for the security check, where the police appeared to want to keep him for a while. This was strange. He kept on ranting and raving and, bizarrely, took his shirt off, throwing his wallet, mobile, keys etc. on the ground and shouting at the top of his voice. Still the polisses did not whisk him away to a comfy cell. And by now he was surrounded by about ten of them. He was going nowhere in a hurry.

When we were all through security and passport control, staff from the shops and café were craning their necks to try and see the cause of all the shouting. It was amazing that the guy had not been locked up. But then Dave explained that the *Militsiya* would be running checks on him just in case he was the prime minister's brother-in-law or was otherwise well-connected, in which case they would apologise profusely for any inconvenience and wish him a pleasant trip, pissed out of his head or not, and perhaps they would offer him a courtesy triple vodka as a token of their deepest respect. You see some strange sights and experience some strange things on the *Toonskaya Armiya's* European campaigns.

Anyway, we boarded our flight okay and saw no more sign of the drunken Russki. Two and a half hours later we disembarked in a very snowy and cold Vienna. We said our farewells as Chris and Sarah headed for the Austrian Airlines transit desk and I made my way to terminal B for my connecting flight to Luxembourg. I was sure I had caught a very nasty cold by now. Austrian Airlines managed to get Chris and Sarah on a London flight that evening after all – so their decision not to spend another night in Kharkiv had been a sound one. While walking through the airport I bought some *Mozart Kugeln* chocs for Wor Lass.

***

When I switched the mobile on, there was a voice message from Barry, who was already making arrangements for Moscow: 'From what I can see it is not going to be easy. It is not going to be easy at all.' That turned out to be an understatement. I was so cream-crackered after such an exciting and tiring trip that I left the plastic bag containing the box of *Mozart Kugeln* on the bus from the terminal to the plane. So I got home late that evening empty-handed. I had brought something with me, however:

A nasty flu.

Anzhi Makachkala away, 7th March 2013

The Retreat from Moscow

'I wrote to President Putin, asking for press accreditation for the match. He said 'Da, da, no problem, Comrade, you can come and pick it up in Siberia."

I just got back last night with all my tin buttons intact despite the incredible cold. No wonder the lads were in black tights and mitts. If Napoléon had had them, he might have come away with a very honourable draw too.

Just a couple of weeks after we made it past Metalist, we were due in Russia to play Anzhi Makachkala – or *Анжи Махачкала* as some might say. The big difference was that you need a visa to get into Russia, while you are welcomed into Ukraine with open arms holding just a passport.

You need a visa to get into Russia. Getting one of those gives you a real taste of Kafka and shows you that Communism is alive and well and still brow-beating tourists into submission. You need to get a travel organisation, which luckily can be a hotel, to give you a booking reference acceptable to the visa authorities and also answer some visa questions for you. I decided to play safe and so, instead of choosing some random Russian hotel, I went for the Holiday Inn as I thought that, being big and well-known, they would be able to give me a hand with the visa details. I must say the Holiday Inn Moscow Lesnaya people were great – very helpful and very fast to respond. Well done to them.

Some of the questions are laughably incriminating and positively sinister. I'll give you a tour of what's in store in case you need to go sometime.

As a silent protest, in answer to the 'have you forgotten your password' question, where a normal country would ask you your mother's maiden name or your favourite pet, instead they give you a string of possible questions to answer such as give the name of the person you first or last kissed, etc. It's like some Russian Inquisition where any answer you give can and will be used to incriminate you. The least innocuous question is 'what was the name of the first concert that you went to see?' Whereas by rights I should have written 'The Beatles', I instead wrote 'Pussy Riot'. They still gave me a visa.

They also ask you to name all the countries you've been in the last ten years, with the dates. Now who can possibly remember that? You might decide on a whim to go and do the shopping in Germany one weekend and in France or the Netherlands the next. Are you supposed to keep a logbook? I settled on some educated guesses. I'd be seriously concerned if they had any way of actually checking whether what I wrote was true:

CZECH REPUBLIC, 05/05/2005, DENMARK, 12/04/2008, FRANCE, 16/02/2013, GERMANY, 20/11/2012, GREECE,10/10/2012, ICELAND, 12/05/2005, IRELAND, 05/10/2007, ITALY, 20/04/2012, LUXEMBOURG, 18/12/2011,NETHERLANDS, 23/12/2011, PORTUGAL, 04/11/2012, SLOVAKIA, 19/03/2012, SPAIN, 25/08/2012, SWITZERLAND,16/02/2011, TURKEY, 12/06/2007, UNITED KINGDOM, 15/02/2013, UNITED STATES, 10/11/2008

Take a look at these other questions, and just ask yourself whether you would seriously think about answering 'yes' to any of them if you were hoping to ever be granted a visa:

Have you ever been deported from Russia?

Have you ever overstayed your Russian visa or stayed unlawfully in Russia?

Have you ever tried to obtain or assisted others to obtain a Russian visa or enter Russia by providing misleading or false information?

Has your Russian visa ever been cancelled?

Have you ever been refused a Russian visa?

Have you ever been afflicted with a communicable disease of public health significance or a dangerous physical or mental disorder? Have you ever been a drug abuser or an addict?

Have you ever been arrested or convicted for any offence?

33. IMPORTANT! EACH APPLICANT MUST READ AND GIVE ANSWERS TO THE FOLLOWING QUESTIONS**

Have you ever performed a military service? If yes, indicate the country, branch of service, rank, military occupation and dates of service

Have you ever been involved in armed conflicts, either as a member of the military service or a victim? If yes, please specify.

** A visa may be refused to persons who are within specific categories defined by the law as inadmissible to Russia.

B@%%@(&$!

Laughably they then say:

'Your answer yes in item 33 does not automatically signify ineligibility for a visa. In this case you may be required to personally appear before a consular officer.'

You could have some fun answering those questions, couldn't you? But I resisted the temptation as I really wanted to go to Moscow.

After all the difficulties to gather together all the documents, rubber stamps and signatures, the actual visit to the Russian Consulate was very easy. No long queue, no filing past a replica of Lenin's tomb. An appointment at a definite time and they actually took me earlier as there was nearly no one else there except a couple of seasoned professionals who were collecting or requesting visas for their clients. Tamara, the straight-black-haired Russian beauty in the tight blue pullover was very helpful, but also very thorough. I began to get some slight flavour of what it might have been like to be interrogated by the KGB back in the 1950s or 60s. I was glad to see that the seat to which I had been ushered had a cushion on it and not just an empty hole like they gave James Bond in Casino Royale. And just as well Tammy was thorough, because if there had been any mistakes in the forms I gave in, she would have spotted them and I would have had time to get them corrected, albeit via another slew of e-mails and telephone calls, I imagine. She carefully cross-checked everything between the visa application form I'd filled in and the various documents I'd had to enclose showing proof of travel arrangements, health insurance, host organisation (meaning my hotel, the Holiday Inn Moscow Lesnaya), passport, and plane ticket. Having to pay for everything before you know that you are going to get a visa is a bit much, but that's the way it works, and you're in their hands. You can even end up paying for the visa application and then they might refuse you a visa because you answered question 33 wrongly, and I bet they don't give you your money back! Anyway, she went through everything, making marks and comments with her light-blue pencil, and then she said the words I wanted to hear:

'Thank you, all seems in order. Come back between two and five o'clock next Tuesday and your visa will be ready for collection, and the price will be the standard eighty-three euros, there is no need for an express application. Please, go over to the next desk and pay my colleague – no cash, just approved credit cards.'

What a relief! She'd said Tuesday. My plane was leaving early on Wednesday morning, so it was going to be just in time. Otherwise I would have had to pay the extra for an express application. Surely Tam knew that too, as she'd checked my plane ticket very carefully, and so I was completely in her power but she'd been very nice and had decided to give me my visa at the cheap(!) price. I thanked her kindly, went over to her colleague, paid, got a receipt, and walked back out of the suburban apartment block's small ground floor office and into the Brussels sunshine with a weight lifted off my shoulders. Just the slight nagging doubt remained that there'd be an unexpected delay, or maybe during their database checks they would find an anomaly ...

But no need to worry: there it was, gleaming on one of the inside pages of my passport when I went back to collect it the following Tuesday. Of course it's all written in Russian Cyrillic characters so you have no idea whether it has all the necessary and correct information on it. This reminds me of a story I was told about misadventures caused twenty years or so ago by visas. Some poor unfortunate had had to go to get a Russian visa, but this was for work, not pleasure, as he was nominated to organise a meeting in I think it was St Petersburg, though it might still have been called Leningrad at the time. Anyway, he got his visa to go to the meeting, but his boss, who was also going, got cold feet and insisted that his man should go over for a reconnaissance visit a week earlier to make sure that all the arrangements were in order. This he did, and he reported back that all seemed fine. So the next week, they went over but on separate planes – I don't think they liked each other that much – with the employee acting as the bag-carrier, taking all the meeting documents with him. Anyway, when he arrived in Moscow Airport, they told him that his visa was no longer valid as it had only been for a single entry and he'd used it up the week before. He tried his best but they just would not let him through and after a whole day spent in the confines of the airport, he was sent back on a different plane to a different country as there were no proper return planes for a couple of days. So the boss ended up all by himself in a meeting with no information and nothing to say as he was relying on his colleague to bring everything with him. He was probably thinking he'd be able to read up the preparatory notes the evening before at the hotel. It would have been an interesting meeting to listen in on, and I wonder what all the Russians thought.

***

Now, let us analyse Anzhi Makachkala, the club, its history, its players, its fans in detail. What? You're not interested? Well, all right, let's not. But a little bit of misinformation does no one any harm. Their ground is situated in one of the most dangerous regions of the world. Think of the scariest place you've ever been and multiply it by a hundred and you're getting close. So instead of using their own stadium, they play in Moscow, sometimes at the Lokomotiv Moscow ground. By the way, I remember seeing the Choo-Choos, which I think is their nickname, getting trounced by a fantastic Valencia team including their great Argentinian defender Roberto Ayala and future Boro star Mendieta while on holiday in Spain, not Russia, in November 2001, just after 9-11 as the Americans would have it. That Valencia stadium certainly has steep banks of seating up in the gods where we were.

Other times Anzhi play at the CSKA Moscow ground, and I remember seeing them win the UEFA Cup Final versus Sporting Lisbon as we'd already bought tickets for the Final the year we should have won it. For us, they have chosen the CSKA ground. You probably saw Mo Farah racing around it in the World Athletic Championships at the end of the summer of 2013. And you will now have an idea of how far away we were in the Toon section from even the nearest corner of the pitch, what with an eight-lane athletics track, long-jump pits, hammer-throwing netting and one of those troughs full of water (or ice at this time of year) for the 3000m steeplechasers to fall in, all between us and the action. It makes you wonder how they train for steeplechasing in winter in Moscow – instead of getting wet once a lap they must ice-skate across the trough, and once in a while some unlucky athlete must crack through the ice and disappear for ever until some Inuit (why are you not allowed to say Eskimo any more?) or a polar bear fishes him out.

***

Wednesday morning dawned bright and early. I wonder who was the first person to write that, as they would be a millionaire by now if they'd copyrighted it. Waiting for the boarding, I found myself sitting beside the very friendly FA officials and young lads of the U-18 England team who were flying back home to East

Midlands Castle Donington head-bangers airport after losing one-nil in the Belgian cathedral city of Tournai. I couldn't name one England U-18 player for you. Apparently their stars were a Liverpool player and a Boro goalkeeper. But daughter Sarah and I did go down to Mons in the bitter winter cold of November 2011 to watch Sammy Ameobi play really well for the England U-21 team, who had been leading one-nil for most of the match until Belgium scored twice in the last few minutes to win.

The Brussels Airlines Airbus only had thirty-five passengers, and three-quarters of them were Toon fans, including many regulars and familiar faces who'd come in on the early flight from Newcastle to Brussels. Until they stopped the Newcastle-Brussels route on 1st April 2013, Brussels was a good hub for Toon travellers. Closing the route was a disaster, and they must have regretted it because now they've started running it again.

Just about everyone had been in Kharkiv and quite a few had booked their planes over the internet while they were still in the Ukraine. Two of the Toon fans had been at the Algarve Tournament with us, and they told me that they had originally been booked on the Tuesday plane along with their friends, but there'd been a mistake with their visas which had only been valid from Wednesday so they'd had to pay extra to change their flights. Others had paid extortionate amounts to get their visas by express post from the London Russian visa office, while others had taken days off work to make return trips to the Edinburgh visa office two days in a row for express visas. Some lucky fans actually worked in a travel agency and they knew all the ropes and had got visas and tickets for their friends and themselves. It was good to have a group of us all together to work out how to negotiate the local travel from the airport to the city, especially considering that by the time the plane arrived, we'd drunk it dry of its stocks of Belgian Jupiler 'Toro' beer and the French and Spanish wine. The passengers on the way back were going to have to make do with vodka, as they could at least stock up with some more of that in Moscow.

It's a shame you couldn't be along on this trip, Pete, you'd have enjoyed the *craic*.

***

'I certainly would have, Barry, and I am still gutted about not getting to Moscow, I really am …'

You know I don't give up easily when it comes to getting to Toon games around Europe, but this time there were just too many bureaucratic hoops to jump through, even for me. I had e-mailed the Cuths Old Boys about all these hoops, and Hearne Minor (a mackem!) mailed back:

'Too many hoops, who is it yer playin? Moscow State Circus?'

Well it certainly was a bit of a circus act the Russia authorities were putting on. I would have had to send off a visa application form to the embassy in Berlin almost immediately after getting back from (the) Ukraine, and with no guarantee of getting the visa on time. Plus, when I got back home on the Saturday evening I was fit to drop, with a severe cold or even flu. And I didn't surface till Sunday afternoon. Then it was off to Belgium for work on Monday and I didn't get back till Friday. If I had been my usual organised self, I would have given the travel agent a passport photo and exact instructions on what to do in the event of us winning in (the) Ukraine and then getting Anzhi Mackleschackle-Dodgytackles in the next round. But who really believed we would beat Metalist?

I had experienced this visa lark back in 1987 when my railway-mad brother Mick and I travelled to Moscow by train, just for the hell of it. We had watched the film 'Gorky Park' (which was actually filmed in Helsinki) and decided, having had a Stella or two, that the thing to do was to go and see the real thing for ourselves, travelling there by train of course.

It seemed like a good idea at the time.

Two and a half days in a trundling Soviet train which we boarded in Essen. But Mick first had to get to Germany from Tyneside. He had to send his passport to me and I had to send both passports off to the embassy. You could get the transit visa for what was then East Germany on the train, but we needed proper visas for Poland and the Soviet Union. It literally took months to sort out!

***

Two and a half days from Essen, eh? So you can add on another four hours from Brussels! Well it's certainly a fair old way away, is Moscow! It is even further east than Kharkiv (by one degree and twenty-four minutes of latitude, or just over a hundred miles).

The in-flight map on the droppy-down screens soon told us we were over Düsseldorf (famous 'Auf Wiedersehen, Pet' location only around twenty miles or so from Essen), and about half an hour later we flew past Hanover, which seems to be about one eighth of the distance to Moscow. One eighth! No wonder Moscow is four hours ahead of Central Newcastle Time. On and on we flew, over the North German plain, past Berlin and over Pomerania – the German and then the Polish bit. Flat lands with their many winding rivers and oxbow lakes, beloved of geography teachers and aerial photographers everywhere.

Leaving Poland behind us, we followed a line taking us between Vilnius (which is in Latvia) to our left and Minsk (which is in what used to be known as White Russia or Byelorussia but is these days officially called Belarus) to our right. At one point I could see a huge wide river which in the distant past must have been even bigger because parts of it were made up of two parallel rivers snaking side by side across the old wide bed of earlier times. As we headed further and further east beyond the by now well-rusted Iron Curtain, the earth got frostier and whiter, more barren and tundra-like. At some point we crossed into former Soviet airspace, a whole new experience for me! Many moons ago, I was at the Turkish-USSR (now Georgian) frontier on the Black Sea coast and my memories are vague but I suppose I must have dipped a toe into Soviet territory or no-man's land. After going such a long way, it would have made no sense not to. In any case that was Georgia, and this is Russia.

The next time I looked out of the porthole, the ground had turned stone grey, the colour you normally see as you fly over the peaks of a mountain range like the Alps on the way to Inter Milan or AS Roma, except these bare mountain tops were flattened down to sea level. They were covered in broad expanses of drifted snow, making a monochrome world of white and grey. I took a black and white photo. Then I thought, are you allowed to take pictures of Russia from the air? They locked up that U2 pilot, Gary Powers, for years for doing that, didn't they? By coincidence, on the way to the airport there had been a news item on the radio about how the Russian police had extracted signed confessions out of three prisoners. They could have my camera if they wanted my pictures.

***

Reminds me of what happened in that train when we were in the sheds at the Brest-Litovsk border crossing in 1987. The two carriages that had come through Germany and Poland had to be lifted up by in-shed craneage to have the standard-gauge bogies replaced by broad-gauge ones for the Soviet railway system, so that at the next station they could be coupled on to a mile-long internal Soviet train. While the bogie-changing was going on our Mick whipped out his camera to make a nice photographic record to show everyone back home what bogie-men look like. *Verboten!* It did not go down at all well with the Soviet border guards, who were already giving us grief because the train had actually got there twenty minutes early. It was about five to midnight and our Soviet visas did not become valid till 00.01 a.m. They were prepared to turn a blind eye on the visa front, but now they presented their Kalashnikovs and promptly confiscated Mick's camera, pointing out that this was an installation in a restricted area subject to military law. We had only been in the country for ten minutes and had already committed two offences, both of which could be construed as espionage activity. Priceless! Gorbachev was busy reforming things with his *glasnost* and *perestroika,* but this was still very much the era of the Cold War.

***

And by the look of things it was also very cold down below us right now. So cold in fact that not only the lakes but also the rivers were frozen. Joni Mitchell wished for just such a river to skate away on and she would have a wide choice here. And the roads were arrow-straight – no nearby villages to tempt them off the straight and narrow. They don't seem to go in for bends in this part of Russia. The roads are laid out in triangles – miles and miles in one straight line then an apex and they head off at a tangent, straight as a die. Tricky to drive on, no doubt – an hour of monotony and then all of a sudden a sharp turn. This was the wilderness, and we were lucky the sky was cloudless so that we could see all this unique landscape. We were flying through the sun and the air of nowhere in particular.

(Back on the train in '87 it was mile after endless tens of miles of forest, then a sudden clearing with a village and road now and again, then more forest, then more forest, then more forest.)

There were some vapour trails very close below, and disturbingly recent they looked to me. We started to pass through mistier air and the captain announced that we were twenty minutes away from Moscow where the weather was currently sunny with a temperature of minus eight. That was a lot colder than the weather forecast had promised. As we approached the Russian capital, the roads began to look more familiar with curves, bends and junctions. We were leaving desolation behind and nearing a place of human habitation again. But still everything was grey or white. No colour. Bleak. Dull.

And soon we touched down in Moscow Domodedovo airport. They have a few airports, but this one apparently took most of the foreign airlines as you could see planes of British Airways, Air France, and so on. There was also an elephants' graveyard of strange-looking planes of unknown makes looking rather shabby with their cheap-looking paintwork and their funny pointy noses. Maybe these were for internal flights, the ones that take you to the home town of Anzhi Makachkala for instance. The passport queue was split into five lines of only about six people each and only took about ten minutes. Much easier and faster than trying to get into America, for instance, where you can easily wait for an hour or more, or even Heathrow. And come to think of it, the questions on the American visa application form are pretty stupid as well – e.g 'Are you a terrorist?' I don't know if they still have the same question, but they used to ask 'Do you advocate the overthrow by force, violence or other unconstitutional means of the Government of the United States or of all forms of law?' Instead of ticking 'No,' one time someone apparently thought it was a multiple-choice question and put a circle around 'unconstitutional means', as it seemed the friendliest way of going about it, and got himself deported.

The nice lady put a slip of paper which I had been asked to sign inside my passport at the visa page and she kept the other copy for herself. Then customs was a breeze – I walked straight through the 'Nothing to declare' lane without being checked at all. They didn't even want to destroy my photos of Russian snow and frozen rivers. They were however carting off bunches of swarthy-looking gentlemen to little side-rooms for further inspection.

The AeroExpress train couldn't be easier either. Head to the left after customs and walk the length of the terminal, following the easily readable signs which are thoughtfully in English too. The only tricky thing you need to know is that you go past the first train ticket stand which is for other trains and go a bit to the right around the corner and there you pay three hundred and twenty roubles for a single. They don't sell returns, a little ominously. Then you go round back past the other ticket booth and keep bearing to the right and half a minute later you're at the platform. Scan your paper ticket on the laser reader and the barrier opens up and you're in. We'd landed at 16.05 and by 16.50 we were sitting in a nice clean red train with white interior walls and seat backs and red seat covers. Very comfortable. The onboard magazine even had a nice colour Metro map with the names of the stations in Cyrillic and our 'conventional' characters which would be very useful when working out journeys so I snaffled it for my inside pocket. Back home I'd tried to find just such a map but had only found maps with Cyrillic-only or international-only station names, so this was a really helpful find.

With it being nearly five o'clock already (though only 1 o'clock Toon-time), I decided I'd go straight from the airport to the *Luzhniki* Stadium and hoped to get there before it turned dark to have a look around and get a possible chance to see the training, if they didn't enforce the secret training session policy again. My new Metro map told me that this would mean switching to the Brown Circle line at *Paveletskaya* terminus, getting off at *Park Kultury* after fours stops clockwise (which could be the tricky bit – how to tell which way was clockwise) and then two stops down the Red Line to *Sportivnaya*, which according to the information I'd printed out off the internet should be right beside the stadium. One thing you'll have noticed from the Metro station names above, and which surprised me too as I had no idea about what Russian was like except it has a lot of shhhs and skis in it, is that once you get past their use of Cyrillic characters, the actual meaning of the words is often quite easy to guess: 'Park', 'Sport', 'Kultur' – what could be easier?

As it set off from the airport, the AeroExpress, more like AeroTrundle, train passed sedately through bare-treed, snow-underfoot forests with occasional sightings of distant dachas straight out of John Le Carré. They've even got railway sidings stocked with drab green old railway trucks full of gravel, maybe hand-crushed by forced labour out in the Urals and Siberia. All it needs is for Michael Caine, Richard Burton and Sean Connery to appear from out of a copse, hotly pursued by Donald Pleasance and a pack of hounds. This view continued out to the right, but as we got to the outermost edges of the city the view to the left changed to industrial buildings, drab housing blocks, and every so often a light-house shaped red-and-white hooped chimney which no doubt was part of their extensive district-heating system. People say that in their blocks of flats there is no way of switching off the heat because it comes down huge great pipes that run overland from the associated industrial plants which work all day, so if the weather gets warmer all they can do is open all the windows to let the heat out and waste it anyway. Closer to Moscow, we were surrounded on both sides by endless suburbs and industrial estates, big power lines, roads and motorways. Mind, to be fair as Peter Beardsley might say, coming into north London on the East Coast line from the Toon is no better.

The AeroExpress comes to an above-ground, dead-end Terminal – what else would you expect, if you're terminal it usually means you're at a dead end – at *Paveletsky Vokzal*. The Russian word *Vokzal* (вокзал) simply means 'station' and it is a corruption of 'Vauxhall'. Apparently a Russian delegation to London was so impressed by the Vauxhall Pleasure Gardens that one of the first railway stations in Russia was named after them, but just Vauxhall (*Vokzal*) for short. That name stuck somehow and came to be used as the word for any railway station.

At *Paveletsky Vokzal*, there's a long, long platform and a big clock above a shabby door which takes you into the down-at-heel station building and down (after a few false manoeuvres and U-turns when I ended up in the separate suburban train station and had to re-enter through a guarded baggage check) into my first experience of the Moscow Metro system. No one's smiling – that's the first thing you notice – and they all seem miserable and caught up in their own concerns. So from what Pete was saying about the good people of Kharkiv, the Russians and the Ukrainians would appear to have that much in common: they look utterly miserable. There was a big queue for the ticket booth and some shifty-looking people hanging around it – I'd been warned about gangs of pick-pockets and worse – so I thought I'd give the automatic ticket machine a try, using some of my loose change from buying my AeroExpress ticket. It was really simple. They sell tickets in ones, twos, fives and tens. I thought I'd buy a ten which would probably last me most of my stay but then I noticed a few machines which were unoccupied and only sold ones and twos, so I bought a two.

It all seemed very normal and easy so far, not much different from going for the first time to some other European town where you don't know the language, so I decided that I should treat this

Metalist Kharkiv 0 - NUFC 1.

Kharkiv - Vlad the Mag Lenin.

They certainly have dirty big balls in Kharkiv.

Misty Metalist Stadium.

Is nothing sacred?

Your Kharkiv taxi awaits, Sir.

Training on the Moscow Luzhniki Olympic Stadium plastic pitch the night before the match.

World's best statue seen from Gorky Park.

Lenin pirouetting in his Red Square tomb.

Anzhi 0 - NUFC 0 It was a very long way from the Toon section to the pitch.

Making history in a posh shop in Moscow.

They had special police on duty for Anzhi.

The Head Magpie chairs a meeting of the Skydive Academy in Cafe Nicola, Lisbon.

Benfica pre-match outside Cafe Nicola, Praça Dom Pedro, Lisbon.

Meanwhile on the other side of the same Lisbon square.

Benfica, just outside the stadium.

Benfica, the Stadium of Light.

A huge turn-out for the Toon Army at Benfica.

Toon Army in the Stadium of Light.

Pilgrimage to Pasteis de Belem, Lisbon.

Ajax Arena for the Final - the three crosses are the emblem of the city of Amsterdam.

Schalke 04 - Gelsenkirchen Pizza-Biergarten.

The Toon Army's corner of the Schalke 04 Veltins Arena.

Niamh - a winner.

A shed in Germany.

NUFC 1 - Malaga 3 at Schalke. The next day was better: Schalke 04 1 - NUFC 3.

Maybe it was Fraser Forster in Palermo after all! Toon Army Poland at Schalke Open Day.

Le Toon Frog und die Miss Schalkes 2013 und 2014.

Home Newcastle.

trip with openness and trust and hope, like I would if I were in, say, Spain or Portugal for the first time. So I'd try to stop thinking 'John Le Carré' and think '*fiesta*' instead, a *fiesta* in the very cold snow. It was a different experience because of it being a new country I'd never visited before, but so far it wasn't as different as I'd expected.

So here I stand for the first time in the indecipherable yet indispensable Moscow Metro at *Paveletskaya*. They have big signs above your head in the corridor between platforms with names in large Cyrillic script along the top and then lots of station names underneath. It turns out that actually these signs are supposed to tell you that if you head in the way you're facing when you're reading the sign, then you're on the often rather lengthy path towards the platform for trains to the stations mentioned in big writing at the top of the sign. But the thing to know is that if you want to go to any of the stations in small writing underneath, then you must absolutely not head off in the same direction down the corridor. Oh no, that would be too simple. No, the sign is telling you that you can reach the stations in small writing from the platform that you're standing on when you're reading the sign. It's not at all obvious. Then you notice there are more signs on the walls and on the columns framing the entrances to the platforms, and this is how you find out which side of the corridor has the platform taking you the direction you want to go. Once you get the idea, after a few trips, it seems sensible enough. But on your first trip, it's bewildering, what with everything being in Cyrillic writing too.

So there I was, trying to work all this out and failing. I was standing in one of these long corridors full of people striding sure-footedly along, when up came a nice young couple, Gary and Tania. They were lost too. At first this seemed surprising as they seemingly were Russian, but it wasn't so surprising at all when they explained, in wonderful English, that they had never been to Moscow before and lived a long way away, but were visiting because they were taking part in a big promotion for the upcoming Winter Olympic Games. I'd half heard about the next Winter Olympics being somewhere in Russia and I thought maybe it was going to be somewhere on the Black Sea. This raised the possibility in my mind that it might be near Anzhi Makachkala's home town. Gary was a lot more talkative than Tania because he was the better of the couple in English, at which he was very assured. He told me they actually were from exactly where the Games would take place,

Sochi. I know it now, but at the time, I got that it started with Sos- or Soc- but after that I was lost. Gary had started up his own company especially for the Games and was actually helping to build the Olympic village, hotels and sports venues.

Gary and Tania sorted out the directions with the locals and it turned out that they were going the first part of their Metro trip in the same direction as me, clockwise on the Brown Circle line, so I tagged along with them down a steep, deep never-ending escalator to the right platform and we jumped into a packed-out, standing-room-only, ramshackle Metro carriage. The state of the carriage was in stark contrast to the pristine, almost cathedral-like Metro stations, of which Muscovites are justifiably very, very proud.

The reason why Gary's English was so good was that he and Tania had worked and lived in England for a fair few years from 2003. He asked me if I knew 'Lambourn', and yes, it sounded familiar, I said, famous for horse-racing. Precisely, said Gary. He had started out working for Ginger McCain's stables. Even I knew that meant Red Rum, though that was a long time before 2003, and it wasn't in Lambourn either. Anyway, Gary had not much enjoyed the working atmosphere there and he had moved on to work at Lambourn for someone who now runs ex-Toon 'favourite' Michael Owen's stables. It's just a pity Owen hadn't been as interested in playing for the Toon as he is in racing horses. The horses usually win by a distance, but he just doesn't have that turn of pace any more, especially after his knee went playing for England but being paid by Newcastle. Gary was head lad, gallops rider, and so on. With all the talking I forgot to count the stops, but luckily Gary and Tania noticed when we got to *Park Kultury* where I hopped out in a bit of a rush, waving them off on the next step of their circular journey.

That was my first taste of the Metro, and it was all going pretty well thanks to Gary and Tania's help. I now had to find the platform for the Red Line in the direction of *Sportivnaya* station. See again, Russian words are often pretty much the same as English. There's a train every couple of minutes to whisk you sometimes the right way, sometimes the wrong way, around the big city. The key thing is that there's a circle line, the Brown one that I'd just been on, that links all the other lines together so you're bound to get to your desired destination eventually, even if you go the wrong way round! A bit like our very own Metro coast line. The other simplifying thing to know is that the Brown Circle line is always the one deepest underground at any junction as far as I worked out. And since the airport terminus station *Paveletsky* and also my hotel station were on the Brown Circle, I could go anywhere with just one change. The easiest is to forget about trying to work out the names in Cyrillic script of the stations as you travel along, and instead use your Metro map before you get on to work out how many stops you have to go to your destination and then just count that number of stops and get off. But be careful with counting the stops, because the maps show double or treble circles where lines join and you can easily get confused about whether these might mean two or three stops when in fact they just mean one. In any case, after a couple of days you even find yourself starting to read the Cyrillic too without thinking. You come to realise that the Moscow Metro is great and not at all scary or full of pickpockets like everyone writes about in internet travel guides. It's probably because they go around dressed up like tourists and taking photos of everything, whereas I hid my little camera and just wore dull clothes as if on my way to work down the salt mine. Just remember that you need to check everything about your route very carefully before you go into the Metro and keep counting while you're on it!

***

Up another big escalator, over and across, and then down some stairs and there was the Red Line. You don't need to buy another ticket – as far as I understand, once you're inside the Metro and you've clicked your ticket through the turnstile, you can go anywhere and as far as you like with the same one ticket. But if you come out past the barrier, you'll have to buy a new ticket to get back in again. In any case, they're so cheap, it's no problem if you make a mistake and have to buy another one: thirty roubles is only about forty pence. A check down the Cyrillic names to find the one that means *Sportivnaya* and then onto the right platform and the right train and count to three and I was there. Outside the station, I looked around hoping to see the stadium or its floodlights but no, nothing recognisable yet. Straight ahead was an open space and a motorway underpass of some kind, so that was where I headed, and when I emerged on the other side there it was right in front of me, the very imposing *Luzhniya* Stadium standing out in the middle of a big park with barriers all around. So I'd chosen the right exit from the station and gone in just the right direction to get to the stadium.

I wasn't sure what to do at the barriers as there was a guard in attendance, but I watched other people and I saw that they just walked straight through the gate so I did the same. It's a public park and anyone's allowed in any time. It was coming up for seven o'clock and still light and as I walked through the park I saw that they have a big statue of Lenin at a respectful distance of about a hundred yards from the stadium itself. I found out why later – it used to be called the Central Lenin Stadium. I took a few photos of the man. We have Wor Jackie and Sir Bobby, and they have Lenin. He's bigger by a long way, maybe thirty feet tall, but he never was any good at football. I know who I'd rather have outside SJP. All three of them, arms around shoulders, thirty feet tall; that would really look good.

There was no sign of the team or a team bus, but I spotted they have a ski-jumping hill looking down on the stadium so I took a walk over that way. It is in the same direction as the monumental edifice of the Moscow State University. Then I took a very long walk around the perimeter of the oval or perhaps even circular stadium. It is huge. So it took me quite a long time to do the full circle and I still couldn't find any sign of a team bus. What I did find though was an entrance marked VIP with quite a few smartly-dressed people milling around outside. I asked a group of three blazered and suited men standing at the entrance door and one of them turned out to be in the know with UEFA and the stadium people and he very kindly phoned them up and found out for me that if I came back at ten o'clock, the team would be there for a training session and I might be able to see the Press and even get into the Press Conference. Sounded good! So plenty time – nearly three hours – to go over to the hotel, report in just in case the KGB want to know I have made the rendezvous, have a bit of a freshen-up and get back down here for the training.

A couple of stops back up the Red Line to *Park Kultury*, then clockwise around the Brown Circle from eight o'clock to eleven o'clock, bandits high, and the *Belorussky* station. That was the station nearest to my hotel.

***

This is spooky, Barry! The *Belorussky* station is where our mile-long train terminated back in 1987, at about nine o'clock on a cold November morning. Weird thing was, we were met by a smartly dressed official-looking type who told us our (black) limousine was waiting to take us to our hotel (the Hotel National – as featured in the film Russian House), right next to Red Square. We had booked everything through *Intourist*, and were probably a bit too individualistic for the system's liking. Maybe the KGB felt they needed to keep a close eye on us! We certainly hadn't ordered a limousine, but our new friend was very insistent and so we went along with him to the forecourt of the *Belorussky* and were whisked through the still-Communist streets of Moscow in great style in a dark Russky limo. Those streets were very pot-holed, however, and the buildings lining them were in some cases literally falling to bits. Some that looked as though they had originally been restaurants or drinking places of some kind had been converted to some other use, such as clock and watch repairs. This was the time of Gorbachev's prohibition – it was his forlorn attempt to sober the USSR up. We could only get a drink in our and other hotels!

***

Well I was rather hoping I would be able to get a drink, that's for sure. When I got back up from the subterranean depths to ground level at *Belorussky Vokzal*, it occurred to me that I had no idea which way to head to reach the hotel, even though it should only be about five minutes away in the right direction. But corporate colours saved the day. I saw some green neon lights straight ahead on the far side of the massive road interchange in front of me, and they just seemed to call out, 'Are you looking for the Holiday Inn? Here we are!' And there they were! But what a drab, run-down path I had to tread to reach the Holiday Inn Moscow *Lesnaya:* shabby wooden boardwalks, street surfaces badly broken up by winter frosts to the point of having major potholes, farm-track ruts, and ankle-breaker pavements. And this was the business district, it turned out. And yes, it did have some shiny office buildings, but the overall impression was of a place where money was too tight to maintain the infrastructure and stave off the ravages of the natural elements. After fruitless attempts to find a pedestrian crossing to get across the mighty traffic of the Leningrad street, I followed the flow of other pedestrians and found a badly-signed hidden underpass whose entrance was concealed beneath a crumbling old concrete office building; otherwise I would never have got across the ten lanes of nose-to-tail cars and lorries. The underpass was full of people who looked like they were refugees straight out of some disaster or other.

Yes, my hotel was in the northern business district, but on a street full of potholes and mud. So not much had changed in that respect since Pete and his brother had been here twenty-six years or so earlier! Adding to the gloom and decrepitude was the mass array of ancient buses, trolleys and trams, Lada-Fiat 124s, and Russian Zil copies of Mercedes saloons, all caked in mud, slush and Siberian salt.

The hotel was like any chain hotel anywhere, no hint of anything Russian. It was pretty pricey too, but that had been the price to pay to make sure that they would fill out the visa application forms properly and quickly. I didn't spend a long time in the room, just long enough to get into a few extra layers for the cold of the night, then back to the Metro and the trip back to the stadium.

I bought another two-trip ticket from the machine and made a rouble profit on the change, and then I noticed a poor old lady trying each of the machines to see if anyone had left any change. I saved her the trouble and gave her some extra. It makes you sad, seeing how some of the people have to live in Moscow. You've seen people on the streets before, but these people on the streets of Moscow looked truly desperate.

It's difficult to spot any station names as you enter the next station on the line because the name plates only seem to be fixed to the walls on the side of the tunnel you don't get out on, and there are very few of them anyway, so you have to be very lucky if your carriage window happens to stop in view of a name plate. Luckily, and unlike the other lines I used, the Brown Circle trains have all their stations listed in a straight line (not a circle!) above their doors, and a red light moves along filling up the row and flashing under the station the train is coming to, and when it gets to the right-hand end it jumps back to the left. It took me a while to get the hang of it, as my station happened to be at one end – on my first trip it gave me a bit of a surprise when it suddenly jumped and started flashing for my station when at the station before it had seemed so far away.

As the crow flies, it was about four miles from the city centre to the stadium and it was three miles from the centre to the *Belorussky* station where my hotel was, so in a car and with all the traffic it would have been a long trip, and even by Metro it took the best part of an hour because my hotel was getting on for ten minutes away from the door of the Metro carriage, and it was another ten to fifteen minutes at the other end too.

A short note for geographers and GPS users: Moscow is at 55 deg 45' North and 37 deg 37' East, while *Domodedovo* Airport is at 55 deg 24' N, 37 deg 54' E. Newcastle is at 55 deg N, so Moscow is on about a level with somewhere between Lindisfarne and Berwick. We are lucky that Newcastle has the heat store of the sea right next door, otherwise we'd also be snowed in for half the year like Moscow with its continental climate. We're in a good spot. I have been to the Turkish-Georgian border at 41 deg 33' E, so further east by quite a distance, but Moscow's further east than Jerusalem, Cairo, Damascus and Nairobi. Makhachkala on the other hand is at 47 deg 30' E, on the west coast of the Caspian Sea and a hundred miles east of Chechnya, famous for all the wrong reasons. No wonder the game couldn't be played there. It's as far east as Kuwait, further than Baghdad and the Yemen, Somalia and Madagascar. I'm not sure how that is still in Europe. And yet there is still plenty of Europe left if you head east from Moscow towards the Urals, the mountain range that is 'generally accepted' as marking Europe's geographical eastern boundary.

***

It took longer than I thought to get back to the *Luzhniki* Stadium from my hotel. From the *Sportivnaya* Metro station, there's still quite a bit of walking to do. The scale of the stadium complex is so massive that your mind plays tricks on you and scales down the size of the surrounding park to what it would be if the stadium were the size of flat-pack grounds like Alkmaar or Reading. But in fact the park, too, is huge. When I finally got to the ground itself, I had to find out where the press conference was going to be held. I'd been aiming to get there at about half-past nine, but it was now already five past ten. The young guard on the door of the Press Centre asked to see my documents – it's in their blood. I said I didn't have any and just kept pointing at the entrance door and saying 'Newcastle' a bit louder and more emphatically each time.

He called a senior guard, who asked in English,

'Press?'

Honesty's the best policy, so I said, 'No. Just Newcastle.'

'Friend?'

'Yes, friend.'

'Come this way.'

Get in! And he led me through the press room past rows of computers and a few people filing their reports, I suppose, and straight out into the stadium. With a 'Thank you very much,' as I shook his hand, I was left to my own devices. It seemed even bigger on the inside than from the outside. It's a very long way down from the stands to the pitch. And there on the pitch was the team doing some training on the all-weather Rustroturf. And there was Steve Storey! I went over for a little chat – he's always got a lot on his plate, especially in an alien land like this – so I didn't want to take up too much of his time. He was standing on the pitch watching the players with his colleague Chris. We agreed when and where I should come the next night to collect my ticket. He had some press returns, but they were not for the away section, so not really the right thing. But tomorrow we three would meet again when I would collect my real ticket.

Steve and Chris, who are better placed than most of us to have seen a lot of grounds in their time, were just as impressed as me by the stadium. Then it dawned on me: this was the Olympic Stadium, the scene of the famously boycotted Moscow Olympics where the absence of the Yanks had allowed Alan Wells to beat Valeri Borzov and the rest of the world and win the hundred metres sprint for Scotland. Powderhall came to Moscow that day. Was it 1976 or 1980? 1980, I think, because the next one was in 1984 and I was in Denmark by then, watching the Los Angeles Olympics 'all night long' to the accompaniment of Lionel Richie and When Doves Cry. Ironic that the USA had already been chosen to host the Olympics straight after they'd snubbed the Russians, which made it all too clear what would happen next. Time flies. So we were standing on the very running track all those great athletes had sped along, steroid-fuelled or not. Blue it was now, whereas I had brick red cinders in my memory, and the surface was quite hard, not at all bouncy like I imagined. The Rustroturf was hard too, and it really didn't seem as good as the high-tech artificial pitches with loose rubber granules to simulate the feel of the soil that I've been used to when coaching kids' football.

After about ten minutes we were asked to leave the pitch so that the private training could start. There'd been maybe thirty cameramen, journalists, officials, and a few locals. And me. What luck to have been allowed the chance to be there. One thing was clear – the seventy-one Toon fans were going to look like a small speck in a giant stadium like this. And if the turn-out was going to be anything like the ten thousand that had turned up for Anzhi's previous round opponents, Hannover 96, then the ground would be seven-eighths empty. This really doesn't seem to be the way to run a competition. If it had to be moved from Anzhi, why couldn't they have moved it to some visa-less venue like, say, Rome or Barcelona or ... Kharkiv/ov!

***

So back I went to the Metro and off I set for the centre of the Russian capital. After all, the night was still young. Because there were so few Toon fans there was no real gathering point, just small clumps of fans dotted around this vast, crumbling metropolis, with not at all the usual atmosphere of away trips.

***

Red Square came as a surprise, literally. I got out of the Metro train where the red and green M lines criss-cross at a station called, working out the Cyrillic, something like *Okotny Ryad* and negotiated the never-ending rabbit-warren of tunnels which eventually reached the never end, and found myself looking up what seemed to be a main business or shopping street. No sign of Red Square anywhere. I knew already from the map that it was a bit of a walk from the M to the Square, but I didn't know in which direction.

Then I heard American voices whose owners were standing beside me at the top of the M stairs and so I asked them, 'Do you know where Red Square is?' Their faces lit up as they pointed behind me and said, 'Here, right behind you!'

I just hadn't bothered to do a hundred and eighty degrees sweep, because there it was in full view, a mixture of deep red/brown, gold and bright colours, towers, giant baubles, spires, and minarets. The Americans had a good laugh, and one said, 'You struck lucky there because we are the dumbest tourists in Russia, but you asked us the one question we could answer.'

Then they asked me if I knew where there was any life in this town? It was true, there was nearly no one around and the very few cafés and bars that you could find were all either shut or empty. All right, it was about half eleven, but it really was closed for business. I said I had no idea either. Armed with their knowledge, I took a giant underground passage past clumps of more stinking tramps and winos and came out again right at the entrance to the Square. What an impressive place. It's huge, with the Kremlin and Lenin's Tomb on one side, and then a block of sparkly-lit posh shops like Gucci and Louis Vuitton on the other. I hadn't expected that – I thought it would be all historic buildings, government offices and museums. It certainly changes your impression of those old grey views of military processions of tanks, missiles and soldiers, as for one thing the scale of the place means that those missiles must have been gigantic, and for another the soldiers must have felt like they were marching past Fenwick's window display.

Yes, there are lots of very posh shops right opposite the Kremlin. Western decadence facing the symbol of Russia. One street behind there is a big department store called ГУМ (pronounced GUM), which looks like it is Moscow's equivalent to Harrods. It's lit up the same way with bulbs all over the façade and hanging from one side of the street to the other. There's another shop called Bosco full of promotional material for the Sochi Olympics, and there was a big fun-fair style temporary arrangement in Red Square including an ice rink with Giant Slidy Russian Dolls with very chatty down-market hoardings around it. It really didn't fit in Red Square. Kruschev, Stalin and Lenin must be spit-roasting in their hellish graves, though Trotsky, or perhaps Tolstoy, might have approved.

At the bottom of the Square is the incredible St Basil's Cathedral, topped with its crazy candy-coloured giant baubles. You can see where Walt Disney got his ideas from. It was frighteningly cold by now and it was way past midnight so I decided to call it a day and catch the last Metro before the system closed at one, I think. And leaving Red Square, who should turn up but a contingent of about eight of the Toon fans who had been on the train with me. They hadn't found much going on either, and were on the hunt for life forms around Red Square. I wished them luck, but told them that as far as I had been able to ascertain, Moscow basically was closed for the night, and had been since eight o'clock. It's strange because there always seemed to be plenty of people in the Metro, but it was as if they lived down there and never ventured up and out into the open air.

So does it sound as though much has changed since you and your brother were here, Pete?

Not really Barry. On our trip all those years ago the place would be absolutely heaving during the day – mostly with miserable-faced people doing what we were soon calling the 'Moscow shuffle.' But in the evenings it was like South Shields on a flag-day, as my Uncle Tommy used to say. There were no tramps or winos to be seen anywhere in those days and the place generally had a very safe feel to it, what with there being a poliss literally on every street corner. In the underpasses and the access tunnels to the Metro, we were often approached by people who claimed they could change money for us at very favourable rates. But as Mick quite reasonably pointed out,

'There's bugger all to buy in the shops. And what there is, is just tourist tat and generally crap.'

'Icons. You can buy icons. And then sell them for beeg money in West!'

'Er, no *spasiba.*'

And although we knew there was officially a prohibition on (except in hotels), we hoped against hope that we would find a typical Russian pub in which to savour the atmosphere of the workers' paradise when everybody was having a pint. But when we asked where we could get a beer, we always got the same answer:

'*Пива нет*' (*piva nyet*), no beer!

***

Hurtling quickly back through the time tunnel to March 2013, match-day Thursday came out beautifully sunny with a brisk wind that put the chill factor to the fore. I asked Olga, the hotel receptionist, for a map and to show me where Gorky Park was. It turned out that Gorky Park was more commonly called *Park Kultury*, so the Metro station which had become my interchange hub and nerve centre for travel operations was actually pushing up the daisies of Gorky Park. I liked the coincidence. The park itself is on the other side of the *Moskva* River from the Metro station so I had the chance to take a couple of photos of the ice-floe strewn river as I walked across the bridge, buffeted by the icy breeze, and with barely a boatman in sight. There was nothing for it, I'd have to put my coat on and deploy the Newcastle-Atromitos scarf to keep a bit warmer.

Gorky Park is right along by the river, with a long car park running along the bank, rounded off with a Russian Space Shuttle at the end. It has the same bare trees as on the trip in from the airport, with snow on the ground, and in the middle there is a small fairground and a rather pleasant wooden café with windowpanes all round from floor to ceiling. I don't remember seeing a Space Shuttle or fairground in the film, but walking between the trees gives you the same atmosphere, and you can almost recognise it, putting aside that the one in the film is actually in Helsinki.

And so to the nice, friendly and very warm café in the middle of the park, beside the merry-go-round, where I tried to order something like breakfast. For me it felt like that because of the jet-lag, but for them it was already lunch time. After reading the Cyrillic menu with a few headings in English and becoming very slightly the wiser, I asked the waiter and settled on a café Americano (a big Nescafé style coffee which came in a normal cup) and minestrone soup which was the closest they seemed to have to breakfast. But then I moved to a table further from the, at first, welcome heat blasting from the wall heater above the entrance door, and took refuge nearer the serving hatch of the kitchen, where I spotted a couple of big bread buns. I asked the waiter if he could hold the minestrone and if I could have a bun instead. 'Minestrone No, Bread Yes, Good,' I said in my best Russian. He brought his colleague, a girl who spoke good English and she told me that they could do me a ciabatta with tomato, olives and ham instead, and that sounded a bit closer to breakfast, so I went for that. And it came out very well. Nice relaxed music, a mixture of Russian and American, in the background too, a view of Gorky Park and the embankment: an hour or so spent very pleasantly.

Wandering away from the café, I could hear they were playing Tie a Yellow Ribbon Round the Old Oak Tree! But I could even forgive that – it sounded like Tony Bennett singing it – because everything else about the place was so perfect. Looking back over to the other side of the river, I could see stylish old apartment blocks where the rich Muscovites must live, with an alternative view over Gorky Park.

From the park I could see a big spiky black thing sticking out of the river. So I decided to investigate. I couldn't work out what it was until I got closer, but it's the most crazy and best statue I've ever seen – Peter the Great perched half-way up a pillar of mini-ships and foreshortened sails above him. All in all I'd say it was my favourite thing in Moscow: a big black weird ship-cum-captain statue, absolutely towering above the surroundings and looking as if it is straight out of Terry Gilliam's imagination, like the start of the last Monty Python film. What a magical and majestic statue and tribute. It really is excellently over the top. In fact I've decided it's my favourite statue anywhere. By good timing, just as I got amidships of Peter the Great's foreshortened ship, a blue hovercraft appeared – a small one for maybe a couple or four people – and made its way over the ice-floes around Peter and away up the river (or down river, it's hard to tell when it's frozen) towards the Kremlin. And not far away I spotted the wonderfully named Red October chocolate factory.

So did you and Mick also actually get to Gorky Park on your trip, Pete?

You bet, Barry. It was, after all, our holy grail – like I said, it was when watching that film that we first hit on the idea of going to Moscow. On the day we finally got to the Park of Parks, we had been wandering about the centre, also visiting Red Square, and we had set our hearts on seeing Lenin in his tomb. And remember, at the time he was a lot less dead – by all of twenty-six years – than he was when the Toon Army were in town, so he was probably still in pretty good nick. But the queue outside his mausoleum on Red Square stretched the equivalent of from the Bewicke pub in Howdon to Percy Main Social Club, so we gave that a miss and went to the red-brick Lenin Museum on Revolution Square instead. The exhibits included the great man's Rolls Royce, by the way. Make of that what you will. After the museum visit we decided it was time to head for Gorky Park and tried to hail a taxi. One duly stopped and I opened the front passenger door, but before I could get in the driver gruffly asked,

'*Kyдa?*' (*Kudá*) (where to)?

'Gorky Park – *Park Kultury'* was the reply of course, but he just shook his head and drove off, forcing me to step smartly back, banging the door shut in the process.

The same thing happened twice more. So clearly it was too short a trip to be of interest to the local taxi drivers. Then we hit on a cunning plan. When the next cab stopped, we got in like greased lighting and waved a ten *deutschmark* note at the driver. That did the trick, and off to Gorky Park we went.

On balance we felt it was not unlike Exhibition Park, and all we could get to eat there was a stodgy, not particularly tasty, ice-cream. It was weird: here we were in Moscow in November, and everybody seemed to be eating *мороженое* (*morozhnoye*) – ice-cream.

***

Well Pete, I didn't see many ice-creams on my match-day wanderings, but I did see a lot of ice-cool, elegant Russian ladies in calf-length fur coats, with matching Kruschev/Brezhnev hats and high-heeled boots. It must be the height of style at the moment – though come to think of it the women were wearing something similar in Doctor Zhivago as well, weren't they? They looked pretty good. But not a patch on wor Julie Christie, mind. You felt like snuggling up into their fur to get nice and warm. One had a snow-white fur on – I don't know how she was going to keep that clean on the muddy, slushy Moscow pavements, but she was looking great while it lasted. And I doubt if she had ever eaten a *мороженое* in her life, certainly not in her adult years! And probably didn't drink that much lager, either.

The roads were chocka all day. You'd take an hour to do what took ten minutes or less on the Metro. Some streets around my hotel seemed to be in permanent gridlock – the lights went from red to green to red with no movement at all so you could cross the road no matter what the sign said.

At one point, I passed a long quayside market of framed paintings, big ones a metre or more wide but with absolutely no one looking at them. Let's face it, who goes out to buy a painting in an open-air market on a freezing cold day?

The next stop on my route after Red October was an imposing white riverside church with big golden onions on top, reached by way of a most pleasant approach across a bridge lined with ornate street lamps. As often with churches, the view from the outside was better than from within, or at least I suspected it would be, so I gave this one a miss and headed up past the Pushkin Museum to the Kremlin. It is impossible to cross the street from the Pushkin side to get to the Kremlin. The street's about the width of SJP and the traffic never stops or even abates. You have to walk a long way up the road until you reach the Lenin Library, where there's an underpass. Now libraries are the opposite of churches, they are much better on the inside, so I had a look but there's a guard and X-ray machines. I couldn't go through all that palaver, or is it *pavlova* in Russia, so I came straight back out.

The underpass is lined with little stalls selling all kinds of practical items like gloves, lighters (they smoke a lot), furry hats and models of the Kremlin, and it eventually leads you out to the entrance to the real thing. Typically, it was closed for the day to visitors, even to me, so I decided I would try again the next day. Though there was a steady stream of people going in and out – *apparatchiks* maybe? So it's closed to the public on Thursdays – a useful piece of information for any budding spies amongst you, as that's obviously the day to conduct your espionage. Thwarted, I skirted the walls and found a memorial to all the battles that they'd won, and at the end they had the WWII section, but for them it only lasted from 1941-45, even if they kept some of their prisoners until well into the fifties. Pete told me a former colleague of his in Germany had remained a 'guest' of the Soviet Union until 1958, though that had been an exceptional case. The person concerned had a Russian mother and German father and had fought on the side of the *Wehrmacht*. That didn't go down at all well after the War, and he could easily have been executed. But they were very forgiving to him and only sent him to a labour camp in Siberia for thirteen years instead. German prisoners-of-war (Pete's father-in-law among them) had been put to work digging tunnels, including for the Moscow Metro, and building roads, including across the tundra that we'd flown over. The Russians don't refer to WWII as the Second World War – for them it was the 'Great Patriotic War'. But don't forget, Soviet war dead – both civilian and military – numbered around twenty million. And the German army suffered around eight out of every nine of its casualties on the Eastern Front!

Anyway, what to do in Moscow on a day when the Kremlin is shut? I went around the corner after the line of battle memorials to an entrance to Red Square, but that was barred so I went to the main entrance. There you have the chance to stand in the officially designated middle of Moscow on a brass circle from where all distances from the capital are measured. I followed everyone's example and threw some coins over my shoulder for luck (and it worked because we didn't lose). When I got up to the square itself, I found that where I'd been able to walk freely last night, it was all shut off with barriers. Lucky I'd already been at midnight. Midnight in Moscow – that's a tune isn't't? Maybe Acker Bilk or Johnny

Dankworth. What is worse, they'd put a tennis-court-style blowy-up white tent over Lenin's Tomb. Last night I hadn't known where it was – clearly the lack of a queue meant it was no longer quite as popular as it had been in 1987 – but today I asked a couple of soldiers manning the barricades and they confirmed it was out of bounds under its pneumatic shroud. So I wasn't able to see the old chap, even if I'd seen a few of his statues, and his library.

I left Red Square and paid a visit to that opulently decadent Harrod's-like 'ГУМ', or to us GUM, department store which I'd seen lit up the night before on my first visit to the square. ГУМ/GUM used to stand for *Государственный универсальный магазин (Gosudarstveny universalen magazin* – State General [Department] Store) in Soviet times, but after the fall of the USSR they decided that sounded a bit dated and made the Г/G stand for Главный (*Glavny* = Main) instead. Did you and Mick visit it, Pete?

But of course! Mind, in those days it wasn't so much Harrod's-like as 1950s Woolworth's-like in quality terms. And architecturally it struck me as being a cross between the Grainger Market and the Central Arcade, but on a massive scale. And yes, quite impressive! But there didn't seem to be much that anyone in the West would even consider buying, except maybe *matryoshka* dolls, which always make good presents of course. Yet the customers we saw there at the time were all wide-eyed with awe, presumably taking time off from being their usual miserable selves. Made us wonder what the 'less glamorous' Russian shops must be like! We couldn't be bothered to queue long enough to find out.

The modern-day, born-again-capitalist GUM is proud to show off, and announce on big 'This way' signs, Russia's first public toilet with its very own history of people's convenience. Apparently it makes Russians flush with pride. After giving it a try, I walked a little further up the shopping street and chanced upon the nearby *Lubyanka*, the old KGB spy centre, a giant, solid, imposing and scary old building on the other side of such a wide and busy road that it was almost like a square. It would have been impossible to cross the free-for-all road so I turned left and found myself walking past a string of very exclusive designer label shops and Ferrari, Maserati, and Bentley showrooms in an enclave encircled by rows of big black chauffeured cars. This must be the Rodeo Drive of Moscow, and it is very handily placed for the *Lubyanka*. Just a little further down is the *Metropole* hotel where a plaque outside tells passers-by that Lenin held meetings in its *Petroso* bar in 1918-19, and then over to the right is the building of the Bolshoi Ballet.

Ludmilla, one of the other receptionists at the hotel, had recommended one last place I might like to visit, the *Arbat*, a mile-long pedestrian street in the historical centre of Moscow. So I made the trek there, thinking that the way she'd recommended it had been rather intriguingly lukewarm and doubtful:

'Some tourists seem to like it!'

I could now see why. Okay, it is cobbled and has some quite nice historic buildings every so often, but basically it is drab and unkempt with a few cafés and lots of souvenir shops, and frankly nothing to recommend it. So I don't.

What's that, Pete?

***

Ah yes, the famous *Arbat*, I remember it well. Apparently in the latter years of the Soviet Empire it had a bit of a name as a trendy, almost Bohemian sort of place. Somebody called Anatoly Rybakov wrote a novel called 'Children of the *Arbat*', set in the early thirties. The book is said to be semi-autobiographical and describes the growing hysteria at the time, when making a basic mistake at work or even just attempting to crack a joke was liable to be seen as subversive and could get you locked up (or worse). It portrayed Stalin as a scheming, paranoid git. It was inexplicably frowned upon by the authorities and was actually banned until Gorbachev came along. But then it became a bestseller of the *perestroika* era because it was so direct in its criticism of the Soviet system. So the *Arbat* acquired a kind of cult status for dissidents of all shades.

Mick and I had a mosey around the place but were mainly on the lookout for nourishment. This was because during our five-day stay in Moscow we lived almost exclusively on the peanuts and Heineken (well its logo is a red star, remember) that we could get in various hotel bars. Our *Intourist* voucher included breakfast, but that comprised only inedible, chew-on-them-forever 'pastries' and a tasteless warm brown liquid which the breakfast menu described as coffee. One morning, possibly after the night before, we asked for a second cup thereof. This wasn't covered by the voucher, and the waiter had to consult his superior, who in turn referred the matter up the hierarchy until a decision was finally taken by a plenary session of the Supreme Soviet. The decision was that we could have another cup if we paid in *deutschmarks*. We could have tried our luck for lunch and dinner at the hotel as well, but we wanted to sample real Moscow food in real Moscow eating places. Big mistake!

Nothing was really nice, except maybe one particular piece of cheese we saw in a very old-fashioned-looking shop with wooden and mainly bare shelves. You had to queue to see what was on offer (very little), then queue again to ask for it, then queue again a third time to pay for it. But hey, there was no unemployment in the Soviet Union! We passed what looked like an early fifties snack bar, and went in and ordered some mince that was being stirred in a great big poss-tub by a huge woman getting on in years and wearing a dirty-white overall and a dirty-white hat like the ones you see Russian doctors and nuclear-power-station operatives wearing. The mince-*ersatz* lookalike tasted pretty much how we imagined maggots might taste. Disgusting. And the dollop of *smetana* (thick sour cream) that the *babushka* had unceremoniously hoyed in for good measure gave it a certain ... *je ne sais quoi* ... oh, what's the word? ... yes ... sickliness. You get the picture.

(Now I do, Pete. And here was me thinking Smetana was a possibly Slovak composer of one of the best pieces of classical music around, 'Ma Vlast'. Now he's just a sickly dollop.)

We were getting hungry, and fed up (quite literally) with peanuts. The lady on reception at our hotel had said the *Arbat* was a nice place and we would definitely find a restaurant. All we found, however, was an outdoor stall selling *shashlik* and sausages. It was actually just outside the Metro station, so maybe we didn't look all that far. If you didn't really focus your eyes, the station did a passable impression of some kind of Chinese pavilion, mainly red with *smetana*-coloured edgings (yuck!). Lured by the smell and sizzling of meat being barbecued, we marched straight up to the stall and ordered *shashlik* (under-cooked Russian-style kebab on a skewer). It was stringy, but filling (and made you want a cool Heineken, sharpish).

***

Pete, that Chinese pavilion-style Metro entrance is still there and I could have fancied one of those *shashliks*, but I didn't see your food stall. Probably bought out by McDonalds. More's the pity, I say. Nevertheless I did buy a few presents to take home, and some postcards. I found that bargaining is the thing to do in Moscow, but my haggling skills were not enough to stop my cash level falling down too low to get through the day, so I was going to have to head back to the hotel to take enough to last the evening. I preferred not to take any bank card with me, just a small amount of cash.

While hunting around for one of their well-concealed and unobtrusive red Metro M signs, I was surprised to spot a *Chez Paul* café and I had just enough left to pay for an onion soup and a coffee. It's a French chain which you see in Belgium and London, and now patently in Moscow too. I sat down within easy earshot of a couple of Froggies who had heard me speaking English and assumed therefore I certainly wouldn't understand them. And what they discussed was all quite interesting to the point where I really didn't know whether they were testing out each other's gullibility or what – talking about buying works of art for oligarchs, unique fifteenth century hand-made maps, statues and icons, setting up deals for famous Russians and their wives, property deals, buying false Puerto Rican and Columbian passports for Russians, and so on. One was a middle-aged podgy-baldy type and the other was young and black haired and at first I'd thought they were father and son until they started talking about how to hide your cash, Swiss banks, and dodgy deals. I should have had a tape recorder.

***

I'd walked a long way and time had flown along and now there was no time to waste, just enough to get back to the hotel and then over to the *Luzhniki*. Moscow's a big place.

Walking through the Olympic park on the way to the stadium, I was in with a flow of Anzhi fans who were really friendly and I got some good photos with them, standing along with Lenin. They'd spent a couple of days on trains and buses coming up from their home town, a mere one thousand eight hundred kilometres away. That's rather like asking Newcastle to play their European home games in Rome! Piece of cake. Just round the corner, really!

I made the rendezvous with Steve Storey and the Other Chris and we had a chat about what we thought of Moscow and the prospects for the match. We agreed that the atmosphere certainly wasn't anything like we'd seen in Bruges or Bordeaux. Steve said that the team had been in Red Square earlier on that day, so I'd just missed them.

It was strange to be in such a huge, empty stadium. We were probably a couple of hundred yards away from the nearest Anzhi fans! Even Alan Pardew, who was also at least two hundred yards away, couldn't hear us call 'Give us a wave!'

I counted seventy-three Toon fans, including many familiar faces who turn up everywhere – they'd just about all been in Kharkiv and many in Atromitos too. And at about half-time, a bunch of about thirty Russian Toon Supporters Club members got moved into the enclosure alongside us, next to about thirty Russian military, who were getting a free view of the game. There was one of them to every two of us.

It really was VERY cold. So I don't blame our players for wearing tights and gloves!

A couple of the local stadium staff had programmes and we tried to get some, but they wanted souvenirs in return. They promised to come back after half-time with more programmes, but they came back with just one scrunched up one. It is strange how you can hardly ever get programmes at European matches. And at this one, there'd been no half 'n' half scarves either.

The weather forecast before leaving had said for at least part of the time it would be 'warmer' than normal, with a Moscow March heat-wave expected: minus one on Wednesday, plus two on Thursday and minus four on Friday but I am not so sure I believe that now. The weather experts said the week after our visit, it would go back to the minus ten degree temperatures that they'd had the week before, but I think the heat-wave failed to turn up, certainly in the *Luzhniki* Stadium and the Kremlin.

When the team came out onto the plastic pitch, it had a bit of a strange look. Not only was it great to see that we were at last wearing proper black and white instead of variegated away strips, but also we had no forwards, what with Cissé being ill and left at home, Demba Ba having long gone as a seat-warmer to cheatski, and new signing Gouffran ineligible as he'd played for Bordeaux against us. So we had a team of defenders and midfielders, with Shola on the bench: Elliot, Simpson, new boys Yanga-Mbiwa and Haidara, Perch, Cabaye, Sissoko, Anita, Ben Arfa returning after a long hamstring injury absence, Marveaux, and Obertan. Anzhi had their thirty million pound signing, Willian the Second (later of cheatski) playing down the right wing and looking their most dangerous player, but Haidara was looking after him pretty well.

After a quarter of an hour Willian took a corner but straight afterwards he bent double as if he'd jarred himself, and wasn't the same after that. It wasn't long after that he went off, which was a welcome sight to us. We were doing pretty well, slowing the game down with careful passing and keeping possession. Just before the half hour Eto'o looked as if he might break away but Haidara blocked his progress, Eto'o complaining that he'd done it with his arm. With about five minutes of the first half left, Eto'o had the first decent shot of the game, but his long-range effort was tipped over the bar by Elliot. From where we were standing it was a long range for sure, as we were probably a furlong away from Elliot. The first half came to an end with our no-forwards line-up conjuring up no shots for us, but we'd contained Anzhi well.

Half time was spent trying to get a programme off the officials who still seemed more interested in begging for souvenirs off us, and who made empty promises about getting some more programmes which never came to fruition. And apart from that, keeping moving to avoid being frozen into position.

The second half began with Anzhi pretty well encamped in our half but without fashioning any real chances at all until Eto'o was the man again with a low shot which Elliot dived well to his right to save. Straight afterwards, Ben Arfa was fed through on the edge of the penalty area by Cabaye. He advanced towards the goalkeeper, tried to chip the ball over him, and just failed. Our best chance of the match had come and gone. Then it was Shola time, with Ben Arfa making way. And then with a quarter of an hour to go, it was Steven Taylor who came on to make his acquaintance with Samuel Eto'o, which would have begun on the island of Majorca almost nine years before if Eto'o of *Real Mallorca* hadn't already been substituted by the time Taylor made his first-team début. The game ran to its end much as the first half had gone, with Anzhi's hardly threatening attacks being comfortably repelled by the lads. Near the end, Tioté took over from Cabaye in midfield and as captain and then Eto'o had another chance but scuffed the ball harmlessly for Elliot to pick up. An uneventful game, but a very good result for us, nil-nil. That was the first time Anzhi had failed to win their 'home' leg in this competition. Well defended and well controlled, Newcastle!

***

The morning after the match was for pre-departure sightseeing. According to the receptionist, Friday was Women's Day, which is a national holiday in Russia, and that explains why everyone was buying flowers the day before and why the girls in the GUM shopping mall were giving them out dressed up in floral Bo-Peep dresses and carrying big wide baskets of flowers. Olga also thought the Kremlin would be closed because of the Women's Day national holiday, but I gave it a try, fully expecting not to get in but it was open after all. It would have been a big miss. I should have remembered of course that the eighth of March is in fact International Women's Day everywhere. How could I forget?

When you pass through the giant heavy wooden doors into the inner sanctum, you're in for a surprise as you enter a new world of calm, spotlessly clean, wide open spaces and it looks a treat in the bright sunshine. The weather turned even colder and the wind whipped up. Being a high point of the city in more ways than one, it is exposed to a bitingly cold wind and there are tiny crystals of ice floating in the air and not just when you breathe out, but everywhere you look. It felt like one of the coldest places I've ever been. My runny nose froze instantly and my breath crystallised in the air and a whole new cloud of tiny ice particles sparkled in the sunlight every time I breathed out. My fingers froze into claws every time I took my gloves off to take a photo.

It is like a peaceful village, a different world from the rest of the city – orderly, beautifully maintained, peaceful, and with just the very occasional car. I'd imagined the Kremlin would be something quite different, a much smaller place and basically just one big old office building hidden behind the perimeter wall. It does have old office buildings but they are spread out along their own streets. There's a lot of space: a park with trees, three literally iconic cathedrals concentrated all together in one area, an armoury and a cannon museum, a conference centre, and a great view over the south (probably) end of the city and the river. I had a quick look in a church full of icons, but when you've seen one church full of icons, you've seen 'em all, and I didn't bother with the armoury either because there were so many cannons on display outside anyway, including quite a few captured from Napoléon. Behind one of the cathedrals, they have the biggest cannon I've ever seen – built, I think it said, in about 1853. If I understood right, it could fire its huge balls of about two feet in diameter a range of 5.4

kilometres. They must have stuffed an awful lot of gunpowder in it to propel its balls that far. The cannon weighed four or five tons, but it must have recoiled a long way even if it was well dug in. I then came upon an even bigger relic, a bell which had a big triangular lump cracked out which was on display beside it too. That must have made one hell of a clang when it fell off. Talk about dropping a clanger! Both the cannon and the bell were the property of Ivan the Terrible. Maybe he tested his cannon out on the bell.

Just time for one last place before going, so partly to get out of the cold, and partly because when would I ever get the chance again, I chose the Pushkin Museum. It is huge so I opted to go only in the nineteenth and twentieth Century Art Annex. It has some of the most famous Impressionist and Expressionist paintings in the world, from a time when rich Russians liked to show their taste by buying art of the period and particularly of French artists or artists living in France. I was surprised you were allowed to take pictures, and I took quite a few. I have them hanging on my wall now. Only joking, you could take photos, you couldn't take the actual pictures. There was that fantastic sculpture of intertwined lovers by Rodin, and then there were paintings by Chagall, a Russian in France, Picasso, Braque, Cézanne, Degas, Renoir, Monet, Manet, Matisse and Corot. Apparently the collection was split in the 1940s and some went to the Hermitage Museum in Leningrad (St Petersburg).

The Pushkin was so good that I stayed too long by going around it twice and then had to head to the Metro sharpish. So this was to be my final trip on the Moscow underground, with one final change at (Gorky) *Park Kultury*, and then the onward journey to *Paveletskaya* Station. Unlike at the airport, you couldn't just pay a lady in a booth, you had to put coins in a machine and mine kept being rejected. The Tannoy announcement said that the train would leave in two minutes but I still couldn't get it working until a ticket man came along and helped. He then pointed the way to the train and I ran up the slope to the platform but I missed it. The train doors closed just as I got on the platform. How long to wait? Half an hour luckily, otherwise it really would have been bad. I was rather keen on catching this particular plane and I was hoping its departure would somehow be delayed, as I was cutting it very fine with my visa. I was really glad that I had checked in and had my boarding pass printed out at the hotel by the helpful man at the reception. Let's hope the luggage checks are quick too. I would have to run to the departure place and hope. I was imagining having to buy a new ticket and also some passport complications as my visa would run out at midnight, and this was the only plane to Brussels for another twenty-four hours. I really didn't relish the thought of being stranded in Russia with an expired visa: if I ever needed to apply for another one I'd have to admit I'd previously out-stayed my welcome.

Sure enough, I had to run all the way through the airport and through the customs and passport checks. But as it turned out, everything went very fast and efficiently, which is not at all what you hear about formalities in Russia. It was easier and faster than in Western Europe. And I could tell I was in the right place as a good quarter of the Toon Army contingent were there at the gate. So all's well that ends well, as the saying goes.

***

All in all, I enjoyed the trip, but apart from the A-grade sightseeing, it is a bit of a dull place, and not what you would call lively. It's not the sort of place where you can settle down in a nice bar like in Bordeaux on our earlier trip and watch the world go by. The Metro stations are something very special, however: underground cathedrals that no doubt were designed to double as huge air-raid shelters, same as in Kharkiv. But as far as I am concerned, I can tick Moscow off my personal list of places to visit. Been there, done that.

So: *Do Svidanya, Moskva.* That's *До свидания, москва*!

Anzhi at home – 14th March 2013

The retreat from Newcastle

Like I said, I was gutted about not getting to Moscow for the first leg, I really was. And I don't give up easily. Barry suggested I try the Russian embassy in Brussels, but from my experience of the Russians in the eighties I knew they would just say Berlin was responsible. And anyway I was working all day. Mission impossible.

So as a consolation prize to myself (well I deserved one, didn't I?), I decided to go to the home leg and duly booked flights with KLM from Luxembourg to Amsterdam to Newcastle and back. I would stay with wor Mick in Tynemouth. Chris kindly said he would sort out a match ticket. The flight to Amsterdam left Luxembourg at 19.35 on the Wednesday, but on the Tuesday Germany and Benelux were still (or rather were once again) in the grip of a Siberian-style winter which I had brought back with me from (the) Ukraine (who had stolen Siberia's winter). We were all bearing the brunt of a cruel Arctic Blast, and that had spelled chaos for air travellers. The German TV news on Wednesday morning showed Frankfurt airport still in the process of sorting out the aftermath of the previous day's cancellations. There would surely be knock-on effects, and it was reasonable to assume that the other big hubs, Amsterdam and Heathrow, would be having similar problems. People had spent the night wrapped in blankets on the floor of Frankfurt's terminal buildings. The scenes were like something out of a Hollywood disaster movie. This did not augur well.

However, the snow storms of the past few days had abated and we were left with the makings of a beautiful winter's day, bitterly cold but no wind and a clear blue sky, and the fields a whiter than white whiteness. The number of times we have blue skies on Toon travel days! So, another good day for blue skies thinking, or even white fields thinking (there's another phrase to add to the thesaurus of managerial claptrap). It was once again going to be a case of travelling light, by my standards, taking only the small pull-along case I had taken to Kharkiv, the maximum size for hand luggage. You see, I am ever mindful of past experience of heading over for the Great North Run with a very tight connection at Amsterdam and with my luggage failing to arrive in Newcastle on the same plane as yours truly. That had once resulted in a mad rush from Tynemouth to the Toon to get kitted out with all the running gear (only the trainers had been in my hand luggage), and then the big case arrived in Tynemouth by taxi late on Saturday afternoon while I was at the match. As a special treat I had taken up KLM's offer, made when I checked in on-line on the Tuesday, for a thirty-euro upgrade to business class. Something I had never done ever before. It was just for a thirty-five minute flight, but still.

After watching the weather forecast on the BBC, I set off on my way to work with the satisfying prospect of ending the day in the Gate of India on Tynemouth Front Street, though it did strike me as a bit far-fetched, as Mick would be picking me up at the airport at 22.10. Ah well, maybe a pint at the Cumberland Arms just as they were calling last orders instead. We would see.

The winter wonderland of snow-covered vineyards along the Moselle valley made sunglasses a must, and all was well with the world as I sped along the motorway towards the world's best run Grand Duchy. Just before the border the mobile rang and I had forgotten to switch the Bluetooth on in order to use the hands-free facility. I had remembered to clean my teeth, however. It was our Tina and I rudely asked her to keep it very short as I was being very naughty indeed using the mobile phone when driving. I had forgotten my case! How stupid was that? The case of the forgotten case.

At the border there is a motorway services with an underpass that allows u to do a you turn under the motorway, so back home I drove. That meant getting to work a good hour late, meaning that the day would be more stressful than planned. Nevertheless I managed to leave the office at half past four on the dot, and was parked up in the Luxembourg Airport underground car park just half an hour later. Just as well, really, because my theory that the airport is far bigger than it needs to be was about to have its credibility undermined. The car park itself was very full for a start. And the super-clean, air-conditioned, all-expensive-looking terminal was far busier than I think I have ever known. Lots of people in their business suits headed for London, Paris, Berlin, Munich, everyone talking about pop music. Talk about pop music? Just as well I had checked in on-line because the queue at the one-long-counter-fits-all check-in desk was a mile long, though how many members of the mile-high club were in it, I don't know. The queue for the security check wasn't much shorter, so really I had not got there ridiculously early at all.

In fact by the time I was through security and had got my belt and shoes back on, there was really just time to buy a bottle of bubbly and some chocs for Mick and Marilyn and get myself a pint before the call came for the Amsterdam-bound to get their arses to gate A14. The thirty euro upgrade had bought a seat in the very first row, with a lot more leg room than on recent flights, and best of all I had the row to myself, so once fully airborne I swopped my aisle seat for the middle one and enjoyed my red wine and sandwich (as opposed to orange juice and a sweet or savoury mini snack in steerage). Well worth the investment, albeit that the experience was a brief one.

We had taken off bang on time, and at a quarter to eight on a mid-March evening in these parts there is still a little light left in the day's sun, especially when you are up a height in a plane. The rolling hills of the Ardennes were at their snow-covered Christmas-card best, the whiteness interspersed with dark pine forest and well ordered villages, the houses clustered around the spire of the church and then radiating out and blending into the snowy countryside. All nicely picked out briefly in a frosty crispness that soon faded into twilight. On went the village lights. Even motorways light up in Belgium, and the odd floodlit sports ground was also to be seen. It quickly got very dark and soon we were over Antwerp's docks, then Zeeland and Rotterdam and a holding pattern over the greenhouses and solar panels of Hellingvoetsluis, before the final descent to Schiphol, flying surreally over the motorway headlights before touching down and taxiing for a good ten minutes. Then we were bussed through the slush, past planes whose wings were covered with snow. Out we got to emerge into the anonymous and international giant terminal. It's a good hike from B30 to D22, and many an opportunity has that provided in the past to get in some last minute training for the GNR, jogging along the auto-walks to get to the gate on time. But this time the connecting flight wouldn't be leaving till 21.50, so there was no hurry at all. According to the departures screens positioned here and there along the way through the giant shopping mall that is Schiphol, flights were not delayed, so it seemed they had sorted things out all right. Mind your step. Off the auto-walk, walk a few steps, back on the next one.

After going through passport control – only moderate queues – and thus leaving the Schengen zone and entering terminal D, there was plenty of time to sup a leisurely pint of the cool Heineken and watch the comings and goings. This place must never, ever sleep, as there are flights departing for and arriving from places all around the globe all around the clock. A strange, timeless and artificial world, run superbly well by our Dutch friends, as you would expect. It makes you wonder what percentage of Dutch national territory is taken up by Schiphol. It really is big and surely must make a dent in the amount of available land. But the Dutch, and their super-efficient ministry of public works, Rijkswaterstaat, are so good at making good use of every single available square metre.

These random ramblings passed the time, and as gate opening time of 20.55 approached I made my way to where a few dozen other Geordies (ex-pats, holidaymakers and business types alike) were headed, gate D22.

We were all aboard by 21.35, so it looked like our scheduled 21.50 kick-off was still on the cards. And mind, there wasn't an empty seat in the house. It's very rare that an Amsterdam to Newcastle or Newcastle to Amsterdam flight isn't full or thereabouts. It must be a gold mine and long may this link continue. Barry had told me that Brussels Airlines were discontinuing their Newcastle link as from April 2013. That is just too bad. Surely flights between Brussels and Newcastle will have to start up again. (Ha, they did, a few months after I wrote this! Just call me *Petrus Nostradamus*.) Poor old Brussels can't be allowed to be cut off from Europe's capital city just like that. What is that airline thinking about?

Anyway, my luggage and duty-free were stowed, and I was strapped into my non-weightist aisle seat and we were all welcomed aboard this KLM Air France South China Airways Aeroflot flight. I was really chuffed as I had never flown either South China Airways or Aeroflot before. In fact I had made a point of avoiding both, and especially the latter. But there you go.

Then came the captain's announcement. That snow on the wings would have to go, and we would have to wait half an hour or so before it would be our turn for de-icing. This I don't like. I hate sitting on the tarmac for such a prolonged period. You get cramp, claustrophobia, you need a jimmy riddle. All those things. And after my South China Airways and Aeroflot débuts, this was another first. My first de-icing. And remember, this was the 13th of the month, though fortunately not a Friday.

Someone had been telling porkies, because it wasn't half an hour we had to wait. No, it was a full hour. Fortunately, we were allowed to use mobiles, so I rang wor Mick, who was just about to leave home to head for the airport. So he was able to delay his departure as well.

Finally, the plane was pushed back and we taxied out to the de-icing experience. And a strange one it was. I craned my neck a bit to gaze past the people in the middle and window seats, out into the dark and the airport lights in the middle distance. Manoeuvring around a neighbouring aircraft about fifty metres to our left were some Martian fighting machines, rearing up on their hind legs and pointing their ray-gun cannons at the plane. These giant arms focused their sprays at wings and fuselage alike, and all was steam and mist, sometimes sparkled by the background lights and the fighting machines' headlamps. From the Mars Attacks cards of my youth, and some American comics as well, I remembered that Martians had weapons that would turn you into one of their own, or at least make a willing slave of you, and clearly the fighting machines had finally turned our plane into one of their mighty flying devices, because at last we were about to take off. We had become Martians. Or maybe I had just nodded off, who knows? It was getting late into the evening after all.

The captain apologised for the delay and promised he would try to put his foot down and make up for some of the lost time. In the event, we landed at Newcastle exactly an hour later, which wasn't too bad in the end. Newcastle Airport isn't quite as big as Schiphol of course, but it is much nicer. When you step off the plane onto the tarmac you are stepping onto your home soil (well, home tarmac). Except we stepped straight into one of those tentacles called boarding bridges (though of course we were alighting) and didn't have to step out into the cold. This makes Newcastle feel even more like an important international airport. A genuine source of pride. Mick was waiting patiently at arrivals as he had done many times before.

In no time we were out of the airport car park, from where I saw what for me looked like new hotels (I hadn't been back for a while) and we were soon speeding towards the lights of the Toon and then across the start of the Great North Run but turning left for Jesmond and on towards the coast, going down past the Park Hotel and along past the Grand Hotel just for old times' sake before entering Tynemouth village. It was too late for a pint and an Indian, so instead we sat talking till about four o'clock in the morning, which for me was five, drinking several pints and eating sandwiches.

***

I was awakened by a text message from Chris saying they were on the train and it was expected to arrive in Newcastle on time. Oh s#1t, I was supposed to be meeting them at 12.41 at the Central with a view to lunch together. But it was already getting on for eleven, so there was no way I was going to make it. So I rang Chris and we arranged to meet at the Monument at three instead, which left time for a leisurely breakfast and some more catching up. Mick then drove me to the Toon, through old familiar streets in Shields, Percy Main, Howdon, Wallsend, Walker and Byker, dropping me off outside the Theatre Royal, and Sarah, Chris and I rendezvoused at the Monument as planned. On the Grey Street side someone was strangling a cat while his mate beat on a drum in a very irregular fashion. We quickly got out of earshot of the (Scottish) bagpipe maniac and headed down Grainger Street to the Central where I needed to reserve a seat on the train from Newcastle to Kings Cross for the first leg of my return journey to Schweigen Deigen Land after the Cuths Old Boys West Highland Way walk in May. I had been able to reserve seats for all the other parts of the journey back in Germany but for some reason not this one. It promises to be a good walk. Three days, at sixteen to twenty miles a day. Manageable, even for me. A few years back we walked the Wall west to east, and the first day over hill and dale was further than a marathon, about twenty-eight miles in fact. The blisters on my heels were so bad that at some points I walked up the hills backwards. After about seventeen miles on the second day I had to give up, the blisters were so bad. Chris and I were picked up by our Executive Logistical Support officer, Big John Lunn Son of Lunn, who very kindly ferried our luggage and was on call to pick up the walking wounded. He took us to the Twice Brewed Inn at Bardon Mill for some liquid recovery. Chris continued the walk the next day and completed it. I had to sit it out and even went to the General for a professional to have a look. It was agony for all concerned and nobody could walk properly again for weeks. Why is it we feel we have to push ourselves to the limits of human endurance? What's wrong with a gentle stroll through the countryside? Anyway, this time it would not be quite so gruelling, and I would be applying the Compeeds before I even started. It would be great *craic*, for sure.

Seat reservation sorted, we made our way to SJP, up through Pink Lane, past the Wimpy and Henry's (which were absent without leave), past Cardinal Baz, whom we glimpsed to our left (he should have been Pope: imagine that, the Pope a Newcastle supporter!), on past the Forth, across to the West Walls, through China Town, past the Irish Centre (which would be heaving this coming Paddy's weekend), and over the road past a kind of Garden of Remembrance for Wor Sir Uncle Bobby. None of us had known about these white memorial stones. What a great idea to commemorate the Great Man in this way.

All Geordie ex-pats will agree that no matter how long you have been away, once you set foot on Tyneside it's as if you have never been away at all. Yes, you are surprised now and then that an old familiar building has been demolished by Tesco or Aldi, but by and large everything is still where it should be. Your feet remember the old walks to the old haunts and the paving stones remember your feet. Even after almost thirty-four years of not living there, it still feels like you never left.

Into the club shop, where I needed to buy a scarf and a woolly hat to replace the hat I had swapped with that Metalist supporter in Kharkov. Although the shop is amazingly well stocked and offers just about every article of clothing you could imagine that is capable of being Toon-themed, they had run out of adult-sized woolly hats. Never mind, I found a nice traditional-style scarf, like the old Mam-knitted ones, a plain succession of black and white squares, but this one also featuring several different crests.

Where to adjourn for refreshment but that most holy of holy watering holes, *La Fraise*, aka the Strawberry. It was only about half past four and so we could easily get seated. Chris had a pint of the Kronenbourg and I could not resist a pint of Rivet Catcher. Sarah had a half of the same. I am a sucker for a great name, and Rivet Catcher is a great name, particularly as that was a job one of my Great Grandfathers had at Palmer's shipyard in Hebburn, or was it Jarrow (aka little Ireland)? Palmer's was an amazing industrial sprawl on the south bank of the Tyne. The steel works and the literally downstream shipyard (spread over Hebburn and Jarrow) sucked in the mainly Irish immigrants, transforming Jarrow from a mere village of six thousand souls at the beginning of the nineteenth century into a teeming industrial hotbed by 1900. A hotbed that was used to hot bunking, too – it was common for a labourer who had just finished night shift to use the bed just vacated by another who was going on day shift. Long gone, Palmer's Shipbuilding and Iron Company, but what a legacy!

***

All that rivet catching makes you hungry, and so we ordered burger and chips as we supped a second one in the very shadow of St James's Park. We were well into rush hour by now and there was a constant stream of cars passing the Strawberry and lots of people were milling around in the gathering dusk, while programme sellers, hot dog vendors and others were readying themselves for the pre-match rush. Gazing over into Leazes Lane, my mind drifted back to those also long-gone days of the '68-'69 glory campaign. My Mam would put up some bait for me and I would take a very early train from Howdon to the Central and then walk up the same route we had taken today to take my place in the already long pre-dawn queue patiently waiting to buy a ticket for the next Fairs Cup game. Eating their sandwiches and drinking tea from flasks on cold winter mornings for the chance to see the likes of Vitória Setúbal – we beat them in the snow five-one. I don't think they would allow a game to go ahead in such conditions these days. The Portuguese players felt the cold so much that some of them wore gloves and tights. Gazing up at the heavens in disbelief, they looked as though they had never seen snow before in all their lives. Happy days.

Our food arrived and who should we spot about to sit down at the table opposite but Paul (another Paul) and Neil, the Toon supporters we had met in Kharkiv (it's in (the) Ukraine). 'What brought you here?' Neil asked. Two planes and a lift in Wor Mick's car.

We ate our scran and saw it was time to move on and rendezvous for (more) pre-match tinctures in the Crow's Nest, so we said our farewells to Neil and Paul, cryptically saying that we would see them again soon, 'somewhere in Europe'. Counter-intuitively, we bent our steps away from SJP and towards the Crow's Nest, passing the Labour Club on our right and an Italian place on our left. For some reason I was reminded of that Harry Palmer video from the Andy Cole era. The plot had been similar to the afternoon we had had. He went for a few pints before the

Liverpool match we won four-nil (afterwards there was talk of possible match fixing, if you remember). Harry, the wandering minstrel who could neither sing nor play the guitar properly, regaled the good people of Newcastle and some very welcome Scouse visitors with such classics as 'Andy Cole, Andy Cole, running down the wing', or 'Terry, Terry, Terry, Terry Hibbit on the wing'. How we enjoyed watching that video in Germany. My daughters were soon word-perfect.

Once inside the Crow's Nest, we saw immediately the impact the new management had had. Gone was the large standing area in front of the giant screen, sacrificed on the altar of selling as much bar food as possible. There were far too many tables. We sat at one, mid-pub, but soon we were standing when we were joined by Peter F. from South Shields, Vince, the Other Clive, the Other Peter and Alan from Gateshead.

***

You will recall that in Bordeaux Alan had told us he was at the crossroads. Naturally we had been very worried about this and were desperate to know if there had been any movement on the crossroads front. Now we all find ourselves at a crossroads at some time, or even several times, in our lives. Sooner or later, there is bound to be a crisis of some sort that has to be dealt with. Sometimes, of course, it can be a case of *chercher la femme*. But as often as not it is about a crisis of faith, faith in *le Toon*. An equally likely scenario is that *la femme* may clash with *le Toon*. How many of us have strayed temporarily from the true path in adolescent years because a girlfriend could not see that the proper place to be on a cold and wet Saturday afternoon in November was the Gallowgate End? Let him who hath not sinned hoy the first peanuts, tanner a bag.

Crossroads can be strange places. You can of course go straight ahead, looking neither left not right. Or you can turn left. Or right. You could always turn right, go as far as the nearest pub, have a pint and walk back again. So many decisions. Some can be wrong, and others right. Look at those crossroads in North by Northwest, where Cary Grant got attacked by a crop-spraying plane and had to run into a corn field for cover. Alan assured us he hadn't been threatened by a crop-sprayer and no tank-lorries had exploded in his immediate vicinity. We looked out at the Haymarket traffic, and sure enough there were no road tankers to be seen. He explained that his crossroads moment had in fact been caused by a string of bad results, and the two-nil defeat in Bordeaux had been a major downer. But he had overcome that and moved on, leaving the crossroads far, far behind. But would there be another crossroads lurking just beyond the horizon?

The Other Clive, true to form, had come up from Sheffield the day before to watch a Northern League game. We were speculating where we might play in the next round, but Vince cautioned against being over-optimistic. I made the mistake of saying tonight's game would surely be a mere formality after the goalless draw in Moscow. That remark rightly met with general disapproval and I was suitably contrite. For my penance I had to promise to sing all six verses of the Blaydon Races during my next shower.

We were all agreed, without actually mentioning that we might not even get through this round, that we didn't want to be drawn against Rubin Kazan, especially as nobody knew whereabouts in Russia it was. Was Rubin the name of the town, or Kazan, for a start? Or maybe Rubin Kazan was a two-word town like Whitley Bay? Someone suggested it might even be quicker flying there via Anchorage, Alaska. Looking at the map later, Kazan turns out to be on a very wide stretch of the Volga River, almost a lake, in the land of the Tatars and five hundred miles even further east than Moscow. Sometimes the weather is so bad in Kazan that UEFA makes them play their home games in Moscow, because it is so 'warm' there in comparison!

If Zenit could beat Basel, Saint Petersburg would be a great place to visit, but there would be visa problems again, though this time there would be a little more time to plan. If not, Basel would be good, as would Milan, but Lisbon would be just brilliant. I had never been. But Clive, Peter, Sarah, Chris, Barry, Neale and the Don had enjoyed the trip immensely back in 2005. I had watched that game in the Cumberland Arms, as regular readers will remember. We didn't want to be drawn against chelski or Spurs. After all, this was a European competition. Mind, chelski could probably make a case for playing their home games in Moscow, just like Anzhi and Rubin Kazan. But no thanks, it would only mean more visa problems.

Match time was drawing closer and so it was time to head back towards Gallowgate. I remembered to get two programmes (one was for Barry) and we made our way past the Trent House, up to

Leazes Terrace and the Leazes End turnstiles. There was a bit of confusion about which access was ours and we found ourselves next to some Anzhi supporters. We were in the wrong queue but we quickly found the right entrance a few yards further along. I squeezed through the overtly weightist turnstile and we made our way up the steps.

You cannot beat the sensation of emerging into the Leazes End and looking out onto the floodlit pitch at St James's Park, especially on a European night. Oh, the memories of those glory days of yore. We took our seats, about a third of the way up the bottom tier, just to the left of the box. The two blokes at the end of our row were dressed as Frenchies, with their berets and curly false moustaches. One of them was holding up a sign that read 'Parlez-vous Geordie?' Looking around, it was striking how many young kids were there with their Mams and Dads. The reason of course was the cheapness of the tickets. For once it was affordable to take the whole family to the match. A lot of the kids seemed to be more interested in running around the place, mind. But it was great that they were there. The presence of families makes for a really nice atmosphere, and encourages everyone to be on their best behaviour. Steve Storey, head of security, made an appeal asking people to be sensible and not invade the pitch, because of the 'Johnny P123' streaker incident at the Bordeaux home game. There was always a danger of getting a ban if that sort of thing continued.

Off to our left in the corner of the Leazes End were the Metalist fans, claiming political asylum for the last few weeks. No, I mean the Anzhi fans. There must have been about a hundred of them, and at first sight their colours gave them the appearance of Norwich City supporters. The Cyrillic writing on their banners and scarves, etc, made it clear that they were Russian, however. But hang on, they are from Dagestan. What exactly is the status of that neck of the woods? Well, it's next door to Chechnya, if that is any kind of indicator of how cosy a place it might be.

The transliteration of Cyrillic letters is a funny business and is certainly not an exact science. If 'rules' were applied by the letter, the Bulgarian word for Bulgaria, for example, would come out as Balgaria. Anzhi is also a case in point. In Cyrillic, the name is *Анжи*, which is pronounced a bit like Angie, but the *zh* is really pronounced more like the *s* in plea*s*ure. How many of you remember 'Add pleasure to leisure with Newcastle Brown Ale. It's the best beer, it's the bottled beer with the North's biggest sale.'

***

Our team tonight was very little changed from the away leg with Elliot, Santon replacing Simpson, Yanga-Mbiwa, Steven Taylor, Haidara, Cabaye, Sissoko, Anita, Marveaux, Tioté instead of Obertan, and Cissé instead of Ben Arfa. At least we had one forward this week.

From very early on in the first half it was clear that Angie were going to be no pushover, and they had a couple of reasonable chances, with Samuel Eto'o again the main threat, dragging one shot just past the post, to be answered by Marveaux shooting just wide at the other end. Steven Taylor was a stalwart in defence, throwing himself in front of the ball on numerous occasions, and he almost headed in a Marveaux cross at the other end, with the crowd chanting 'Taylor for England.' It was a big blow when Cabaye went off with a groin injury to be replaced by Gutierrez, as we were losing the battle in midfield. And then Ahmedov, who was arguably Anzhi's most tricky and skilful player, missed a pretty easy chance to put them ahead towards the end of the half and only managed to find the side netting.

At half time, we went back down the steps to get the beers in but quickly discovered that under UEFA rules it was the non-alcoholic stuff only. No alcohol. No thank you. In Kharkiv we had not been allowed to buy any beer, but the home fans had certainly been buying plenty of the stuff. In fact it had been brought to them on trays. Even those who had patently already had too much to drink were able to buy it. Did different rules apply? Surely not. It's just that in (the) Ukraine they don't apply the rules, whereas in Newcastle they do.

We were a whole lot better in the second half and put Anzhi under sustained pressure. Mid-way through the second half they had Carcela-González sent off for a second yellow-card offence, so here was our big chance. Taylor gestured to the crowd to get really behind the team. And yes we did our bit. There was a lot more singing and encouragement coming from the 'terraces' than I could remember from any of my recent home games. Mackeltackelshackel were good even with just ten men, however. They were really organised and tight at the back, and at times it was hard to believe they were a man short. But going forward they were also sharp, letting themselves down with some dodgy passing now and then. Samuel Eto'o, who as you know played against us for *Real Mallorca* many years ago before he became famous with Barcelona, was a constant thorn in the side of our defence and very nearly scored at the Gallowgate End when he hammered in a near shot from a tight angle, but Rob Elliot managed to palm it away. Anita made a rash tackle and everyone waited with baited breath to see if the ref was going to make it ten a side. Luckily for us, he decided a yellow card fitted the bill. Then one free kick from just outside our penalty area on the left looked for a brief half second, from our vantage point, as though it could be going in. Fortunately, it hit the bar instead. And with the very last touch of the game, at the end of three minutes of injury time, Papiss Cissé headed home Marveaux's excellent curving right-wing cross into the Leazes End goal and we were through to the quarter final for the first time since 2005 when we went out to Sporting Lisbon.

So Alan Pardew had triumphed over Guus Hiddink. Quite a scalp.

It was a joyous post-mortem back in the Crow's Nest, and now we had certainty about who we could be drawn against. The eternal opti-pessimists, we had visions of visa nightmares and a trip to darkest Russia, or, even worse, London. After all, there was a two in seven chance of us playing Spurs or chelski.

Similar speculation was to be heard on the half-full last Metro from the Haymarket to Tynemouth, and mind those new ticket machines are a bit hard to fathom when you encounter them for the first time. After such an exciting evening it was impossible to gan straight to bed, so Mick and I sat up again into the small hours. Benfica had beaten Bordeaux, so there was no chance of an early return to that peerless city, though Lisbon would be a perfect alternative. The other continental options were Basel, Lazio, Fenerbahçe or Rubin Kazan who'd unfortunately beaten Levante, Obafemi Martins' latest team. That would have been a nice place to go, Valencia.

***

Again, I was awakened by the beep of the mobile telling me there was a text message. It was Barry to say we had been drawn against Lisbon. Yes, I had dossed till mid-day. This was brilliant news – they were pretty much our ideal choice. A Panglossian moment. The best of all possible draws. Friday was spent tootling around Tyneside. A trip through the new Tunnel. And the drive back, through the old one, was amazingly free-flowing for a Friday afternoon rush hour.

What used to be Saint Aidan's Church and Junior and Senior Schools in Willington Quay is now a housing estate and it was great fun trying to work out where we were in old terms. We're on the football field. No, this is where the Parish Hall stood. Then the position of Howdon gas tanks and the line of the old Black Path helped us get our bearings and pinpoint the location of the old dining hall. It's a nice estate and dead handy for the Metro, but what a pity none of the streets had names like Saint Aidan's Way, or Parish Hall Drive. A great pity, that. On the way back to Tynemouth we took in a Polish car wash. The car was hand-washed by a team of four. All for six quid, not including a Polish polish. Great value.

And no trip back home would be complete without a visit to the Gate of India. It was only six o'clock, so we were the first in. But within half an hour the place was half full. The front page of the menu told us the Gate had been there since 1976. We reckoned we had been patrons from about that time, too. No need to read the menu on the inside. Onion Bhaji, please, then Lamb Rogan Josh, Basmati rice, stuffed paratha. A beer? Hadn't thought of that, but what a great idea. A Cobra please. By the time we left the Gate, Tynemouth Front Street was stepping up through the gears, though things weren't yet going full tilt. Taxis were dropping people off and taking others on to their next venue. The groups of lasses all looked great and were dressed for the French Riviera in July rather than North Shields in mid-March. What a great atmosphere. A timeless Friday night on Tyneside.

The return journey the next day was pretty much the outward one in reverse, and I got home in time to watch the *Sportschau*. Dortmund whipped Freiburg five-one after going a goal behind, while Schalke lost three-nil at Nuremberg, in what must surely have been a trial. A week earlier Schalke had beaten Dortmund two-one in Germany's derby of derbies. It is the nearest thing Germany has to the Tyne-where? derby, in the German region that comes closest to matching Geordieland in terms of mentality and industrial heritage (coal and steel). Don't forget, Schalke play in Gelsenkirchen, Newcastle's twin town. At this point, little did we know (though Nostradamus could have told us) that Schalke would hold a pre-season tournament in August 2014 and invite NUFC to play in it, and you will read all about it anon. But back in March 2013 it was time to get back on the internet to book the flights for the Lisbon trip.

Benfica away – 4th April 2013

The best of all possible draws

'Benfica wrote to me in advance asking me not to write asking for press accreditation.'

When we flew down to Lisbon for the quarter-final second leg against Sporting the best part of a decade ago, the plane banked just over the Stadium of Light – the real one – with its endless rows of red seats and rounded shape. I remember thinking it would be good to play there one day. At the home of Eusebio. That's who comes to mind when I think of Benfica. The hero of the 1966 World Cup to me. He dragged Portugal back from the North Korean maws of defeat in Middlesbrough and I wanted him to go on and win the Cup. But it all went wrong, and two years later it all went wrong again in the 1968 European Cup Final when George Best's Man Utd defeated Eusebio's Benfica. But now that Eusebio's retired from playing for them, I want them to lose. Especially when they're about to play their biggest game since 1968 as far as I know as I haven't actually followed their progress since then. I was disappointed to hear that the great man wouldn't be leading the line for them tonight, because he must be around seventy now and that would have given our defence an easier time, but at least let's hope he's somewhere in the crowd. Maybe we'll see him.

But don't forget that the young Eusebio did play against Newcastle once, Barry, in a pre-season friendly at Saint James's Park on Saturday August 7th 1971. That match also happened to be Malcolm Macdonald's début. Gibbo scored the only goal of the game, at the Gallowgate End. And I wasn't there. Believe it or not, a very close relative got married that day. Bloody cheek! Meant I couldn't get to the match of course. Mind, I was at Palace a week later for Supermac's league début. Unfortunately we lost two-nil. But then a week after that it was his home league début against Liverpool, which I witnessed from the Leazes End. We won three-two and, as everyone knows, Supermac scored all three before being carried off after colliding with the goalkeeper when trying to make it four. Still, I would also have liked to see Eusebio play. It just goes to show you should be very careful about marrying in early August. Make sure you only ever tie the knot before the pre-season friendlies start! Otherwise, you'll never know whose big day you could be spoiling!

That's sound advice, Pete. But with a bit of luck we might just bump into Eusebio over the next few days!

It promised to be a great occasion, and the weather was fine for take-off in Brussels. Somehow it always seems to be a crisp blue sky when I'm heading off on these trips. On the last one I'd been burdened with a wadge of visas, hotel documents, insurance papers, official tourist office papers, plus downloaded advice on how to use the Metro, and dual-language maps in Cyrillic and our own script to negotiate my way around Moscow. But this time I could relax as I would be on familiar ground, and all I had with me was a home-printed boarding pass and a passport. I could even have got away without the passport as Portugal is in the Schengen free-movement-of-people zone where all you need is some less official form of photo identity such as a driving licence. I must admit, however, I've never risked it and I always take my passport.

(Just as well, Barry, because those arrangements only apply for citizens of the Schengen zone countries, not to Brits or other non-Schengenites who happen to live there! But hey!)

Whatever! The one fly in the ointment was that I made the mistake of checking the Lisbon weather forecast. Rather than the sunny and mid-twenties for which I'd fondly hoped, it was for thunderstorms and just fourteen degrees. Still, that's almost thirty degrees warmer than Moscow. So I had to change my packing plans from snorkel and flippers to my 2004 UEFA Cup Final windcheater which I got courtesy of some generous officials the morning after the Gothenburg Final between Marseille and Valencia which Didier Drogba had shot us out of with his twin-barrel blast. Can you still see him and Hugo Viana against the backdrop of those floodlit white cliffs of Marseille? It's etched on my memory.

And this trip wasn't a cheap one either, what with it being the school Easter holidays, and it took me some time to find a combination of flights to bring the price down from over five hundred euros to a more reasonable three hundred and thirty euros, but at the non-cash expense of having to get up before five o'clock for the seven o'clock Saturday morning flight back. And you were setting off bright and early on the other side of the Ardennes, weren't you, Pete?

I certainly was, Barry, and it was a crisp cold start to a beautifully sunny day. It looked as though the winter was finally giving up its valiant attempt to strangle spring at birth. Easter at the Dutch coast the weekend before had been cold, and the weekend before that had been positively Siberian and definitely not a good place for brass monkeys – appropriately enough, there were none to be seen. Even the beach remained covered in six inches of snow, unimpressed by the salty sea air. The drifts along the sides of the Zeeland roads covered the ditches and fanned out onto the carriageway itself. And piled up against the German bunkers still dotted around the dunes and coastal countryside, they gave the place an eerie, even menacing air. But hey, we were now Portugal-bound, and how does that old Beatles song go? Here comes the sun.

I was tremendously looking forward to seeing Benfica at long last after missing out due to fraternal matrimonial shenanigans forty-two years earlier. Still, I am a patient guy, and with or without Eusebio this promised to be one hell of an occasion. Having the away leg first was of course a huge added bonus – and all in all this surely was the best of all possible draws. Well look at the alternatives. Kazan, the place in Russia no-one could find (and with the same visa rigmarole). *Nyet, spasiba* (though in fact we would of course have played Kazan in Moscow, as cheatski did). Or cheatski themselves or Spurs? Hang on, this is a European competition. No, Pangloss was right, this was the best of all possible worlds, temporarily at least. Barring earthquakes, of course, Candidely speaking. Bring it on.

***

On this ever-brightening morning Luxembourg airport was back to its best – all sleekness and plate-glass light, unhurried and stressless. The on-line check-in facility airlines now offer is wonderful, and you can turn up that little bit later, unless of course you're paranoid like me and turn up just as early as you would have anyway – if not a bit earlier for good measure. The light that flooded into the terminal was symbolic of the fact that later that day we would be entering the light in the original Stadium of Light, the *Estádio da Luz*, home of Benfica. To be truthful, a few of us had thought that Benfica and Sporting played at the same stadium. Not true at all. We were getting mixed up with the likes of Rome and Milan.

On Look North the previous evening (God bless the miracle of satellite telly) they had shown the players training on the *Estádio da Luz* pitch. And then an interview with Alan Pardew. He had said it was a privilege to be playing against such a massive club as Benfica and that the Europa League campaign had provided the fans with some *luz* relief during what had been and still was a somewhat 'sticky' Premiership season. Well, all of that was true of course. But it wasn't exactly the fighting talk you might expect – in fact it sounded rather like apologising before the event ...

But a sticky season it certainly had been, and the previous (Easter) weekend had seen us lose four-nil at Man City and slide to within just a few points of the drop zone. Benfica, meanwhile, were running riot at the top of the *Primeira Liga*, having crushed Rio Ave six-one in front of a 46,000 home crowd. The form team we were not. They were. Plus, our next two home games in the league would be against a hungry Fulham, whose sights were still firmly set on a European place, and then the mackems.

safc was in deepest gloom after the club had quite spectacularly shot itself in both feet by sacking Martin O'Neill, after a one-nil home defeat at the hands of Man U, and appointing in his place one Paulo di Canio. While we were heading for the original Stadium of Light, the mackems were quite rightly going on chat shows and websites to say they wouldn't be visiting their version again until he no longer darkened its doors. (Message from the future courtesy of our time machine: they didn't have to wait long, did they?)

My fellow travellers all looked as though they were looking forward to escaping the Luxembourg winter for some Lusitanian spring warmth, and their Portuguese sounded great, and really fluent. It's a funny thing, isn't it, but a lot of us – and all of the usual suspects on this trip – can pretty well cope with reading Portuguese at an everyday level. Well it is so close to Spanish and also has lots of similarities with French. But speaking it or understanding the spoken word? No way, José Mourinho! Still, that wasn't going to stop us having a bash, now was it?

A little bit of chalk-and-cheese telly the night before (late on, a lot later than Look North) had helped a bit ... helped us to realise just how impenetrable spoken Portuguese can be, that is. Helpfully, they had also shown an interview with Alan Pardew. It wasn't the same interview as on Look North, but he said pretty much the same inspiring things. The subtitles were a doddle, especially listening to

Pardew's original English at the same time. But when the Portuguese presenter came back on – wow! With its nasal sounds and syllable contractions, Portuguese can at times sound almost like Polish!

Funny you should say that, Pete! To me it sounds a bit like Russian. Lots of ssshhh noises. The CSKA Moscow supporters must have felt right at home when they came down to watch their team win the 2005 Final against Sporting Lisbon. When I tune in and start to pick out some Spanish-ish words in the Portuguese I can tell them apart, but it always takes a while.

A colleague with excellent Portuguese said that Brazilians were far easier for a learner to understand as they pronounce the endings (and the beginnings and middles) of words more fully and speak that little bit more slowly. Ah well, one day we may well be playing São Paulo in the Final of the World Club Championship ...

***

My very first flight with Portuguese airline TAP (another début after Aeroflot and South China Airlines from Amsterdam to Newcastle in the previous round) proved to be a very enjoyable experience, and the safety video on the flap-down screens was great. The people telling you how to fasten your seat belt, etc. were genuine TAP passengers, and it was a young lad wearing a pilot's hat who did the intro. Mams and Dads and teenagers then shared the rest of the video, showing you where the emergency exits were and all the rest of it. What a nice touch, and a very nice way of making you feel at ease. They even showed some take-outs in a making-of section at the end, with people fluffing their lines and getting fits of the giggles. Best of all, it was in Portuguese with English subtitles so you could start to get a feel for the language even before take-off. During the flight that trusty old Langenscheidt *Sprachführer Portugiesisch* (bought pre-flight at the airport) explained all the basics, and the essential differences between Portuguese and Spanish quickly emerged. The former seemed indeed to have a lot more *sssh* sounds and nasals, and the *m* at the end of words like *quem, tem* or *viagem* seemed to be completely redundant.

In the on-board announcements, even the word Portugal seemed to be reduced to *Ptgl*. Presumably they would pronounce Constantinople *Cnstpl*, or Barnstaple *Bnstpl*. Ah well, perseverance is a virtue, or so they say. Understanding some of this as yet unlearnt lingo was helped a lot by a couple of glasses of *vinho verde* (green wine, as in fresh, not yet ripe), so that by the time we began our somewhat turbulent and rain-lashed descent towards an overcast Lisbon airport, the whole experience had the feel of a kind of homecoming. Yeah? More like Newcastle's pigeons coming home to roost!

This was my very first trip to Portugal. My Mam passed away just before our game against Sporting in 2005, so I of course rushed back to Tyneside. This time, though, I would be joining all the usual suspects for a happy gathering. Sarah, Chris, Barry and I would be staying at the same hotel, the *Lisboa Tejo*. And looking out of the plane window there was the eponymous river *Tejo* right now, and that famous, geet long bridge you always see on any TV or magazine report about Lisbon. Apparently, the English name for the *Tejo* is actually Tagus, reflecting its Ancient Greek name (Τάγος – Tagos). It is just over a thousand km long (the river not the bridge, it's not THAT geet long), has its source in Spain and its mouth very near Lisbon. The Don (not the River Don, but THE Don, and may I take this opportunity to once again express my undying loyalty) and Steve and his partner Jenny from Whitley Bay would be staying in Madrid (only kidding, they were staying in a Lisbon hotel really), while the Other Clive, the Other Peter and the latter's better half Liz would not be far away, together with Alan from Gateshead. And we were sure to be bumping into lots of other familiar faces in what promised to be a wonderful coming together of the Toon Army clan. Apparently 2,800 tickets had been sold through the club. And all of our little gang had theirs. In fact it looked as though Barry and I would have four between us thanks to our usual belt and braces approach. The Don had two for us and so did Steve Storey. But as always we were ultra-confident of finding a good home for the spares.

***

Another glimpse out of the window, this time at the other side, revealed some brightly coloured topple-box houses, cast like dice by the gods and changing hues through red, green and blue. Was it that green wine or maybe the turbulence and lash of rain we had felt during the descent? Or would we be joining the waifs and strays and would-be Hemingways? Was our destiny to be the Lisbon version of *la vie bohème*? Who knows? And yet the pull of

Portuguese shower poetry would soon be working its magic. A gentle bump, some applause, and that was it. We had landed.

***

We were about ten minutes late, so it was around 13.20 local time. Isn't it funny how Portugal has the same time as Britain, yet is so far away? Is it maybe some kind of statement along the lines of, '*¡Hola!* we are not Spain, we have our own time thank you very much'. Well whoever made time certainly made a lot of it. So why not share it around?

Barry's flight had landed shortly before mine (which meant our plane had had to brake hard to avoid running into the arse-end of his) and had also been a lot cheaper. In fact with hindsight it turned out it would have been cheaper for me to drive to Brussels and leave the car at Zaventem. The Grand Duchy of Luxembourg does not have a huge population, it is true. In fact it amounts to about half that of Tyneside. But the biggest immigrant group is the Portuguese community, and as a result there is always a high demand for flights to Portugal. Higher demand means higher prices, and we were of course in the middle of the Easter holidays. But what the heck, shrouds have no pockets, etc.

No sooner had I emerged into the arrivals hall than Barry appeared, dressed maybe not for sunbathing and snorkelling but certainly more for spring than winter, and it already felt a lot warmer than in Luxembourg. Maybe I wouldn't be needing that winter jacket after all. We were soon in the spanking new Metro and armed with our tickets to ride. The Metro system is in fact so spanking new that the website Sarah and Chris had consulted said it was still being built, and recommended taking a bus into town. The system was definitely operational, however, and after a journey time of about half an hour, including one change from the red line to the green one (you can take the blue one too as they all criss-cross), we duly got off at *Rossio* and emerged into a slight drizzle in *Figueroa* Square, which was already buzzing with the Black and White. The equine monument immediately evident in the middle of the *Praça* prompted us to call it Horsey Square for the sake of convenience, and – eerily or conveniently enough – we were later to see that horse's pedestal being used as a convenience by one or two people under cover of darkness (and quite possibly under the affluence of incohol).

We asked the way of a couple of Black and Whites who were as disoriented as we were, and then of several Portuguese, all of them with very good English. And it turned out we were only a couple of hundred yards away from the *Tejo* hotel. We just had to turn in the opposite direction from the one in which we were headed when we came out of the Metro, walk along one side of Horsey Square, turn left, following the tram lines set in the cobbled street, and there was the hotel about fifty yards away on the next corner. As we approached that corner, we raised our heads and could see the Castle of *São Jorge* up a height. Our attention was brought back down to street level by the ding-ding of a street-car called something or other. The trams in Lisbon really are great. Old-fashioned and single-waggoned, they look like something from the 1900s, which quite possibly they are. And like Lisbon houses, they come in all sorts of colours, but mostly sandy. At the front of them is what looks like a cow fender. So here was a town where you really could say 'mind the trams,' what with its winding tight streets and very narrow pavements. The overall tram image in Lisbon is spoilt just a bit by the sight of the ultra-modern yellow and bendy ones, which would not be out of place in Berlin or Amsterdam. But, in fairness, they seemed to be running just during the rush hours, so as not to offend the senses too much.

So we entered the *Lisboa Tejo* Hotel, and there right on cue were Sarah and Chris waiting for us in the lobby. We just needed to drop our bags off in our rooms and freshen up a bit. While checking in we asked how to pronounce the name of the hotel (and hence of the river) and the answer was *Tejo* with the *j* pronounced like the *zh* in Anzhi, i.e. like the *s* in pleasure. Now if that wasn't a good omen!

Then we had a little bit of comedy as my card failed to open my room door. Have you ever been in that situation? Annoying, isn't it? Back to reception I tappy-lappied.

'Oh, we knew there was a dodgy card knocking about. Now we know it's this one. Thank you very much.'

'My plea*zh*ure'.

That sorted, I was able on my way back to the room to admire the hotel's sheer blueness. Everything seemed to be a shade of blue. And it turned out blue is a very popular colour in Portugal, especially for tiles. That's why they call them *azulejos,* as in azure blue. This time, the card opened sesame, but I have to let off steam again and ask: what is wrong with conventional keys? They have so much more character and, what is more, they always seem to work. If they were good enough for the Romans ...

Then came a surprise. A room with no window. But wait a second, those full length shutters over there. Ah, they are cunningly designed to conceal French windows giving on to a kind of small, ten by ten foot atrium-type thing. Not a lot of light, what with there being another few floors between this one and the top, but I suppose this arrangement could be most welcome at the height of summer. Another surprise: no mini-bar. And another one: no wardrobe, just a couple of racks to hang things on. But then the best feature of the lot: the bathroom featured a shower-wall poem! The first three lines read thus:

'O Tejo é mais belo que o rio que corre pela minha aldeia

Mas o Tejo nao é mais belo que o rio que corre pela minha aldeia

Porque no é o rio que corre pela minha aldeia'

(The *Tejo* is more beautiful than the river that flows through my village

Yet the Tejo is not more beautiful than the river that flows through my village

Because the Tejo is not the river that flows through my village).

Wow! Well this finally was it. My on-the-road-to-Damascus (while-in-Lisbon) moment. I suddenly knew that I would now be devoting the rest of my life, and possibly some of the time thereafter, to the study of Portuguese shower poetry. Maybe I could even become a Portuguese shower poet and my work would be admired by thousands of showering tourists, who would then probably say 'what a shower'.

Back in the lobby, my enthusiasm for, and ardent love of, this new and wholly unexpected manifestation of the poetic muse must have been blindingly obvious, because before I could open my stammering mouth, Chris said:

'Ye divvent hev te say anythin', bonny lad. Ah knaa what ye mean.'

And then he recited:

'Tudo de repente um pudim preto grande voou pelo ar

Mas não atingiu a minha mãe, conheceu meu pai

E empurra-oda cadeira'

So pure and so mournfully beautiful were the rhythm and cadences that we were instantly moved to tears – though we understood only the odd word. The effect was further enhanced by Chris endowing the lines with a merely suggested, barely perceptible, almost whispered, very northern Portuguese accent. Rich it was with melancholy. We implored him, begged him to give us the translation, to put us out of our misery, end the heartache, the longing, the …

'Oh all right, then', he replied, and after taking a deep breath in preparation for a truly Shakespearean delivery, thus did he utter:

'Aal of a sudden, a geet big black puddin'

came flyin' through the air

it missed me mutha but hit me fatha

and knocked 'im off eez chair …'

Beautiful, just beautiful.

***

Uplifted as we were by all this wall-to-wall poetry, we sallied forth to join the Toon Army.

And the Hotel *Lisboa Tejo* really was the perfect location, for in just a couple of minutes we were back on *Praça Figueroa,* or Horsey Square. By now the sun was giving us some more *luz* and despite the fact we were all wearing *luz* glasses we were approached several times during the first hundred yards by people of various nationalities offering us that very commodity. When we declined, they asked if we would like some hashish or cocaine instead. Er, *obrigado*, but no thanks. A woman has to say *obrigada* of course, and a mixed group, even if it includes more women than men, has to say *obrigados*, whereas a female-only group says *obrigadas*. So the same *macho* rules apply as in French, and presumably Spanish too. As we crossed Horsey Square, minding the trams, we saw more Black and White leaving it at the far end so we followed them and could hear chanting come from what turned out to be the next square, quickly christened Column and Fountain Square on account of, well, a great big column and fountain in the middle of it. Its real name apparently is *Praça Dom Pedro IV* (in honour of Peter Beardsley, obviously), though we were told most people call it *Rossio*. Confusing, isn't it. And the only thing we saw bearing the name *Rossio* was the Metro station on Horsey Square!

Interesting that what would be an *l* in Spanish and an *i* in Italian becomes an *r* in the Portuguese word for square (*Praça*). Sound shifts are fascinating and funny things, aren't they? In Italian they seem to avoid an *l* in the words for flowers (*fiori*) or rain (*pioggia*). If you put an *l* in the latter you would have something that sounded like 'plodga' (let's gan plodgin') and not far off the French word *pluie*.

The two squares really are the spitting image of each other (ignoring the fact that one features a horse and the other a column and fountain) – for a start they're both oblongs, not squares, and they both have old off-white buildings all around them, and they both have some very welcoming bars. The *Figueroa* is the one with the *Bacanas*, the smallest bar in the square, where we'd drowned our sorrows and sung all those old songs, magnificently led by the Other Clive, after the four-one quarter-final defeat to Sporting Lisbon all those years ago. We couldn't do as badly this time, surely.

The Peter Beardsley/*Rossio*/Fountain/Column Square was stowed out with the Toon Army. It was a fair bet that the Don, Steve and Jenny from the Bay would not be far away.

(By the way, did you know that Whitley Bay used to be called just Whitley. But then a former resident of the town died in Edinburgh. It had been his dying wish to be buried in his native turf and so the body was transported south. Unfortunately it ended up in Whitby, not Whitley, and thereafter the local council decided a name change would be in order. So it consulted the local population, and the most popular suggestion for a new name was Whitley Bay. This was a fortunate coincidence, as there happens to be a bay at that very spot.)

A phone call told us our friends were in fact just yards away and we quickly rendezvoused on our side of the Square. We could barely hear ourselves speak, however, as the Toon Army – massed at two bars facing each other across the breadth of the square, the *Pastelaria Suiça* and the *Café Nicola* – were in fine voice. No-one had had lunch yet so we thought it would be a good idea to cross to the other, slightly quieter side of the *Praça* and seek out a suitable venue. It was now about 14.45, so there was plenty of time. We always seem to think there is plenty of time, somehow. (Discuss!)

So across the Square we went and then bore left, turned right and then right again into a quiet side street called *Rua 1° de Dezembro*. A couple of kilted Celtic fans left over from the 1967 European Cup Final came along the way and spoke a few sentences to us in a very friendly and welcoming manner. These Lisbon lions had clearly stayed on and gone native. Unfortunately, we couldn't understand a word they were saying, so we asked them to switch from Glaswegian to Portuguese for ease of communication. Their eyes glazed over even more and they went on to recite some beautiful poetry, comparing the *Tejo* with the Clyde. They wove along on their romantic and melancholy way and we soon found ourselves outside what turned out to be the rear entrance to the *Café Nicola*, which in turn turned out to be a nice restaurant-cum-*bistro*. Check it out, we recommend it. We went down a couple of steps and were very impressed by its *art déco* style featuring lots of marble. It was truly marbelous, in fact. Most importantly, *Café Nicola* offered excellent acoustics, a fact not long lost on our little group. We were fortunate in finding a table just the right size set back a wee bit to the left at the bottom of those steps, and it also happened to be an excellent vantage point from which to view the gannins-on at the front, where plenty of our brethren were quenching their thirsts in the entrance area in groups that were spilling good-naturedly onto Column Square. Some were sitting outside on *brasserie*-style chairs. Most were standing, many were singing. A few were, not to put too fine a point on it, well and truly scuttled. Plus, we were just a few yards from the steps leading down to the facilities so there was a constant to-ing and fro-ing in Black and White.

A Ronaldo-lookalike waiter quickly appeared with menus in hand and we were immediately able to at least order the drinks, mainly beer. While perusing the menu we learned that it would be Jenny's birthday the very next day. Another good omen. Ronaldo brought the drinks, ably assisted by his colleague, Stan Laurel, who otherwise just stood around looking miserable, a bit like that security guard in the bank in Kharkiv. Ronaldo certainly needed the assistance as the beers were all of the one-litre *Oktoberfest* variety. But hey, we were thirsty after all the poetry and culture we had consumed. I had been told that I had to have *bacalau* (cod) when in Portugal, and in view of the size of the beer I decided to order the salted cod, with roast taties. Barry opted for what looked like a bowl of assorted animals in soup.

That's right, Pete. It was called something like *'feijoada'* which was possibly a fava bean stew featuring various dubious pieces of meat and sausage of indecipherable genetic make-up. Very popular in Portugal. Some fragments were surprisingly tasty, but these were few and far between. One large piece of fetid skin and bone, I have no idea what it was, was bossing dish midfield so successfully that all the other gristle and jellified morsels were crammed together on top of each other in an undignified scrum. I just didn't have the heart or strength to pry them apart so I left them to get to know each other in their eco-diverse soup. The chips were all right. Everybody else's food looked better than mine. Anyway, no one should hold an ill-chosen dish against the *Café Nicola* which in all other respects was an excellent place to while away the hours.

Agreed, Barry! It was a steady place all right. And the nosh was grand (well, apart from yours). The Super Bock and the Dao were flowing freely, and the afternoon passed by swimmingly. But who was that on his way to the facilities? None other than the other Paul of Karkhiv and Strawberry fame. Well we had said we would meet again 'somewhere in Europe' and we had been right. Unfortunately, his marra Neil had been unable to make this trip.

Barry suddenly remembered he still had to ring Steve Storey.

Yes, and I was just about to when our little group was supplemented by the very welcome presence of my twin (we have the same birthday) Paul English and his pals who'd travelled up the day before by train from Faro. That's a bit like flying to Exeter then catching the train back to London to watch Fulham. Paul specialises in circuitous routes, as you will remember from his Bordeaux round-the-world trip. After failed attempts to meet up in Bruges and Bordeaux, we had finally succeeded following a series of international (Portugal to Belgium to Geordieland then back to Portugal) text messages and calls.

So it was then mid-to-late afternoon by the time I finally rang Steve Storey, and by chance he and the other Chris had just arrived beside the fountain in the *Rossio/Dom Pedro* Square right beside our *Café Nicola* to rendezvous with a few other Toon fans who had made the same arrangement or who needed duplicates for delayed tickets. As ever, Steve was our stalwart and dependable *amigo*. We invited the other Chris and him over to meet *Café Nicola* and all the crew, but they had to head off to meet up with the team and make preparations for the game. They were looking forward to a great game in a great city. So back I went into the café, where the waiters told us that Alan Pardew had been quoted as saying something along the lines of Benfica being like an eighth-placed Premiership team, and that this had certainly fired up their players. Though, had they taken a look at the current table they would have seen that this was actually a big compliment as Alan Pardew would have given his eye teeth for the Toon to be an eighth-placed Premiership team too.

Anyway, our ticket problems were more than sorted, as we now had too many, but we had no worries about getting shot of the extras.

Don said he was expecting our old school mate Ian Rosenvinge to appear together with some 'para-marras' of his, including Jerry Greeves, Rachel King, Jamie Dobson, and Gareth Johnson, who were going to be dropping in. He explained it was seven parachutists, mainly Geordies and one Benfica supporter, making their way up from Skydive Algarve and planning to head back south straight after the match. The Don texted them and told them to be careful not to get tangled up in Ronaldo's Mam's washing hanging out between two nearby blocks of flats. They must have heeded that sound advice because they all appeared just a few minutes later, one of them wearing a giant Magpie Head. The gods were clearly on our side. The auguries were good.

After we had enjoyed a, well, very enjoyable lunch, and ordered another round of beers, our thoughts turned to testing out the acoustics. Sarah said she remembered another line of Portuguese shower poetry which she had quickly translated and thought would make some good lyrics that needed a tune to go with them:

'There are no mackems in the Stadium of Light'.

Well of course it wasn't long before we came up with a suitable tune, namely that of 'Harry Redknapp, you should be in jail' (somewhat unkindly sung at White Hart Lane last season when we were trounced five-nil). Do you think 'Sloop John B' would have been as big a hit with these words:

'The Stadium of Light,

the Stadium of Li-ight,

there are no mackems …

in the Stadium of Light.

The Stadium of Light,

the Stadium of Li-ight, …'

Well, the acoustics were perfect, and so was the song, and the constant stream of facilities visitors joined in, as did the other end of the restaurant. Soon the whole place was a feast of song. Both Ronaldo and Stan looked on somewhat bemusedly, yet approvingly. Old favourites inevitably made their appearance, and we had Bertie Mee talking to Joe Harvey, the Blaydon Races of course, and even Benny Arentoft was deservedly mentioned in our choral dispatches.

We made up a few more songs based on the week's news of the new sunderland manager's political tendencies to add to all the usual old tunes, and a great time was had by one and all. Kick-off wasn't till 20.05 (strange sort of time, isn't it?), but we wanted to be in no rush (remember Bruges?) so we set off for the ground at about six. It was a short walk to the *Restauradores* Metro station, from where it was a nine-stop ride to the Benfica stadium. There is a station en route called Benfica, but that is just there to confuse the away supporters, in the same way that visiting fans from the Smoke who arrive at the Central Station may well be told to travel to St James's via the Coast.

Here, the station you really need is the one with the long name ending in *Luz*, and beginning with *Collegio Militar*. The train was packed to the gunwales, filled mostly with the chanting Toon Army but also some utterly bewildered rush-hour commuters and shoppers, and not a few Benfica fans. They were all enjoying the fun. The acoustics at our station of destination were also good and the Blaydon Races got another resounding rendition.

***

The final few hundred yards to the ground were lined with booths selling the usual souvenirs, so we bought some half-and-half scarves – at a very reasonable seven euros fifty a time – and, for good measure, some Benfica-only ones too. We passed a queue at a ticket office and so we offered our spares for sale, happily prepared to welcome a couple of local fans into our fold. We saw no problem there. But some home fans were a bit wary, perhaps understandably. One guy showed some overly keen interest, and the general consensus was that he must be a tout, so we blew him out (if he's a tout, blow him out). Undeterred, we asked a young couple in Benfica colours if they would be interested in two tickets, five euros a piece, the only condition being they had to come into the Toon end. They readily agreed and after about five minutes of small talk we realised that Rosie and John were in fact Scottish. We had originally supposed they must be Portuguese and kept on believing they were during the aforesaid five minutes. Isn't it funny how it can often be a struggle to overcome preconceived ideas even when those ideas are overwhelmingly refuted by the facts (such as thick Scottish accents)? Our new friends were both from Dundee, but Rosie's parents hailed from Newcastle. They (Rosie and John, that is, not Rosie's parents) already had Benfica tickets but were happy to pay a little extra to be able to savour the sights and sounds of the Toon end. So once again, we had found a good home for spare tickets. And as usual, we'd been happy to have too many tickets rather than too few. As we have seen, not only had the Don come up magically with two tickets but our official application to NUFC had been unexpectedly successful. The club's new ticketing system had just started up whereby, as well as still having to fill in the Word form giving your passport details and travel arrangements and sending it in by e-mail, you now had to pay online through the website, as is the case for Premiership matches. This all got quite complicated as there was no option on the website to ask to collect the tickets in Lisbon rather than have them sent to my brother's office, which would not have helped at all as there would have been no time for Ian to send them on to me. Luckily, a phone call to the ever-helpful staff at the NUFC Box Office had sorted that little problem out.

In the company of two Scots, the subject of the independence referendum inevitably came up. Their considered view was that Mr Salmond was a manipulative bar steward but would not win. They accepted, however, that giving sixteen year-olds the vote had been a very shrewd move by a very shrewd man. Young folk can often be swayed by pure emotion while economic and other considerations, well, hold no sway at all. Time would tell.

***

Aal of a sudden, not a geet big black puddin´, but Alan from Gateshead appeared as if from nowhere – well actually from the midst of the throng of black and white forming a queue in front of the entrance. A happy reunion, and an even happier one for learning that he was definitely no longer at the crossroads. After briefly looking right, left and then right again (you must always remember your kerb drill), he had crossed the crossroads and made his way straight ahead. In fact now he was not very far away from a level crossing. The lights were flashing and so he would probably have to stop to let a train pass. But maybe there was a subway, or perhaps even a footbridge. He could not quite see yet, as it was a bit foggy. (Deep, huh?) He was wondering whether or not to go to Brazil for the next World Cup. Not to swell the ranks of cockneys singing En-ge-land. En-ge-land, En-ge-land, but just to be there, be a part of it, listen to Portuguese spoken at a human pace and with all the syllables and vowels left intact. Should he go, what did we think? Wheyaye, man. Life's too short not to. And think of the poetry. Right, that sealed it.

***

Into the ground and into the light we went. A majestic, truly magnificent Stadium of Light, the original Stadium of Light. The huge bowl, the undulating upper fringes, the net in front of us. The poetry on the toilet walls. This surely was what it was all about. Mind it was a bit on the red side, and adverts for *Sangres* beer were just about everywhere. So that was the Benfica sponsor. In town we had been drinking *Super Bock* (and singing *Super Bock*, superstar, how many beers have you drunk so far?). Turns out that SB sponsor Sporting. We wondered if the two breweries worried about losing the custom of the respective other club's fans. After all, in Glasgow Carling had eschewed the idea of sponsoring just one of the Old Firm for that very reason, and ended up sponsoring both! But we reckoned that things could not possibly be as polarised here as in Glasgow. For one thing, they are virtually all left-footers in this neck of the woods!

We were high up in the corner which at SJP would be the meeting of the Leazes and the East Stand, but without the sudden change in height, as the Stadium of Light is symmetrical all the way round. There were clearly a lot more Toon fans here than had actually got into the ground in any of the previous rounds (more had certainly travelled to the city of Bruges, however) and we were spread out over two large, tightly-packed sections. The rest of the ground was maybe two-thirds full. We would be able to read the details in the copious pages of print, diagrams and photos in the two sporting papers the next day. The Portuguese certainly go in for extremely detailed coverage of their football – you get nothing like it back home.

242

***

Look, here come the Other Clive and Peter and Liz, bang on cue. And there's the other Paul again, a few rows down. Photo opportunities time. A few rows behind us was that serious-looking grey-haired chap we had seen in Kharkiv and who had been on the same plane from Vienna. Someone said he looked like a spy, no, like John le Carré. Crikey, yes. Maybe it was John le Carré and he is writing a new novel based on the Toon Army in its quest for a new footballing order in Europe. The mind boggles. We must try and have a chat sometime if we get the chance. The more Toon tales we can collect, the better!

Pre-match entertainment was laid on by a giant bird. After all that's what birds do, lay things. And it wasn't Dolly Parton either. No, this was what looked at first view like a radio-controlled replica of a big black stork with white legs trailing out behind, it was so still and perfect, calm and graceful as it circled on the thermals within the stadium. There were a couple of people out on the pitch and maybe they had a radio transmitter to guide the flying machine around. Then I thought, no, it's a real bird, isn't it? Maybe it had somehow got caught roosting inside the canopy of the stadium and had been scared by the lights and the crowd. Wrong again. What had seemed like its trailing legs were actually long white and red ribbons of Benfica's club colours. This was the official eagle mascot of the Benfica club, and what a magnificent sight it was as it swooped down to perch-land on its owner's gauntlet to great applause. It is so good that Crystal Palace got themselves an eagle too a few years ago, though it only swoops from one end of the ground to the other. A magpie flapping around SJP couldn't hold a candle to the Benfica eagle. A magpie can't hold a candle, full stop.

Kick-off time was now rapidly approaching and the Toon Army were all inside. And what a fantastic sight to behold. The massed ranks of the Toon Army, a packed and cascading kaleidoscope of black and white and a cacophony of Geordie sound and song awaiting the start of the first leg of a Europa League quarter final. Does it get much better than this?

***

Newcastle were in the black and white again and were kicking away from us in the first half. It was difficult to see from where we were, miles away from the action, but with some difficulty we made out the starting line-up to be Krul and Santon back from injury,

Simpson, Yanga-Mbiwa, Perch, S Taylor, Cabaye, Sissoko, Gutierrez, Marveaux, and Cissé. The grass looked so green, wet from the rain. We began well, and just after the ten-minute mark Simpson played a perfectly-aimed pass into the right of the penalty area for Sissoko to run onto and square it beautifully through a bunch of defenders to Papiss Cissé who side-footed it in from a couple of yards out. Cardozo had claims for a penalty waved away and then just a few minutes later we could even have made it two-nil when Sissoko played a ball across to Gutierrez on the left who moved forwards into the penalty area before passing to Cissé whose shot from the edge of the area deflected off a defender and crept agonisingly towards the goal line before being pawed onto the post and then, trickling along the goal line, pounced on by the goalie (probably, though it was hard to tell from such a distance away). A two-nil lead would surely have changed what was to follow; such are the margins between triumph and defeat.

We hung on until about twenty-five minutes when a bit of a mix-up allowed them to get an equaliser when Krul parried away a powerful shot from the edge of the area by Cardozo only to see the rebound guided in by the in-rushing Rodrigo. Within a minute Krul made a fantastic double-save as Benfica had three snap chances to score a second, and then we had Krul to thank once again a few minutes later for preventing a second goal from Rodrigo. From then on it was constant pressure from Benfica who really got on top of us.

The second half began more brightly, with the Toon now kicking towards our end, and in a fantastic breakaway Cissé on the centre circle headed a long Gutierrez pass out to Marveaux, who then took it on smoothly with one touch and crossed it back to Papiss, who was by now approaching the penalty area. He controlled the ball and made to lift it over the keeper and it lobbed slowly in our direction and goalwards. If it had gone in, it would have been a goal-of-the-season contender. With the Cissé of last season's unerring aim, it would surely have gone in but this season, as so often, it hit the post. After that, Benfica got more and more on top, though you would never have guessed from the lack of any sign of life from their crowd who were drowned out by the Toon Army. On the hour, Perch, who had done well in defence, had to go off injured to be replaced by Anita. Then came their goals, both of which could have been avoided. The second, by Lima, just after the hour was the result of a misjudged Santon back-pass which left Krul stranded, and the third on seventy minutes was a twice-successfully-taken penalty by Cardozo after Taylor was seen to have fended the ball away with his right arm. On the other hand Benfica had loads of corners and lots of good chances but a number of excellent saves from Tim Krul kept it down to a respectable and possibly retrievable score-line of three-one. The additions of Shola, our second-highest European goal scorer, and of Gosling a couple of minutes later were to no avail. Santon tried to make amends with a powerful shot which flashed narrowly wide and Ameobi was almost the victim of play-acting by a Benfica defender who tried to get him a red card for what he made out was a Mick McManus forearm smash, but was in fact just a light push. Mick might have been watching the match but sadly passed away a week after the Final. RIP Mick. And so the game ended. It wasn't a knockout, and it certainly wasn't a submission, but it was looking like the first fall.

Well, we agreed, it wasn't over yet. If the goal posts had been curved a little bit differently it would have been three-three. The only certainty was that three-one was a funny score in Europe! Chris said that three-two would have been even funnier. And four-three, the Don reminded us, would have been absolutely hilarious. Sarah pointed out that, had we lost five-four, we would have been creasing ourselves with laughter. Emerging from the shadows, collar turned up, John le Carré cryptically told us that had the score been six-five they would have had to call an ambulance, as we would have gone into fits and spasms of hysterics.

The next morning's papers were literally full of themselves about the great result for Benfica: twelve pages including the front page news and a column analysing who had swapped shirts and why they'd chosen with whom to swap in the '*Record*' and ten pages in '*A Bola*'. They don't do things by halves in the Portuguese sports press. Action photos, diagrams of the route the ball took from one player to the next for each of the goals, interviews with everyone and his donkey, they put anything they can think of in the paper. *A Bola* and *Record* both had nice tributes to the Toon supporters, remarking on the good spirits, the strength of the singing, and the round of applause given for the Benfica eagle's regal display before the match. One thing they were very much in agreement on was that it wasn't won yet, and they were well aware that but for a lick of paint on the goalposts it could so easily have been us leading two-nil in the first half and then three-one early in the second. So there was still everything to play for in the return.

***

Now comes a not so nice bit. In fact a very nasty bit that still leaves an equally nasty taste in the mouth. All during the match, there had been the usual banter between the two sets of fans, including some rather strange gesturing on the part of the Benfica supporters. But that had been all. There had not been even the merest suggestion of any violence. No-one had thrown anything at anyone else. Nothing at all. *Nada.* And the numerous police and security people had basically looked on benevolently the whole time. At the final whistle, the two sets of supporters very sportingly applauded each other. People exchanged scarves and hats over the dividing fence under the friendly eyes of the smiling policemen. We were kept in detention of course. Then the stadium announcer kindly thanked us for having come to their ground to support our team. And as a special treat they would be showing us a 'Rivalries' video on the two giant-giant screens at both goal ends. The video showed goals from past Tyne-where? and where?-Tyne derbies. And since we usually win them, this was good entertainment. This was a very nice and friendly touch on the part of our host club!

However, there is a however. This detention lasted a very long time, and for no good reason. And understandably, people were beginning to get a bit fed up after half an hour or so. But again there was no nastiness anywhere among the 2,800 travelling Geordies. Finally the *policia* began to let the fans out, and our little group patiently shuffled along with everybody else. By the time we almost reached the concourse with only a couple of flights of steps to go, there was some shouting and gesturing towards the thin blue line. We thought it was because fans were not being allowed to use the toilets beyond that line and the police were insisting they leave the stadium perimeter directly. We initially thought no more of it. Sadly, however, we later heard that a Portuguese policemen had for no reason at all (and what possible reason could there be, for that matter?) struck a seven-year-old lad (!) on the head with a truncheon. No wonder people had been shouting and gesturing at the police. How on earth can such things happen? So often on European trips we have seen a completely over-the-top riot-police presence. And we have often had the impression that some of those policemen have been waiting for any excuse to wield the baton. But what excuse can there possibly be for striking a seven-year-old laddie? To the club's credit, Newcastle United officials later advised the family to institute proceedings against the Portuguese police. But will that do any good?

Unaware of these events, we made our way back to the Metro and back into town. We got separated along the way but mobile technology enabled us quickly to re-assemble.

***

Wandering unbridled into Horsey Square at less than a canter, we found ourselves in the same nice, unpretentious late-night café that we'd congregated in after the loss to Sporting Lisbon and installed ourselves there for a night cap and some scran. Our waiter was Speedy Gonzalez, who played the clown for us when asked to take some photos of our group, taking pictures of himself instead. He was so quick off the mark in pursuit of his waiting duties that he took our order and left again before we had even told him what it was. Whatever it was, we didn't get it. But we did get a selection of chips, sausages, cheese and fish, plus some rather excellent red wine, beers and soft drinks. It was fine, and at ten euros a head it was pretty good late-night value. The Other Clive gave us, amongst other songs, a marvellous rendition, to the tune of the Lambton Worm, of an account of our Fairs Cup campaign of '69-'70. As the Don put it, Clive is a great singer and has the knack of tantalisingly ending one verse in a way that makes you think it is over but also making you want more, and then he gives you more. Great stuff, well done Clive! A fitting follow-up to your similarly excellent performance after the Sporting game. It went down well not just with our group but also with the numerous locals, who joined in our applause.

Clive, Peter and Liz took their leave. And as they were leaving, Clive told us he would be off to see the Celtic v. Rangers game at the weekend: Gatesheed Leam Lane Rangers v Cleator Moor Celtic in the Wearside League. For the record the score was (unfortunately, from a left-footer's point of view) Rangers two, Celtic one.

So farewells were said and soon afterwards the rest of us also started to make tracks, and before the Don, Steve and Jenny headed off to their hotel we arranged that we would meet at the station at eleven the next morning for the trip Sarah had planned for us. So the four of us went back to the *Tejo* for a final night cap in the bar that was still serving at what was now just after one in the morning, even though the midnight hour was its official closing time.

***

We *Tejo* residents duly met in the lobby at ten-thirty, Barry having breakfasted at the *Nicola* on Column Square and read the opening twenty or so pages of the match report in a Portuguese paper, Chris and Sarah having breakfasted at the hotel, and Pete having stayed in bed an extra half-hour. Sarah showed us a very becoming picture she had taken of Chris through their frosted-glass bathroom door. Clad in his black and white top, there he sits bent over slightly, intently reading Portuguese toilet-wall poetry.

What is it about modern hotels? Why can they not fit common-or-garden, non-see-through doors (that lock) in their bathrooms? Most people, I would humbly suggest, do not want to be seen at all when using the bathroom (never mind photographed). One hotel in Mainz where Iris and I stayed a while back had a shower that featured a kind of port-hole, with clear glass, enabling you to look into and be seen from the bed-room while you showered. Who wants that, for goodness' sake? Maybe some seventies television personality?

Our route to the station took us first to the *Praça do Comércio*, a beautiful large square, one side of which gives a wonderful open view of the *Tejo*. To get there we only had to turn right as we left our hotel, walk past our side of Horsey Square and left down one of the wide avenues that make up the grid-like layout of this part of central Lisbon. Apparently, the streets around here date from just after the Great Earthquake of 1755. After the quake it was decided to do away with the old higgledy-piggledy layout in favour of grander, broader streets. The buildings are certainly grand but somewhat faded. Yet that fadedness adds to their charm, as do the numerous cracked and chipped blue tiles on their facades. We soon came to the arcades lining the near side of *Praça do Comércio,* and immediately to our left was the *Restaurant Café Martinho da Arcada, Praça do Comércio 37.* A Portuguese colleague, Luisa, had said we had to eat there. Not only is it one of Lisbon's oldest restaurants/cafés (check it out, together with the rest of *Praça do Comercio*: http://www.youtube.com/watch?v=zhuLEkL0Ue4), but it was also a favourite haunt of one of the country's most famous twentieth-century (shower?) poets, Fernando Pessoa. Clearly, this was a place for us. So we popped in to have a look at the café section, very impressive and evocative of a time long gone. The waiter said there was no need to reserve a table for that evening, and we said we would be back for sure.

The *Praça do Comércio* vaguely reminded even those of us who had never been there before of the pier head in Liverpool. It has an open-space feel about it that conveys the same sense of maritime adventure and purpose. As we crossed it, some young people were distributing leaflets. It turned out they belonged to the Dortmund *Studentenorchester* and were in Lisbon to give a concert. We asked the young musicians if they had been in Malaga that week for Borussia's champignons league game. They hadn't.

By the way, did you know that *Borussia* is neo-Latin for Prussia? Me neither.

Just before we got to the station the Don rang to ask where we were, probably suspecting that Pete was still in bed. But no, we were just around the corner and so we rendezvoused, bought our tickets and boarded the train, which took us nicely along the bank of the *Tejo*. Soon we passed a district of former warehouses which had been converted into bars and restaurants. A Portuguese lady was passing through our carriage so we asked her to take a photo of us all. She did, and then, in wonderful English, gave us a detailed account of twentieth century Portuguese history. She kept up her narrative even as we alighted in the suburb of Belém. From the platform, Chris asked: 'There's more?' As the train pulled away, we could still see her lips moving as she thoughtfully continued her lecture, attended only by the ghosts of what had been our presence.

Sarah took us to the famous claggy-cake emporium *Antiga Confeitaria de Belém*, where they serve the equally famous *Pastéis de Belém,* sweet mini custard pies originally made by the monks at the Monastery of the Hieronymites. They surely rank among the tastiest claggy cakes known to man. At first we were put off by the long queue in front of the shop, which in turn is at the front of the café. Undaunted, however, Barry led us past the queue, through a labyrinthine network of blue-tiled (as ever) and old-fashioned rooms of what must formerly have been several residential houses, to a back room with loads of space at the tables. For the first time we encountered a waiter with no English at all, so it was great fun practising our dodgy Portuguese, and we got our claggy cakes and coffees nae bother.

But this sunny day's adventures were not over yet, and back we went to the station to get the next train, taking us to the resort of Cascais, on the Atlantic coast. Logically, the train ride took us right to the mouth of the *Tejo*, and when we caught our first glimpse of the Ocean we also had our first view of some very impressive rolling waves. Groups of surfers were also in evidence, making the most of the rollers and creating a wonderful sight for all to enjoy. We passed through the resort of Estoril, catching a quick glimpse of its famous casino. Between us and the Ocean were some very impressive old villas, some of which had no doubt been the homes of rich Englishmen in times gone by.

At Cascais we made our way through a pedestrian zone paved with wavy black and white patterns that made us feel a bit dizzy – *Moiré* fringes, physicists apparently call them. But pints of Super Bock at the Irish Pub soon restored our equilibrium. How pleasant it was to sit outside the Irish bar sipping our beers, soaking up the sun and gazing out beyond the palm trees onto the surfy-foamy Atlantic Ocean.

***

Our paradise moments were briefly put on hold by a call on my mobile from the German chappie whose GTI Golf's rear bumper my car had recently kissed during a moment's inattention on my part at a roundabout in Trier. Honestly, you could barely make out the alleged scratch on the photos we'd taken immediately after the automotive snogging match. The damage was going to be about a thousand euros (!), he said. The reception wasn't too good due to the salty air and he seemed to be saying something about claiming a Porsche Cayenne as a replacement car during his inconvenience, plus a villa with swimming pool in Marbella, and a lifetime pension of four and a half thousand euros a month.

***

Ah well, time for lunch.

A few winding streets through the fishing village later and we came into a lovely little sunny square offering the welcoming sight of several restaurants along one side. We chose one called 'The Palm Tree' and enjoyed a relaxed and blissful lunch of omelettes, fish, red wine and Sangres in the sun. During our noon-tide repast we were gently entertained by a wandering minstrel who must have gauged our ages just right and accordingly offered us a wonderful selection of seventies favourites. Simon and Garfunkel, Dylan and friends all joined us for lunch. Does it get much better than this?

After lunch, the Don, Steve and Jenny had to get back to Lisbon and on to the airport for their flight home, so they took their leave, while Barry, Sarah, Chris and I lingered a bit longer over our wine and then coffee. An ice-cream at Santini's (the best ice-cream in the (Portuguese) world, their adverts said) rounded the afternoon off nicely. And the train got us back to Lisbon in time to have a little rest and freshen up at the hotel before heading back to *Martinho da Arcada* for supper. When we got there just after eight we automatically headed for the section we had seen in the morning, but the waitress guided us to the back part where the actual restaurant was. The walls were adorned with pictures of the poet Fernando Pessoa, who to us bore a striking resemblance to James Joyce, himself no stranger to drinking places strewn around the continent.

The menu was a bit challenging as it included lamb with roasted taties, and lambkin with roasted taties. The waiter assured us it was the same thing and that we should not worry about eating little lambs. In fact we should have no sympathy with them at all, he said, as the restaurant's supplier only slaughtered the ones that were vicious little bastards. Chris and I duly opted for the vicious-little-bastard lambs, Barry for cod and Sarah for a bowl full of fish. It was nice food, and the house red recommended by the waiter complemented it beautifully. This place was a bit pricey compared to the other eateries we had been to, but it still wasn't too bad at thirty euros a head. On the way out we bumped into two Belgian girls (from Bruges, appropriately enough), who told us they had enjoyed our pre-match chorals in *Café Nicola* the day before. The Toon Army were thus probably already more famous in Lisbon than the Dortmund Students' Orchestra, though we are sure they are really good.

***

Speaking of *Café Nicola*, a night-cap there might be a good idea, so thither we went. We had an interesting conversation with a fellow Geordie who informed us in long-winded detail about his perception of the evils of Europe – the Toon Army had certainly perfected the art of joined-up drinking. Then we headed back to the hotel. Barry had to go straight to bed as he had a very early flight and it was now just after midnight, while Sarah, Chris and I could manage another night-cap at the hotel bar if that bunch of very rude French tourists would make their minds up what they wanted and make room for us.

So Saturday arrived, and Chris and Sarah's flight was late afternoon. Mine wasn't till Sunday. There was time for more sight-seeing, and our task for the morning was to take a tram up the hill to Saint George's Castle. There was a big queue at the tram stop and no sign of any trams, but five euros got us a taxi up through the winding cobbled streets. Just short of the castle Sarah spotted a marvellous *mirador*, or viewing point, so out we got on the spot. We bought some nice coffees and pastries at a little booth-type café and enjoyed a sunny view that took us across to the river and then swept us back up past the brightly coloured houses to the cathedral of saint somebody or other with its under-stated colonial-style twin spires. (Oh to write for a Sunday supplement!) Moving on to what was basically a big patio affording equally superb vistas, we pondered some paintings and artefacts offered for sale, and a Georges Moustaki look-alike kindly played *la Paloma* – Pete's all-time favourite tune on such occasions. Oh yes,

... la Paloma ohé. Seemanns Braut ist die See, und nur ihr kann er treu sein ...

We wandered on foot (what choice did we have?) through more winding alleyways to the grounds of the castle itself. The streets all had very holy names. *Rua da Spirito Santo*, etc. but we reckoned you didn't have a prayer if you wanted a pizza delivery man to come all the way up here.

Back down we wandered slowly into town and stopped for lunch at an open-air restaurant in one of those wider avenues in the grid-layout quarter. Then it was time for Chris and Sarah to head for the airport, and for me to head back to the hotel for a wee siesta (well, a wee and then a siesta) before fulfilling my final Lisbon wish: to have a ride in one of those old trams. Yes, a nameless street-car was the object of my desire! That wish duly came true around eight, and the old tram clattered and dinged its way through the darkening narrow streets till I got off not far from the station where our happy little gang had met up the day before for our coastal outing. From there it was a taxi to the *Barrio Alto*, the up-a-height quarter diametrically opposite the castle. The bright lights of central Lisbon stretched out and shimmered enticingly between the two hills. It is on the *Barrio Alto* side that you will find that famous old elevator that adorns many a postcard. I decided to walk down into the centre, however, and had a pint at *Café Nicola* for old time's sake. Then it was time to head back to the hotel for a night-cap and then beddie-byes.

Sunday mid-morning saw me take a taxi to the airport. Then it was duty-frees and all the rest of it – and a big silver bird took me back to the Grand Duchy. It had been a grand, fantastic, brilliant trip to Lisbon. This simply had to rank among the all-time very best away venues. When would the Toon be here again, I wondered.

***

Between the two legs, on the 8th of April to be exact, 'baroness' thatcher died, probably still wondering whether the Toon would stage a comeback in the home leg. There was some mention in the media of her remaining 'somewhat controversial to the end' but all the rest was about her being one of Britain's greatest ever Prime Ministers. It is true that Look North was a notable exception where the many critics were given due air time. All credit to the good people of Easington, who would be commemorating the anniversary of the colliery's closure on the day of thatcher's burial. If there were street parties, well that is a true reflection of the low esteem in which she will always be held by many. Let this little joke from that week have the final say on the matter here: 'Breaking news: thatcher in Hell less than a week, already five furnaces closed down.'

Then there was the second leg ...

Benfica at home – 11th April 2013

The worst of all possible results

We'll keep it short, so as not to prolong the agony. Our exit from Europe (Geordiesootxit) took place on Thursday the 11th April 2013.

Let's begin at the end. Alan Pardew was quoted afterwards as saying 'We nearly pulled it off.' Well we'll go along with that. Yes we nearly did it. But sadly we didn't. Have we maybe heard that before?

'If you're a Newcastle fan, you want to see your team having a real go and I think they were acknowledging that. In the second half, we put on all our big-hitters. We probably had the most attacking side I've ever put out and we nearly, so nearly, got it.'

So close, yet so far. Yes, par for the course again.

And when the final whistle blew, there was a brief period of silence while people let it sink in that here was another glorious European campaign over without a trophy. But then everybody applauded, as surely only Geordies can. We are great losers, let's face it!

But let's also face the fact that in the end we weren't good enough and Benfica thoroughly deserved to be in the Semi-Finals.

And who could stop themselves from looking back and deploring some very poor defending in the true Stadium of Light? If we had played our cards right there we could have come away with a draw or even a two-one victory. But we didn't. Yet on the night, back at Gallowgate, it looked at times as if we could do what only two teams before us had done at this stage in the competition: come back from a two-goal first-leg deficit.

We had a good view from the Platinum Club seats near the half-way line that we'd got especially for this game. It was going to be a great few days in the Toon wasn't it, what with this game on the Thursday and then the derby on the following Sunday. Wasn't it? What could possibly go wrong? Well, quite a lot, really. The team came out with a starting line-up of Krul, Simpson, Williamson, Yanga-Mbiwa, Haidara, Cabaye, Sissoko, Anita, Gutierrez, Bigirimana, who was making his first appearance since the away leg against Metalist, and Cissé. Ben Arfa, Shola and Marveaux were held back for the second half. We looked pretty lack-lustre in the first half and there was no sign of that vital spark which would liven things up. Bigirimana was one of those trying the hardest, and just before half time it was he who made the cross for Cissé to head into the net, only for it to be declared offside, as so often this season, and not for the only time even in this game. Shola Ameobi came on for the second half in exchange for Bigirimana, and got one of the first shots of the game on target. On the hour, Cissé was ruled offside a second time after putting a ball from Shola into the net. Then mid-way through the half Shola was joined by back-from-injury Ben Arfa and Sylvain Marveaux. Of the three of them, Ben Arfa made the biggest impact, running at defenders and generally putting himself about. But it was a headed goal from Papiss Cissé in the seventy-first minute that suddenly gave us hope aplenty. An inexplicable mix-up in the Benfica defence had allowed Ben Arfa and Shola to combine and Cissé to nip in and score from point-blank range, making up for his two disallowed efforts.

One more and we would be through provided we kept a clean sheet. Not beyond the realms … So there was every reason for optimism with the Magpies in full flight and wave after wave crashing down on the Benfica defence. Ben Arfa suddenly cut in from the right and could so easily have made it two-nil but blasted his shot into the crowd. Pardew was later quoted as saying 'That was the moment I really thought we might get it … I really thought we would get a second goal.' But we didn't.

Committing so many players into attack naturally comes at a price. It's called vulnerability at the back.

Hope springs eternal, and hoping is what we kept on doing, right into stoppage time. But then came Eduardo Salvio's break-away goal. Up to then we had refused to believe it was all over, but now it certainly was! Curtains. And overall, you had to admit that Benfica deserved the draw on the night. Then that stadium-wide standing-ovation applause set in. And rightly so! The lads had done us proud over another great and memorable Euro-Campaign.

***

Okay, it was over.

We only got as far as the quarter-finals, but we had given Europe a run for its money all right, criss-crossing the continent from pre-season victory in the Algarve to the sweltering summer heat of Athens, and from there to the cooling breeze of Portuguese islands out in the Atlantic swell; from the Flemish canal tapestry that is Bruges to the wine-red *savoir-vivre* of Bordeaux, where we all became *bons vivants*. Wider still and wider were the bounds of the Toon Empire set, as we went well and truly over the top on UEFA's Eastern Front. Industrial Kharkiv's austere snowscape was juxtaposed in what seemed like an instant with the frosted spires of the Kremlin, a fitting stage for Midnight in Moscow. Then back to the Ocean's edge we went for the most glorious of two-legged finales, in the wonderful cities of Lisbon and the Toon.

All in all, it was the best of all possible worlds for the ever faithful Toon Army – the best of all possible football supporters!

Benfica v cheatski, The Final – 15th May 2013

I don't want to go to Chelsea, but Amsterdam will do

Well you have to be optimistic, don't you? We had put our names down in the UEFA lottery for Cup (or should that be League?) Final tickets before we were anywhere near the quarter-final, and we'd come up trumps. Pity the lads hadn't had our luck too.

I nearly missed the train at the Brussels *Midi* station – walking in all relaxed, thinking there was loads of time (this sounds familiar, Barry!) and looking up at the departure board to see my train to Rotterdam was leaving from platform 18, I suddenly realised it was leaving in one minute's time at 10.18. I'd thought there was at least ten minutes to spare, but no. So I raced off down the central concourse past all the deadbeats and *gendarmerie* on the lookout for cheatski 'ooligans coming off the Eurostar and planning to do like me and take the train up to Amsterdam.

I charged up the escalator and the train was still there so I jumped straight on it. I'd have surely missed it but for the lucky chance that one of the carriages had had a problem and the passengers had had to be evacuated. I think I understood from the Dutch on board that the air conditioning had been overloaded by the stench coming off blue-shirted tramps. Maybe I misheard. Anyway it all worked out, and I settled down nicely, only to be told after we'd got going that my carriage had to be shut down too as it was dangerous to be isolated at the back of the train as the stinky carriage in front was impassable. So we had to get out at the next stop, Mechelen, home of KV, and go up to the front end of the train. I think they call it the prow.

And I think I am right in thinking that Arriva is/was a mackem bus company? Then they expanded to other areas. Well, I have just seen an Arriva train running past mine between Dordrecht and Rotterdam. Speaking of Rotterdam, as you go through the outskirts take a good look to your right and a hundred metres away you will see *De Kuyp* Stadium, scene of our last-minute Bellamy goal triumph in the champignons league, getting on for ten years ago now. He would be playing again the next year in the red (!) of the bluebirds. It did turn out to be their Chinese-inspired lucky colours after all (at least for one season, anyway).

Ha ha – all the cheatski supporters who disappointingly were occupying seats in the first class carriage from Brussels to Rotterdam were all kicked out when the ticket inspectors came along. Ah, fresh air! After that there were none of them in my carriage and as far as I could see there were nearly no cheatski or Benfica fans at all on the train, and the few who were seemed very discreet. Good. In fact it was very pleasant – a Dutch Railways (*Nederlandse Spoorwegen*) train in red and black leather. Stendhal would have loved it. The plan was to get off at Schiphol airport rather than go to *Amsterdam Centraal*, take the local train over to base camp at the Holiday Inn on the edge of town near the Ajax stadium, make the rendezvous with Pete, then head into the city to soak up the spirit of the day.

If this Final had been in January, there would have been lots of fun and games on the trip because this was when the shortest-lived-ever super-fast twenty-first century Fyra train 'ran' for a couple of weeks, in the loosest definition of the word 'ran' as it was mostly stationary. There are lots of stories about this Italo-Belgo-Dutch scandal but it goes something like this: the train was ordered from Italy, the home of trains obviously, and to save some money the Dutch (obviously) and I suppose the Belgians too, asked for a knock-down version of the Italian high-speed train as it didn't need to go really fast as the distance between stops in the most-crowded-place-in-the-world *Randstad* triangle was too short to get up to top speed. The Italians apparently warned them that they'd be better off buying the full Monty, but on the other hand they still built them a train which the Eyeties said would be fit for purpose. It turned out to be fit only for the knacker's yard and now they are in an international court case, I think, blaming each other.

So the Fyra, which the operators said was chosen to mean 'proud', has been consigned to some sidings and they have gone back to using the old trundly trains, which at least work, even if you have to change in Rotterdam and Schiphol. Sometimes you even have to change in Antwerp, Roosendaal, Rotterdam and Schiphol! When I got out at Rotterdam to swap trains, there was a train with 'Fyra' written on it, but it was a nice, normal train that worked. I took a couple of photos of it. There is a French-built twentieth-century Thalys TGV train, and that alternates hour by hour with the old train (which is still called Fyra to save face and maybe in the vain hope that someday it will work), but the Thalys costs two and a half times as much. Why pay that to get there less than an hour earlier, when the old trains are so nice and comfy and olde-worlde? There's another funny story about the Fyra: it is said that one of the trains went missing from the factory. Can you believe that – a whole train? Guess where they found it. Go on, have a go. Did any of you say Libya? No, I thought not. Some people say so. I don't know if I believe it either, but some say jailbird Berlusconi made a gift of it to gamebird Colonel Gaddafi. The Fyra's not running in Libya either.

***

This had been a memorable week. I'd been across in a rush to Shepherd's Bush, mush, to support the lads in the vital match at QPR where our one-two away win had helped to save us from relegation with one game to go, but QPR were now confirmed as going in the opposite direction. Meanwhile Wigan were heading towards winning the FA Cup but had run out of time in the league and were losing their Premiership status, leaving the mackems hanging on in fourth-bottom place. More derbies next year after all. We haven't played QPR very often in recent years and one of the few times that we've been to Loftus Road was to play non-league Hayes and Yeading in the FA Cup 3rd Round one New Year, and that had been a great trip.

My ticket said 'restricted view' but everyone was just standing wherever they felt like (I mean the fans, not the players) in the away end behind the goal, and I ended up with a very good view directly in line with the penalty box from where I could definitely see that Debuchy did not commit his foul inside the box, so Rémy should never have got his penalty against us. He scored after about ten minutes so we had plenty of time to recover and Ben Arfa equalised with another penalty after having had his shirt stretched to Triple XL, before Gouffran first-timed a loose ball rebounding out of the penalty area and back into the goal. Then we had to hang on for the rest of the first half and all the way through to the end. It was good that Joey Barton was still away in Marseille, as otherwise I could just imagine things would have got out of hand one way or the other. I half-suspect he would have scored an own goal to make sure we wouldn't get relegated. He'd already helped us to get relegated a couple of years earlier so he'd have wanted to make amends.

There's nothing like going to away matches – the atmosphere in the Toon section is always great, and this time was no exception with songs like 'We're winning away, we're winning away, you must be $#1t if we're winning away,' and 'I like Debuchy, Buchy' and 'De Gouffran ran, ran, De Gouffran, ran.' We really weren't very good, but luckily QPR were worse. And that was on and off the pitch: the QPR fans raised a few chants when they went ahead but after we equalised and right through to the end, we did not hear a peep out of them – prompting chants of the obvious 'Shall we sing a song for you,' and 'Give us a song ... Shhhhh.'

At half time they brought on half of their '82 Second Division Championship-winning team, of which they were incomprehensibly and inordinately proud. When you've had so little recent success you tend to magnify any small upward curve into a major triumph. Sounds familiar, doesn't it? Amongst the string of names, they announced Wayne Fereday, briefly of Newcastle when he'd already seen better days. I'd have been much more interested to see their real stars like Rodney Marsh and Stan Bowles but they were from the late sixties and seventies – when QPR really were pretty good. Or of course they could have brought on Sir Les – that would have been the choice of choices.

The final minutes were very tense. QPR had a fierce shot very near the end which looked like it was going in up at the far end away from us, and everyone held their breath for an eternity. And of course Cissé had his habitual offside-ish goal disallowed. At the end of the match there was a pitch invasion – QPR were obviously expecting it as loads of security guards came out and sat facing the stands ten minutes before time and tried to stem the flood of refugee Premiership fans as they headed for the Championship, but the security effort was completely ineffectual and they flooded onto the pitch. Some came down to our end and started gesturing, and were answered with 'We'll meet again, don't know where, don't know when,' and rounded off with '%@*$ off to the Championship.'

Coming back, I got off the Tube at Hammersmith and walked back down river – to where son Brian was staying at the time in Fulham – in contra-flow to the thousands of Fulham and Liverpool fans coming upstream from Craven Cottage. Their scoreline had been a predictable three-one to the visitors. Fulham could easily have gone down if the season had lasted another couple of weeks as they'd lost about five or six in a row.

***

But enough of this. Today is all about the Europa League Final. It doesn't seem like Final time – the weather is more like mid-winter than mid-May.

We checked in at the Holiday Inn at a very unreasonable football final special price of a hundred and sixty euros plus twenty-two euros each for breakfast. At least it was a big room. Other hotels had prices in the several hundred euros range, even getting on for a thousand euros.

We took the Metro for the fifteen-minute trip to *Amsterdam Centraal*. It is amazing that they can even think of having a Metro in Amsterdam, what with all the water and the sunken piles (oo-er) that hold the buildings up. Surely the Metro must be under water? They must have sealed tunnels and pumps working away full blast to drain the water away, but to where? It must only come straight back. The trams are more like submarines than Metro trams. Surfacing from below sea-level, we walked out across the station's wide piazza, past the serried ranks of thousands of upright Dutch bicycles, and headed along Damrak towards Dam Square. We met quite a few decent supporters selling tickets for seventy euros face value. Even with our luck, you can always just turn up at a Final and buy a ticket at a sensible price.

Like the packs of Celtic fans who turn up at all the finals, I brought my Benfica/NUFC half 'n' half scarf and Toon top to show we had made it to the Final even if the team hadn't. Like us, the ever-optimistic Celtic fans buy their tickets in the Christmas-time lottery, but never (or hardly ever) get through. As the day went along we saw fans in the town and in the neutral section of the stadium from just about all of the clubs that had been in the last sixteen, including probably around twenty of the Toon Army.

Can you credit that cheatski sent back some of their tickets? They started by complaining that only twelve thousand tickets was unfair out of the fifty-three thousand capacity of the Ajax stadium, but then they couldn't even sell them! 'S#1t fans' indeed.

The Don had two tickets, too, but what with Brighton making such a brave attempt at reaching the Premiership he decided against it, and offered his tickets to Steve, but he was unable to come as well. Apparently tickets were offered on ebay for two thousand pounds a few weeks ago when cheatski qualified, but seeing they couldn't even sell their own tickets, I doubt there were many takers for them at such a price.

The *Damrak* was full of supporters, mostly Benfica it seemed, though there was a fair sprinkling of cheatski too. And we saw many shirts of other clubs that had fallen by the wayside – the Toon of course, Liverpool, semi-finalists Fenerbahce, but strangely no one from Basel, the other semi-finalists; it was probably too illogical to a Swiss to buy a ticket before being sure of qualifying for the Final. Nor were there any Spurs fans. Clearly no one from there had any interest in, or stomach for, watching cheatski have a chance to go even further ahead of them in the silverware department.

After Dam Square, which was encamped by the Portuguese too, we asked a policeman, as you do, who turned out to have been shipped in especially for the day from up north in Groningen (Newcastle's twin town in the Netherlands) and had no idea how to get to *Leidseplein*. Another eventually took us through to the next street and told us to take a tram from there. Our twenty-four-hour Metro pass for seven euros was working a treat. The tram took us from what had turned out to be Amsterdam's stamp street, the famous Red Stamp District, I think you've all heard of that before. There were some street stamp sellers doing a roaring trade who tried to sell us some Nazi-era stamp books, but we told them we were not from Antwerp.

Some say philately will get you nowhere, but the nice blue and white stamp-street tram worked for us and took us out across all the picturesque canals and famous arcs of streets including *Prinsengracht*, *Herengracht* and *NZ Voorburgwal* and eventually we found ourselves on *Leidsestraat* leading, naturally enough, to the *Leidseplein*. You can't go wrong as the trams have electronic notice boards telling you the next stop and they read them out too. One funny thing about their trams is that they have someone who looks like he ought to be the driver but he is stationed in a little cubicle about half-way along the tram. We worked out that he couldn't get a very good view of the street from there, and sure enough, there was another driver up at the front of the tram too. If it had been a ship out of Francis Drake's or even Moby Dick's time, you would of course steer from the back, and as a famous sea-faring nation it seems like the Dutch are having difficulty in adapting to the realities of city-centre traffic and have compromised by putting a second driver amidships.

The *Leidseplein* had more of a blue colour so we shifted briskly to our real goal which was the American Café of the American Hotel. This has quite possibly one of the best ambiances of any hotel café in Europe, and hence the world.

The American Café has been one of my favourites for thirty years. I even tried to persuade my daughters Emilie and Sarah to go there for their snack on their school trip a few weeks earlier to Amsterdam museums, but it seems they and their friends disappointingly chose Starbucks and MacDonalds. The youth of today, when will they learn? You may be asking what is so good about this American Café if I'm not keen on Starbucks. Well for a start it's not in any way American. The first time I chanced upon it, I went in on a cold mid-afternoon to get into the warmth and found myself in a place of theatre. Full of arty, party people. What lodged in my memory was an impeccably, not to say flamboyantly, dressed man with a trimmed beard in an extravagantly large brown, or was it maroon fedora. Swirling the camel cape draped insouciantly over his shoulders, and twirling his cane, he swept into the room and surveyed what to him was clearly his 'audience', 'his people', as if bounding onto the stage, making his entrance before being shown deferentially to his primely-positioned table at the centre of the scene, I mean room. It's an image that has stuck with me. Pure theatre. It was great. And when I looked around that first time, I noted that many others in the room were of the same ilk. Now I go back every time I'm in the vicinity.

Today was a little more subdued but you still could sense the atmosphere and feel the style. The room itself is a gem of *Art Nouveau*, of Dutch genus and genius. And what is more, the menu is very welcoming and reasonable. We favoured the three-egg *uitsmijter* with ham and cheese, a Dutch/Flemish delicacy, and the large flagons of Grolsch. The afternoon passed by marvellously and soon it was time to head back along one of the Amsterdam bicycle-spoke streets which cut across the arcs of the canals to the Central Station hub. From there we took the packed-like-sardines Metro out to the Bijlmeer Amsterdam Arena, which was an excruciatingly-squashed yet mercifully short quarter of an hour or so away to the south, near our hotel and the motorway to Brussels and beyond.

***

When you get out of the Metro at the Arena stop, it looks like you are in an out-of-town shopping and office centre which just happens to have its own football ground too. The place was thronged with supporters of both sides and the aforementioned clubs that had been knocked out earlier, and even more neutrals. In one of the shopping mall pre-match bars, we met a very pleasant couple from Cork, Liverpool supporters of course, and as we walked over to the stadium we bumped into a bunch of Toon fans singing songs and waving banners. Home from home indeed.

Making it feel even more like a shopping centre, the football stadium has an underground, and therefore underwater too, multi-storey car park. The pitch itself can be rolled away under one of the stands and out into the open to maintain the quality of the surface, and maybe to allow the stadium to be used for concerts without ruining the pitch. Just like Schalke's Veltins Arena.

There was no Benfica eagle flying around Ajax's Bijlmeer Arena. Benfica weren't allowed to bring their own with them – too much risk that it was a homing eagle and that it would use its pigeon-like innate sense of direction to fly out through the little gap in the almost roofed-in Ajax Stadium and head back down to the warmer climes of Lisbon.

We were sitting in the neutral section one row down from the roof, close to the Benfica fans' end which was below us to our left. They had hung up a giant banner all along the upper stand behind the goal saying *'Acreditimos Nos'*, which means 'We believe', can you credit it? Even in with the neutrals, we were surrounded largely by Benfica supporters with big voices who were all jumping up and down in time with the main block of Benfica fans. There were a few very quiet cheatski fans, including two sitting right beside us who hardly piped up at all. After yet another of his blunders, I asked them why on earth they have Luis in their team. It became obvious that they were foreigners, and maybe even Brazilians as they had a completely unrealistic opinion of Luis's abilities. Speaking of foreigners, it might surprise you to learn that the cheatski starting eleven with its three Englishmen contained two more home-grown players than Benfica's which contained only one Portuguese player, the right back Almeida.

Even when cheatski scored, their fans hardly stirred from their slumbers, in marked contrast to the exuberant and excited Benfica fans. The Benfica noise totally drowned out the puny squeaks emanating from the cheatski end. The support for Benfica was far superior and so was their play, and the neutral sections were soon all on their side.

The match itself was full of hope throughout, yet ultimately disappointing. We hadn't come all this short way just to see Benfica lose ... or cheatski win. As we told anyone who cared to listen, we didn't care which team won as long as it wasn't cheatski. We can't stand them. It will not have escaped your notice from the Benfica chapter that I have a soft spot for Benfica because of the 1966 World Cup and the magnificent Eusebio. How Benfica could have done with him tonight. Their Paraguayan centre forward Oscar Cardozo wears number seven and is a very good player and had been the downfall of the Toon, but he just doesn't have the killer goal instinct of Eusebio. He was the real hero of the 1966 World Cup, not Bobby or Jack Charlton or whoever else.

Benfica gave cheatski a lesson in football on the night. Close control, accurate passing, speed of thought and movement. They could and should have been two or three up within the first half hour. But as so often happens, a team might be on top but if it does not take any of its many chances, then it will later rue its failure to capitalise on its superiority. And that is how it played out; cheatski recovered a little and in patches held their own and on a break-away scored a goal. This was cancelled out by a penalty by the Benfica number seven, but unfortunately Benfica then had another goal disallowed, Cissé-like, for offside. Then cheatski got another goal in added time from an excellent parabolic header from their number two, Ivanović, who was later named man of the match (maybe in sympathy for being bitten by Suarez, a Liverpool attacker in the true sense of the word), and then the Benfica number seven had the ball on his toe with thirty seconds to go, but somehow failed to kick out his foot goalwards and the chance evaporated. Eusebio would have done it, even now at probably a bit over seventy. He was sitting alongside Platini, probably slightly uncomfortably for both of them as they are both rather satisfyingly plump these days, but he was looking good still. (Note from the future, courtesy of our time machine again: sadly, he died not long after. One of the few players whose club career shows he scored more goals than he played games. RIP Eusebio.)

So there it is. Benfica lost, very unluckily and cheatski spawned another lucky win. Money talks, even in a russo-cockney tongue.

Mind, you have to admit that Frank Lampard Junior is a good player, even without the benefit of Senior's beard. He whacked two great shots at goal during the game. The first was luckily flapped away by the goalkeeper's outstretched and flailing left hand when his whole body was misguidedly heading the other way. The close-up video showed the goalkeeper hanging his tongue out afterwards, betraying his relief that he'd got away with that one. The second shot came near the ninety minutes when he slammed one against the junction of the right post and crossbar from way outside the penalty area. The rest of the cheatski team was unimpressive, Mata having a very quiet time without any influence on the game, Luiz a liability as ever in defence, Mr Wor Cheryl just plain annoying, and Torres stuttering and stumbling to their first goal in a very hesitant and apologetic break-away. Really, Benfica only had themselves to blame for coming out of this the losers as the trophy was theirs for the taking.

Repeating the pantomime of the previous year, the shameless John Terry, who had played no part whatsoever in the game, came onto the pitch dressed up like a little boy in his replica kit supporter's outfit and pretended that he'd done something to win the match and the trophy. Like last year, he even had the gall to go up the stairs and collect a medal, though this time at least he went up last, not first. Their manager, Benitez, might as well have done the same, got dressed up in Samsung blue and shown us all his nobbly knees.

And now cheatski are the first club to sack two managers in a row after they've won them the two major European competitions. Ungrateful wasters!

So there we are – another European campaign comes to an end. Here's to a rapid return.

Toon auf Schalke – 2nd and 3rd August 2014
Ye cannit gan wrang, bonny lad

When the Schalke Cup tournament was announced on 1st April 2014 and Newcastle United were among the four participants (we were through to the semi-final already!), we reckoned it had to be an April Fool's joke. But no, the Toon really would be playing *auf Schalke* at long last – in Gelsenkirchen, Newcastle's twin town in Germany. Joining the twins would be Malaga and Everton. So that would be fine – there's never any bother between Geordies and Scousers (they have too much in common) – but then the Toffees were, unfortunately as it turned out, replaced by the Hammers. From the outset, it was clear that things could get confusing, because only 60 clicks – about 40 miles – or so to the north-west of Gelsenkirchen lies a town called Hamm, and a native or resident of Hamm is called a Hammer. So if President Kennedy had gone to Hamm instead of Berlin he wouldn't have said *Ich bin ein Berliner* (which of course means 'I am a doughnut'). Instead he would have said *Ich bin ein Hammer*.

Within three days, the match tickets and the hotel accommodation had been sorted. There was simply no way we were going to miss this one, we had waited long enough for such an occasion. Mind, we discovered that the Toon had in fact played Schalke once before, in May 1960, when Len White got two and John McGuigan one to give us a 3-0 away win at the (in Germany very) famous *Glückauf Kampfbahn*, the place Schalke called home from the 1920s to 1973. To many fans, the *Kampfbahn* is still their spiritual home. *Glückauf*, by the way is a traditional miners' greeting, wishing a safe return to the surface after the shift. And Schalke's equivalent of the Blaydon Races is a mining song entitled '*Glückauf, der Steiger kommt*'. In the *Ruhrgebiet* nowadays, saying *Glückauf* is a way of wishing someone all the best. A politician making a speech in the area will always end with those words. It would be almost unthinkable not to.

Anyway, May 1960 was a long time ago, and we weren't going to wait another 54 years for the chance to see the twin towns clash again. The lady I phoned at the Maritim hotel in the centre of Gelsenkirchen – just minutes away from the main pedestrian zone – said we could also book the match tickets through the hotel. I had hoped as much because I had been there a couple of times before and I knew they arranged tickets for *Bundesliga* games, for which there is even a shuttle bus laid on. But the bus would not be available for the Schalke Cup. Never mind. We really can recommend the Maritim. It is a 1970s tower block about fourteen storeys tall, right next to its twin residential tower of private apartments. A low-rise but large-area bungalow-type structure joins the two towers at ground floor and basement level. In that complex you have the reception and lobby area, restaurant/breakfast room, an 'English pub' giving onto a beer garden, another bar-cum-restaurant, and a fitness centre complete with swimming pool and sauna. To one side of the Maritim is the nearby city centre, to another the *Stadtpark* or city park – an extensive Leazes-Park-type affair providing a green oasis woven into the urban fabric. Yes, we heartily recommend the hotel with its friendly and efficient staff. But there is one small blemish – there is no air conditioning. That was to prove a less than welcome surprise in the summer heat, the tournament dates being Saturday the 2nd and Sunday the 3rd of August 2014.

***

Just so yiz can get your bearings: Schalke is a district of Gelsenkirchen in the same way that Byker, say, is a district of Newcastle. And the *Glückauf Kampfbahn* stands in the Schalke district, about five km from the city centre. When the club moved to the *Parkstadion* in 1973 it actually left Schalke (in body though not in spirit) and settled down further away again from the city centre, maybe eight clicks or so. One city district of Gelsenkirchen is called Bismarck, and we were rather hoping that like the *Bismarck*, Schalke 04 would be sunk without trace – if not without a fight – when the Toon destroyers steamed in for the kill. Whoops, sorry, we weren't supposed to mention the war. As an aside, Schalke's arch rivals are Borussia Dortmund, and the city of Dortmund has a district called Scharnhorst. That's a lot of naval firepower (all sunk) for a region so far from the sea.

But don't put your sextant away or abandon ship just yet, because we are still getting our bearings, remember? Gelsenkirchen, population around 260,000, is located in the northern half of the Ruhr area, which is in the west of the country, roughly half way between Germany's most northerly and most southerly bits (so it is in the country's West Midlands, as it were). The Dutch and the Belgian borders are not far away (about seventy-five and a hundred km, respectively) and the nearest North Sea beach is roughly a three-hour drive away, Dutch traffic permitting. In German the area is known as the *Ruhrgebiet* and colloquially it was affectionately known for decades as the *Kohlenpott* (coal scuttle). Today it is still often referred to, equally affectionately, as *der Pott*. The *Ruhrgebiet* is simply gi-huge. It is one of Europe's largest conurbations, with a total population of around five million. When travelling around the place, it is difficult to tell exactly when you have left one town or city and entered the next, even though there are plenty of green spaces dotted around the place. A bit like Tyneside in fact, but on a much bigger scale.

At the beginning of the nineteenth century, the towns and cities were mere villages; in 1840, Gelsenkirchen had just six thousand inhabitants. So what happened?

***

The steam-powered industrial revolution started in England, of course, though Flanders can rightly claim that its cloth industry was also pretty revolutionary well before the steam age got under way. Germany's first operational steam locomotive, *der Adler*, was built in (you've guessed it) Newcastle upon Tyne, at the Robert Stephenson locomotive works in 1835. Industrialisation as we know it thus took off a bit later in Germany. The Germans therefore had a lot of catching up to do, and boy did they catch up! Krupp in Essen achieved its first breakthrough by copying English cast steel, and other makers, shapers and processors of steel set up shop all over the, well, shop – though on an as yet comparatively modest scale.

It had been known for a good while that the Ruhr valley sat on a coal field, and people had been scraping coal from the surface in makeshift strip mines since the middle ages. As the likes of Krupp and Thyssen expanded their steelmaking activities, demand for coal naturally rose, and from the mid nineteenth century on, the industry enjoyed what can only be described as explosive growth. And the region's population exploded with it. The *Ruhrgebiet* literally became the powerhouse of the German economy, and immigrants were sucked in by the train load, and no doubt plenty of them walked or hitched lifts on carts as well. They came not only from the surrounding rural districts and from the Eifel and the Westerwald areas (both around a hundred and fifty km away), but also to a huge extent from regions of what is now Poland. At the time, Poland as a state was missing altogether from the map of

Europe, having been partitioned between the Russian, Austro-Hungarian and German Empires. One part of the German Empire was Silesia, where the population was a mix of German and Polish speakers (even to this day there is still a small German-speaking minority there). It too has a rich heritage of coal mining and steel-making, and over the decades tens of thousands would come from there in search of better wages, while many thousands of others came from all over what were then the Eastern provinces of Germany in search of any work at all, usually at a pit or a steelworks.

(The parallels with Tyneside are striking, aren't they? In the decades that followed the Great Famine, tens of thousands of Irish poured into Tyneside to work in the pits, steelworks and shipyards. Jarrow, for example, became known as 'Little Ireland'. It went from being a village with a population of just a few thousand in the early nineteenth century to a bustling and booming industrial town of about forty thousand largely exploited souls by the time the Kaiser, the King and the Tsar (three first cousins) were more than happy to take their grandstand seats to watch a spot of pan-European carnage.)

Well what the Irish were on Tyneside, the Poles were in the *Ruhrgebiet*, but again on a bigger scale. And to this day, just as the phonebook at home has plenty of Irish names in it, so you'll find any number of Lewandowskis, Szymanskis, Kowalczyks and Koslowskis in the *Pott*. Come to think of it, you'll now find a good few such names on Tyneside as well! The Poles and the Irish have a lot in common, and it's not just their fondness for the drink. The majority of Poles at the time of their great emigration to the Ruhr Valley were Catholics, just like their Irish counterparts moving to Tyneside, Merseyside and Clydeside.

Immigrants tend to stick together, go to Church together, drink together and play football together. And it wasn't long before churchgoers in the Parish of the Holy Trinity in Dortmund founded Borussia Dortmund (probably over a pint or two). Most of those involved were Poles, a lot of them from Silesia and from the area around Poznań, or Posen, as it is known in German. Meanwhile, Gelsenkirchen had likewise attracted thousands of Polish-speaking immigrants to work in the mines and other industries. In the early twentieth century, it was the most important coal mining town in Europe. Indeed, it was known as the *Stadt der tausend Feuer* (city of a thousand fires) because of the flames of the mine gasses being flared off at night. But the Polish speakers who came to Gelsenkirchen were for the most part not from Catholic Silesia, but from the largely Protestant *Mazury* Lake District (which unlike our Lake District is fairly flat). At the time that area was better known by its German name *Masuren*, and the Polish-speaking population there largely regarded themselves as Germans who happened to speak Polish. The immigrants to Gelsenkirchen were true-blue Prussians, whereas the Polish Catholics who settled all over the *Ruhrgebiet* were largely of a nationalist persuasion. Another thing that set the Polish speakers from *Masuren* apart was the fact that a lot of their names ended in –a, and not –ski or –czyk, for example. And to this day, you will find many such names in and around Gelsenkirchen: e.g. Przygodda, Pustolla, Dudda, Gruza, and Borutta. Schalke's most famous player of all time was Ernst Kuzorra, the son of immigrants from *Masuren*. We'll be hearing more about him a bit later.

And it was the sons of such immigrants who founded Schalke 04 in, well, 1904 – in the very shadow, as legend has it, of the pit-head gear of a mine called *Zeche Consolidation*. The name they originally gave the club, however, was *Westfalia Schalke*. One of the Schalke fans' mottos is *Auf Kohle geboren* – born on coal. So we really do have a lot in common! There is even a tradition of breeding and racing pigeons in the region.

Though originally founded by Catholics and Protestants, respectively, Borussia Dortmund and Schalke 04 have never been regarded as clubs with bigoted sectarian followings. Thankfully, they never went down that particular road to Hell. The rivalry is fierce, of course, again just as it is between the Toon and the mackems, but it has never had the nasty edge that is to be expected at the Old Firm games, for example.

***

Coal and steel provided employment for hundreds of thousands and they made the *Ruhrgebiet* great. And they made the coal and steel barons very, very rich. They also provided the raw materials for armaments and hence for wars. Krupp in Essen became known as the weapon-smith of the Reich (*die Waffenschmiede des Reichs*). But here too, look at the parallels – for Krupp, read Armstrong. One war led to another, and of course the Ruhr region was one hell of a target for the RAF. The destruction and the civilian casualties were huge, but actually the production of coal, steel and tanks and locomotives just went on rising till well into 1944. After that, the *Ruhrgebiet* was no longer a force to be reckoned with. Till the early fifties, that is, when the *Wirtschaftswunder,* or economic miracle, kicked in. That continued until maybe the early to mid-seventies, when the first of the big oil crises made everyone *wunder* if the good days were gone for good.

One after another, the mining wheels that once did spin no longer turned around, and now there is not a single pit left in operation in Essen or Gelsenkirchen, though to the north of the *Pott* there are still a few. You can still see plenty of pit-head towers dotted around the place, but none of them are actually in operation in the *Ruhrgebiet* proper. The spoil heaps may have returned to nature's verdant embrace, yet mining and steelmaking remain very much part of the region's rich industrial heritage, and of its psyche. Again, does that sound familiar?

***

The dialect of the *Ruhrgebiet*, with all its variations and nuances, is a bit special too, just like ours. It has been influenced of course by the Poles. For example, the German word for hammer is *der Hammer* (it loses a lot in translation, doesn't it?), but in parts of the *Ruhrgebiet* the word *Mottek* is used, which as near as damn it is also the Polish word for hammer. So maybe we should call West Ham 'the Motteks'. And in most places in Germany, the way of saying 'at Schalke' would be *bei Schalke.* Here, however, it is *auf Schalke.* And they also say *auf Rot-Weiss* (Essen or Oberhausen, take your pick – provided it's Essen!).

So all in all, Newcastle is well twinned with Gelsenkirchen (and sunderland with Essen, and Middlesbrough with Oberhausen, and Mülheim an der Ruhr with Darlington).

And at long last, the Toon would once again be *auf Schalke.*

***

So we had the tickets and accommodation sorted, and we were set for another great European adventure. Many of the usual suspects would be in attendance. Me and Wor Lass would be travelling the two hundred and fifty km or so from Trier, while Barry and Brian would be covering a similar distance from Brussels. The Other Clive and the Other Peter would be of the party of course, and as usual they were in the market for some local football as a supplementary counterpoint to the Toon soap opera. This time it would be Fortuna Düsseldorf's opening game of their 2014/15 second-division campaign against Eintracht Braunschweig. Düsseldorf is only around forty km to the south-west of Gelsenkirchen. Chris and Sarah would be flying from Heathrow to Düsseldorf and then taking the train to Gelsenkirchen. And Peter F, Joanne, Pauline, Caroline, Vince and Wilf would be flying from Newcastle to Amsterdam, getting the local train to *Amsterdam Centraal*, then an InterCity to Utrecht, another InterCity to Oberhausen, and a suburban train, or *S-Bahn*, to Gelsenkirchen. I had told Peter F. that when they got off at Gelsenkirchen *Hauptbahnhof* they just had to walk through the pedestrian zone and keep a look-out for the Maritim's twin towers – 'Ye cannit gan wrang, Bonny Lad.' I had given Chris the same advice.

***

That's another great thing about the *Ruhrgebiet* – the public transport system and communications in general are outstanding, so you really cannot go wrong! From the main stations of the Ruhr cities you can get to just about any other major city in Germany in a matter of hours (Cologne in one and a bit, Hamburg in about three, Berlin in five or so, and Munich in seven-ish). There is a formidable grid of autobahns and urban expressways to keep motor traffic moving, and the whole area is criss-crossed by a dense network of *S-Bahn*, Metro and tram lines. And if you are into cycling, you are in luck. When the pits and steelworks closed down (the latter just about everywhere except Duisburg), so did the industrial railway lines serving them. The tracks have made way in many cases for cycle paths, and the northern half of the *Ruhrgebiet* is, thankfully, as flat as a pancake. Oh, and did I mention the canals, and of course the great River Rhine itself, that have also helped move the goods and keep the wheels of industry turning over the years?

So there would be no excuse for getting to the match late.

***

When the big weekend finally arrived, the logistics worked like a treat. Chris and Sarah were in Gelsenkirchen and checked into the hotel by mid-afternoon on the Friday, and they were joined a couple of hours later by the party travelling from Newcastle via Amsterdam, Utrecht and Oberhausen. The Other Clive and the Other Peter were in their Düsseldorf digs and getting ready to head off to their second division match (a two-two draw before a crowd of forty-one thousand and, according to our reliable eye- and ear-witnesses, a fabulous atmosphere). Barry and I were both unable to leave work till four, unfortunately, and probably reached the outskirts of the *Ruhrgebiet* at about the same time. He and Brian got to the hotel a good while before we did, however, as Iris, our Tina and I had some memory lanes to wander down first. Iris is from Mülheim and Tina was born in Essen, our Stephie four years before her in Mülheim, like her Mam. And in all, I must have spent about twenty years of my life in the *Ruhrgebiet.* So we made a couple of detours – this *kindergarten*, that school, this restaurant, that place of work... we lived there... then we moved there... you know the kind of thing, and you know the kind of roadworks and detours you inevitably encounter when you are hooked on nostalgia. And then we dropped Tina off at Norbert's and Andrea's place in the Essen district of Altenessen, very close to Gelsenkirchen's city limits. Tina's been friends with Norbert's and Andrea's Stephanie and Caroline, and other neighbours' daughter Wiebke since kindergarten days in Altenessen. The younger generation were happy in their own company and Norbert and Andrea followed behind in their car as we drove the final six or seven clicks to the Maritim Hotel in Gelsenkirchen.

By the time we arrived at the hotel it was about ten-thirty on a muggy first of August evening. After checking in we made a bee-line for the beer garden which had become a corner of Geordieland in a foreign field. The Saint Cuthbert's crowd all knew Norbert of course, as he had been on several of the Cuths Old Boys' cycling and walking tours, including the *Camino* from Burgos to Santiago de Compostella, and the *Cuths Waak the Waal* trip along Hadrian's Wall from West to East, not forgetting *Cuths Gan Dutch – Operation Wor Allotment* (Amsterdam to Arnhem and back), *Operation Rheingold* from Trier to Cologne and *Operation Rheingold Zwei – Cuths on the Bummel* (from Freiburg to Strasbourg on the German side of the Rhine and back to Freiburg, via Colmar, on the French side). Unfortunately he hadn't been able to make this year's cycle trip, *Cuths escape to Colditz – Back on the Bummel*, which took us from Berlin to Leipzig and then to Colditz and Dresden. We actually spent a night in Colditz Castle, fulfilling a boyhood dream and soaking up the atmosphere of adventure and derring-do. Who says Biggles flies undone? Only after the trip did we discover that one of the original Colditz escapees was a Cuths

Old Boy himself – Flight Lieutenant Dominic Bruce from Hebburn. On 8th September 1942, POWs in Colditz were told to pack their excess belongings into boxes for storage. In true Cuths Old Boy fashion, Dominic Bruce immediately seized his chance and was packed inside a Red Cross packing case, three foot square, with just a file and a forty-foot length of rope made of bed sheets. He was taken to a storeroom on the third floor of the German *Kommandantur,* from where he made his escape during the night. The next morning the German guards discovered the bed-sheet rope dangling from the window, and Brucey was gone! He made it as far as the port of Danzig, (now Gdańsk in Poland), where he was caught trying to smuggle himself on board a neutral Swedish ship.

On our cycle tour, we of course all did something similar (i.e. we escaped not just to, but also from Colditz) but didn't get any further than the beer garden of the pub a couple of hundred yards away from the Castle. Mind, during the night we did manage to emulate Douglas Bader. (What, Pete? Don't tell me, you all got legless?) No, like Douglas and the rest of the RAF chappies we built a two-man glider which we launched from a ramp we'd built on the castle roof using only some firewood and a few pipe cleaners from our Red Cross parcels. Unfortunately, our two chaps caught a bit of flak from Jerry shortly after takeoff; and dash it all, it looked for a minute as if they would end up in the drink (the nearby river Mulde). But Lady Luck was with them. An unexpected thermal sent their kite soaring heavenward, and Ginger very deftly feathered back on the old sammy, looped the loop and bally well managed to avoid taking a waspy. Far from having bought it, he and his rear gunner bailed out of the flaming cabbage crate using the single but highly effective parachute we'd made by stitching together our newspaper rations. They pulled off a perfect *pas de deux* landing in the exercise yard, right in front of the *Kommandant's* nose. To a well deserved round of applause, they were escorted forthwith by the goons to a five-star suite laid on specially for them in the old slammer. Good show, chaps. Carry on! Sweet dreams.

But here we were now in the Maritim Hotel *Biergarten* in Gelsenkirchen having a canny sup till past midnight. Norbert and Andrea went back to Altenessen, and the arrangement was for Norbert to be at the hotel the next afternoon at one o'clock, together with Harald. A new player on the scene, Harald had a key role to play in *Operation Schalke 04* as he is a Schalke supporter. And he has a *Knappenkarte*! That is the bit of plastic you need in order to buy beer and sausages and the like inside the Veltins Arena. You pay some money onto the card at a cash desk and then queue up for your food or drink and pay with the card. Sounds a bit of a silly idea, but in fact it does seem to speed things up nicely. *Ein Knappe*, by the way, is a pitman. Born on coal, remember? As part of our preparation for our visit to the Veltins Arena we had even been drinking Veltins beer in the beer garden. The Maritim used to serve Stauder, brewed in Altenessen, but they must have switched allegiance sometime over the past few years. But no complaints, because Veltins – brewed in the *Sauerland* region with water taken from the Dambusters' reservoirs – is, in my humble opinion, Germany's best beer (and that is saying something).

Before turning in we enjoyed the views from the thirteenth floor. Towards the west you can see the lights of Essen and beyond, and to the east and north there is a great view of a Christmas Tree oil refinery and the Veltins Arena, looking quite majestic like a great white oyster dominating the sparkle-lit skyline.

The buffet breakfast at the Maritim is copious and tasty – anything you like, basically, including *sekt* (sparkling wine) and smoked salmon. And the bacon and eggs are pretty good too. Looking out into the *Stadtpark* we could see the damage that had been wrought by a Whitsun storm. Trees had been snapped or even uprooted wholesale, including a magnificent old weeping willow down by the pond. And there were still loads of them lying around waiting to be cut up and removed. The scale of the damage must have been amazing, because the Germans are pretty efficient at clearing such things away and getting back to normal in next to no time. But Whit was about two months ago so they must have had plenty of clearing-up to do.

None of us had slept very well as the night had been so hot (mid twenties) and the lack of air conditioning was not appreciated. Still, it was matchday so everyone was in good spirits. Vince had already been to the Schalke fan shop in the pedestrian area and bought himself a Schalke cap. And, being follically challenged myself, I decided I also had to have one of those caps on the sunny summer's day that was in it. So off we meandered to the pedestrian area. It was just a few minutes' walk away so we couldn't gan wrang.

After a few wrong turnings we finally found the shop and before long I was also the proud owner of a Schalke cap and scarf. As it was past opening time we wandered along in search of a suitable watering hole. We had noted that we had to get the No. 302 tram to the *Veltins Arena* and also noted that we were close to an underground station at *Heinrich-König-Platz* so we decided not to stray too far from there. And our match tickets also counted as tickets for the tram – brilliant! Everyone remarked on how few old buildings there were – the RAF had done a thorough job here too. After a few minutes we came to a nice open part of the pedestrian zone at the broad junction of two shopping streets. There were various cafés with tables outside in the sunshine, but thankfully with big parasols, and there were still plenty of empty tables so we grabbed two of them and ordered our beers. Everything was nice and peaceful, with a fair few good-natured Toon and West Ham supporters in their colours, and a few flags of both clubs on display. One said 'Toon Army Poland'! Those Polish Geordies were presumably also visiting some of their cousins in these parts. I rang Clive, and he and Peter were on the train headed for Gelsenkirchen. He told us there had been some trouble in Düsseldorf last night caused by some West Ham supporters out to pick a fight, for reasons best known to themselves and their cockney brains.

And just then it became clear that the train ahead of Clive's and Peter's had arrived in Gelsenkirchen a few minutes earlier because about thirty or so middle-aged cockneys wearing no colours, but plenty of tattoos, soon approached our little square from the direction of the station. They probably thought they were completely inconspicuous, but in fact they stood out like a sore thumb. At first there were no police to be seen, but a few minutes later there was an impressive presence and it looked as though things would be okay with a bit of luck. The cockneys tried to take over the cafés and draped their England flags all over the place, duly getting on other people's nerves by securing their colours to seats and tables.

It was getting on for half past twelve, so I needed to be heading back to the hotel to meet up with Norbert and Harald, and we all supped up and set off in that direction. We later heard that there had in fact been some skirmishes on our previously idyllic little square. Hopefully a few of the cockneys were arrested. On the way back we turned left after the *Heinrich-König-Platz* underground (*U-Bahn*) station to head along the lane that led to the hotel. On the left was a nice pub/café with seats outside, and it looked very inviting so we had a pint there before I rushed back to the hotel and came back with Norbert and Harald in time for another before we set off for the match. While we were having that pre-tram-ride pint, the Other Clive, the Other Peter and two mates of theirs arrived and joined us. It really was a pleasant atmosphere at the *Altstadtcafé*. That was the name above the door, and the name means 'old-town café'. So presumably we were in what had been the old quarter before the bombs fell. Certainly everything around us now was post-war. We had thus found a wonderful watering hole away from the cockney intruders in what was a quiet side street. We decided to keep it Gelsenkirchen's best-kept secret and to come back here after the game for a meal because it looked so inviting inside as well. Confusingly another sign said '*Kaffeeklatsch*' so we weren't sure what the place was called, but we were happy with *Altstadtcafé*. It is in the Robert-Koch-Strasse and we recommend it.

So it was time at last to head off to the match. We took the lift down to the platform at the *Heinrich-König-Platz U-Bahn* station in two groups, the second group finally remembering to press the button to actually call the lift. The tram was about two-thirds full, mainly Schalke but also quite a few Toon. We once again bumped into Philippe from Paris (we had seen him at breakfast in the hotel). He was very inconspicuous in his beret and a T-Shirt that said 'Toon Frog'. *Vive le Toon*, we say! There was some good banter on the tram, yet bizarrely the Schalke fans at one point started singing 'Glory glory, man united,' to which we of course replied, 'Who the f*@& are man united?'

Almost immediately after pulling away from *Heinrich-König-Platz* the tram went up a ramp and came out into the sunlight. It soon swung past the *Musiktheater* and round towards *Schalker Markt*. We were coming into the original territory of Schalke 04. Very soon we were hurtling along a low-rise street of two- and three-storey buildings, a stretch known as the *Schalker Meile*. All the shops, pubs, insurance offices, banks and other high-street facilities were decked out in blue and white, with the words Schalke 04 to be seen literally everywhere. A bit further along, just before getting to *Ernst-Kuzorra-Platz*, we could see the *Glückauf Kampfbahn* to our left. We were in the Schalke heartland. The stadium has the look of the typical German *Sportplatz* of the 1920s and 1930s, low-slung terracing and oval in shape, with the ends behind the goals set quite far back and with a covered stand along the length of one side. As mentioned earlier, this is where the Schalke legend was born (on coal).

***

If you have seen the film *Das Boot*, you may remember a scene where *Bootsmann* (Boatswain) Lamprecht, played by Uwe Ochsenknecht, shakes his head in front of the radio set and goes to pass on some important information to the crew. 'Bad news, I'm afraid, men.' Of course you expect the bad news to be maybe about the presence of the Royal Navy nearby, or perhaps another devastating air raid on a German city. But no. Lamprecht goes on to explain, to the groans of all the ratings: '*Schalke hat verloren*' (Schalke have lost).

The reference is to the 1941 German championship final between Schalke 04 and Rapid Vienna, played before a crowd of ninety thousand in the Olympic Stadium, Berlin. The final took place on the very day that Nazi Germany launched its invasion of the Soviet Union – Operation Barbarossa. Whereas in Britain competitive football as we know it was suspended for the duration of the war, in Germany it continued as normal for a number of years. This was all part of Dr Goebbels' propaganda effort. Things were to stay as normal as possible for as long as possible – that way the population would be ultra-confident and sure of victory. Morale (and of course industrial production) would remain sky-high. Such was Goebbels' reasoning.

Schalke had been firm favourites to win the game against Vienna as they had been champions several times in the 1930s. In fact, under normal circumstances, the result would have been a foregone conclusion. But 'it was felt' that Hitler would be happier if the Austrian club won, and so that was what happened – after leading two-nil, Schalke lost three-two. Even in those days, the club had iconic status in Germany. And they still have that status today. The local support is one hundred per cent, but they have fans throughout Germany and beyond. There is even a Schalke UK fan club whose members make the pilgrimage to Gelsenkirchen for home games.

The key figure in the Schalke success story of the 1930s was Ernst Kuzorra, as already mentioned. The Gelsenkirchen-born son of Polish-speaking immigrants, he spent his entire playing career at Schalke, leading them to six championships and one Cup victory over the period 1934 to 1942. He was the lynchpin of the *Schalker*

Kreisel, the Schalke 'spinning top', a gyrating system of quick, short passes that confused and overwhelmed the opposition. (Sounds good, Pete, maybe the Toon should try it.) He was recognised as the best German striker of his era but was capped only twelve times. On the other hand, I don't suppose there were that many countries that wanted to play against Germany in those days!

***

Our tram trundled along on its way, past the stop named after the great man and over the Rhine-Herne canal. We were very much in the industrial north of the *Ruhrgebiet*, though the really heavy industry has all but disappeared. But as far as the eye could see to our left, there were industrial estates and admin buildings and very few dwellings. A couple of stops more and we arrived at the Veltins Arena, surrounded by all manner of sports facilities and general greenery. It is often the case in Germany, but also in other continental countries, that the stadia of the big clubs are a good way from the city centre. In the case of Germany, clubs like Eintracht Frankfurt, FC Cologne and Borussia Dortmund spring to mind. You travel there by tram and then you alight at what looks like a huge set of sidings or even a railway station concourse, and sometimes you have to cross over a pedestrian bridge to get to the actual ground, a good fifteen- to twenty-minute walk away. And so it is at Schalke.

So we went up the escalators and crossed the bridge heading towards the Arena. We passed people selling cool beers (Germany is very much a beer-based economy) and scarves and other souvenirs. Unfortunately, there was nothing resembling a match programme. Over to the left we could see the floodlights of the *Parkstadion*, which hosted five matches of the 1974 World Cup and two matches of the 1998 European Championships.

***

Hang on a minute. Germany have now won the World Cup four times, right? Well actually Germany had two teams playing in the 1974 Finals – is that not called cheating? East Germany beat West Germany one-nil in Hamburg, and 'beaten finalists' Holland beat East Germany *auf Schalke*. So for my money the Dutch can claim to be the 1974 World Cup winners, not Germany at all. And while we're on the subject, Germany are also in the record books as having won the 1954 World Cup, yet in the qualifiers they played the then 'autonomous' Saarland. Saarland lost three-nil in Stuttgart, and three-one in Saarbrücken. But Saarland is an integral part of the Federal Republic of Germany, having been German up to 1918, then again from 1935 to 1945 and now again since 1957. So the only way Germany won the 1954 and 1974 World Cups was by playing against (and in 1974 actually losing to) a part of itself! Call me Mr Pedantic, but I'd say that's cheating. Some people might conclude that perhaps some kind of deal was made with Saarland in the 1954 World Cup qualifiers along the lines of 'Let us beat you and we'll see about getting you back in with us in a few years' time!'

***

We were coming ever closer to the Veltins Arena, which was itself the scene of five matches in the 2006 World Cup. (It sounds to me, Pete, as if Gelsenkirchen might be able to lay claim to being the city which has hosted more World Cup games than just about any other.)

Our super-duper tickets were for the third tier, just about on the level of the half-way line, but it turned out that because the crowd was not going to be that big we were being upgraded to one tier below, with an even better view! We went through the turnstiles and duly queued up in the concourse behind the stand for our beers and sausages. The only trouble was we only had one *Knappenkarte* and Peter F. was standing in the sausage queue while Chris and I were in the beer line. It wasn't clear who was going to get to the front of the respective queue first and there were some Laurel and Hardy moments as I dodged back and forth with the *Knappenkarte* as sometimes Peter F. and sometimes Chris and I edged ahead. For the record, the sausage queue won in the end and Peter F. took the *Wursts* to our seats while we got the beers.

Brian and I were taken by surprise by this separate beer and sausage queue lark, Pete. It was only when we'd stood together for a quarter of an hour in what turned out to be the food-only queue that we found out we couldn't order drinks. Luckily we side-stepped the problem and saved ourselves another quarter of an hour by spotting a couple of Toon fans at the front of the beer queue who'd run into the same problem and we got them their sausages and they got us our drinks. That is one aspect of Teutonic efficiency which hasn't really been thought through, because just about everyone wants a *Bier* with their *Wurst* but you don't really want to have to queue twice.

Mind, it has to be said that the Germans have sorted out most things on the beer front, and at Schalke you get a cardboard beer carrier to avoid spillages. The lassie serving at the bar lays out the cardboard *Bierträger* flat on the counter, places the plastic glasses of proper Veltins in the holes that are provided and disposed accordingly, lifts up the handles in the middle, and, hey presto, you have your perfectly balanced six pints in your carrier, as level as a spirit level, which you can then carry, free of worries, to your seat. So good we took them home as souvenirs. Simple, yet brilliant!

The beer carrier, like everything else, is in the Schalke blue. As you emerge from the access steps into the seating area and look around this magnificent Coliseum of a ground, you cannot help but feel a sense of awe: opened in 2001, it was known until 2005 as the *Arena auf Schalke*. It cost €191 million to build and has a capacity of almost 62,000, with 15,000 of those standing. The stadium is reckoned to be one of the most technically advanced in Europe. It features amongst other things a retractable roof, a slide-out pitch, and a movable South Stand. Suspended over the pitch, and clearly visible to everyone in the ground, is a giant cube with screens on all sides. On it they showed clips of previous games, adverts, team line-ups and replays of goals and other key moments during the actual match. And to think that at SJP we haven't even got a scoreboard any more! (Breaking news: now we have, but it flaps in the wind!)

Our views were perfect. To our left the bulk of the Toon Army present were in the standing area up from the corner. Clive and Peter were there, as was Paul English. The Toon had sold about six hundred tickets and then there were lots of Toon fans who like us had got themselves tickets through other sources. There must have been getting on for a thousand Toon followers, not bad for a pre-season friendly in Germany. Our first game, kicking off at three-fifteen was against Malaga, but there cannot have been more than a handful of their fans around. Some of the proper football supporters among the West Ham presence were already in the ground to watch our match, and the Schalke standing end away to our right was filling up nicely and looking very colourful in a blue and white sort of way. Their support was great with a lot of noise and songs and flag-waving and razzmatazz. When the stadium announcer reads out the team, he just says their first names and the crowd roar back with their surnames and cheer like crazy. And to build the atmosphere, they blast out the tolling of AC/DC's 'Hell's Bells' which shake the Veltins from its foundations to its rafters. It's nearly as good as 'Local Hero'.

In the end there were about 15,000 in the ground on the Saturday. We went three-nil down in eighteen disastrous minutes in the first half, with Sergi opening the scoring on twenty-five minutes with a long-range shot that went in off the woodwork. That was followed by a Samu Castillejo volley at the far post in the thirty-second minute and the same player made it a brace as the clock was just a couple of minutes away from half-time. At this point, Chris underwent some kind of Damascene conversion and decided that from now on he was going to be a lifelong Malaga supporter. Most man utd and cheatski supporters got there by the same road. He and the rest of the Malaga boot boys would easily sort out the West Ham bovver boys if they got out of order. Personally I put it down to the summer heat and the German *cerveza*.

The consensus in the Geordie, German and German-Geordie half-time beer and sausage queues was that NUFC had done bugger all in the first half and would probably do the same in the second. The beer queue was the scene of a not-so-surprising coincidence, as where else would he be, but Paul recognised Sarah from meeting up in Lisbon and he came down to join us for the rest of half time and the start of the second half. Paul said that Marcus and Steve who'd been with us at the Heerenveen and Alkmaar matches were going to be at the Sunday game but unfortunately we never found them for a reunion.

Like Paul, the Other Clive and the Other Peter joined us in seats nearby, so it looked as if the security people weren't too bothered about fans moving around the stadium from the Toon corner. We sincerely hoped that they would keep the West Ham contingent well away from us. To be fair, we know of course that the vast majority of West Ham fans, like the vast majority of football fans everywhere, are decent, well-behaved and civilised people. We had in fact been chatting with some really nice West Ham fans in our hotel, including a couple who had travelled for these friendlies all the way from Northern Ireland (via Damascus).

Newcastle were not much better in the second half, with Gabriel Obertan's bright performance overall being one minor highlight. And he thoroughly deserved his goal on the one-hour mark that prompted the Toon Army to briefly chant his name. Alan Pardew was later quoted as saying something to the effect that Obertan may still have a future at Newcastle United. We could clearly look forward to another glittering league campaign.

Towards the end of our match, West Ham fans started pouring into the standing area reserved for them behind the goal to our left (where Obertan had scored). We later heard that fifty or so of their 'fans' had surged through the concourse below the stand and tried to provoke the Toon Army into a fight. But the Geordies sensibly chose to ignore them, and the very unwelcome intruders were kept well in check by stewards and police. Alan Pardew was later quoted as saying that the Newcastle supporters had 'conducted themselves superbly under some provocation. Well done to them.'

***

Norbert and Harald (who would not be able to come on the Sunday) decided they were going to make a day of it and stayed on to watch Schalke and West Ham play out a goalless draw, with the Londoners then winning on penalties taken immediately after the ninety minutes (no extra time). The rest of us decided we would head back into town on the tram, however, and went back to our new local, the *Altstadtcafé*. The place was nearly empty and they were clearly glad of our custom. We re-arranged the tables and put them all together in the conservatory, and a fine repast was had by one and all. The Veltins went down well with our *Currywurst* and chips and other specialities. We lingered a good while, being joined in due course again by Norbert and Harald. Everyone was in good voice, and the Blaydon Races and many other old favourites were duly sung. Clive gave us his brilliant Fairs Cup song to the tune of the Lambton Worm (Aal tell yiz aboot the Cup). And Wilf sang some brilliant Irish ballads, including the Fields of Athenray. The staff and other customers were very impressed, no doubt about it. At the end of the night, Clive and Peter had to head off back to Düsseldorf, and Norbert and Harald to Altenessen. So the rest of us repaired to the hotel for a nightcap. The beer garden was closed by now, but the bar inside was still open, so there we tarried till about one in morning.

***

Along came Sunday and where better a place to meet in Gelsenkirchen for pre-match tinctures and a limerick contest than the *Altstadtcafé*? We were joined in due course by Clive and Peter and company from Düsseldorf, and Chris and Sarah's friend Holger, who is a Borussia Mönchengladbach fan but lives about a hundred km away from Gladbach in the south of North-Rhine Westphalia. Holger had parked up very close to the *Veltins Arena*, and gave some useful tips to Barry, who then set off with Brian with a view to parking as close as possible to the ground so as to be able to make a quick get-way after the match.

The night had not been as hot and humid as the previous one and we had all slept a lot better despite the thunderstorm in the middle of the night. It was now nice and sunny again but the forecast was for more electrical storms in the course of the day and night. We had been warned. This part of the world is at the interface of some hilly countryside and the start of the North German Plain. Somebody once explained that that made for some spectacular storms around this area. And I can vouch for that – in my time I have seen some absolute crackers in and around the *Ruhrgebiet*. *Donner und Blitzen*, as they used to say in the Hotspur. Though to be honest, I have never actually heard a German say that! *Donnerwetter* I have heard often enough, however.

We had heard that Schalke were holding a big open day (*der Schalke-Tag*) in the green spaces between the tram stop and the stadium, and a total of about a hundred thousand people were expected to turn up over the course of the day. So we naturally headed there before going inside the stadium. The plan was to watch the second half of West Ham vs Malaga ahead of our match starting at five-thirty. At the open day, some Schalke players appeared on a stage between performances by bands. And, to our delight, we discovered there was a *Miss Schalke* contest going on, followed by a keepie-uppie competition – but to make it more interesting the contestants had to skip at the same time. There were plenty of places to eat and drink, of course, and most of our crowd had *currywurst* and chips with a beer. Once you have had a *currywurst*, there is no going back to a plain old *bratwurst*. It is a life-changing experience. People always remember when and where they had their first *currywurst* in the same way they remember where they were when they heard that President Kennedy had been assassinated (even if they hadn't yet been born) or when Andy Cole was transferred. For the record, Barry's first *currywurst* was at the *Schalke-Tag* in Gelsenkirchen in August 2014. Mine was in Cologne in July 1974.

Isn't a club open day of this type a brilliant idea? No wonder Newcastle United have never thought of it. They have a half-hearted open training session at SJP on a mid-week day when most people can't go, but they could do so much more. Leazes Park would make a great venue. Maybe the supporters should organise one themselves and invite players to come along.

***

On display in a nice green and pleasant spot at the foot of a tree was the banner in honour of John Alder and Liam Sweeney – 'One City. One Club. One Family. One Love. RIP John Alder and Liam Sweeney.' We stood silent before it for some moments, along with many others. All around, people were sitting in groups on the grass, chatting, supping their beers, being part of the Toon Army thing. It was good that there were rounds of applause at seventeen, twenty-eight and sixty-three minutes in both our Schalke Cup games.

All credit to the people who had that banner made. It is a fitting and respectful tribute to the memory of those two lads. And we would like in our humble way to echo those sentiments here. We didn't know either of them at a personal level but, like everyone, we knew the Undertaker to nod to at European away games, including most memorably for us in the forty-degree heat of Athens when we played Atromitos. What a great trip that was, and there were so few of us present that everyone shook hands with each other and chatted. That will stay a lingering and fond memory. They would both of course have been at Schalke as well, enjoying the fun and the *craic*. They will be sorely missed. Let this chapter be dedicated to their memory.

And all credit also to the Sunderland fans who joined in the tributes, and especially to Gary Ferguson who organised the fantastic Just Giving online charity collection which raised well over thirty thousand pounds for the two families' chosen charities: the Sir Bobby Robson Foundation and the Marie Curie Hospice in Newcastle. This tragedy has brought the North-East football family closer together, no doubt about it.

***

By the time we got to our seats (in the upper tier this time, but still with really great views) the second half of West Ham's game was under way and Malaga were two-nil up. Life-long Malaga supporter Chris was of course delighted, but so were the rest of us. Our Veltins tasted even better for that!

On about fifty-five minutes the Spaniards looked like they were going to get a third, but Adrian pulled off a great save to deny Rescaldani, pushing over from point-blank range. And then he did the same again after the resulting corner. Late on, however, the same Adrian provided some comic relief by fumbling the ball, but West Ham's Juampi missed an absolute sitter. With under five minutes left West Ham could and should have pulled one back when Matt Jarvis somehow stole the ball on the half-way line and went one on one with Kameni. But he didn't control the ball well enough, and the Malaga keeper rushed out of his box to clear.

So Malaga were duly proclaimed the winners of the Schalke Cup even before our game began, though we didn't actually see a Cup being presented, which was a bit strange.

As we had hoped, the vast majority of the West Ham following left the stadium when their game was over, with just a handful of the true football fans among them staying on to watch us play against the hosts. With a bit of luck, there would be none of the undesirables still infesting the city centre by the time we headed back there after the match.

As our kick-off time approached, the end behind the goal to our right was filling up nicely and both the Toon Army and the home fans were in fine voice. And with our Schalke scarves and hats prominently on display, we joined in both sets of songs as best we could, much to the amusement of the Schalke fans sitting near us. They included a couple of supporters who had travelled from Leipzig to watch these friendlies. That is quite a hike, a good four hundred km in fact.

Just before kick-off there were around 25,000 in the ground. That left the 62,000 capacity stadium looking and feeling less than half full, of course, but there was nevertheless a good, friendly atmosphere with plenty of singing. Before the actual kick-off there was a minute's silence for John and Liam, but it turned into a minute's applause from the Toon Army. This initially surprised the German supporters, but they then joined in as well, as did the two teams, led by Tim Krul.

In stark contrast to the previous day, Newcastle had something about them from the start and had clearly found the vital spark that had been missing in their lacklustre performance against Malaga. The main difference of course was that instead of being faced with the excellent Malaga, they were now playing a pre-season, out-of-sorts and injury-weakened Schalke side. With a quarter of an hour passed, Rolando Aarons ran half the length of the pitch towards the goal away to our left. He ended his run, checked back and sent in a well-weighted cross to set up an excellent header by Emmanuel Rivière for the first-half opener. But there was more, and better, to come from Jamaican-born Aarons. Once again he tore down the left wing and when he looked up he couldn't find any likely candidates to pass to. So instead he floated a great big cross over towards the goal, and it sailed past Schalke keeper Ralf Fährmann and into the far corner. Aarons was later quoted as saying he meant it to be a shot on goal, so let's give him the benefit of any small doubt. Newcastle's third came in the second half after new boy Ferreyra was brought on and almost immediately set up his fellow sub Cabella. The latter raced clear of the pack and hit home a sweet low right-footer from just inside the box.

Schalke's Donis Avdijaj pulled one back for the hosts with the last kick of the game. It received only muted applause from the home fans, however, as many of them had already left. The Toon Army had stayed on to the bitter end, of course, determined to savour every moment of what would, after all, be the only European trip this season. But at least we ended up 'Runners-up in the Schalke Cup, Runners-up in the Schalke Cup!'

The roof had been closed during the second half for a thunderstorm. That was now over, but the dark sky held the promise and threat of more to come. Barry and Brian and Holger took their leave and headed off for their cars, while the rest of us took the tram back to the city centre. Once back in the pedestrian zone, Clive and Peter set off for the station and the train back to Düsseldorf, and the rest of us went to our local, the *Altstadtcafé*. To our disappointment, however, the kitchen was closed, so we had to make other arrangements. Not far from there, only half a kilometre or so away, is a really nice *Pizzeria* called *La Tombola*. So called because at the end of your meal you name a number between one and a hundred and then pull a numbered ball out of a bucket. If you get the right number, you don't pay for your meal.

On the way to the *La Tombola*, it started spitting on again and we could hear the rumble of thunder in the distance. We later heard from Barry that his journey home was a stormy one. Yes, Pete, we went through three separate storms, including one which was so bad that some cars stopped on the hard shoulder and a poor lad on a motorbike who passed us when we slowed then himself stopped under a flyover when he could take no more. His leathers and boots must have been filled to the brim. It was so bad that we took a wrong turning down a motorway which appeared from nowhere on our GPS and we ended up driving back into Germany from Holland and then spent a half an hour bumping along farm tracks until we got back on course. Over to you, Pete.

As it was still quite warm when we got to our restaurant and the rain wasn't heavy, we decided to sit outside at one long table under the awning. The food was great, and after our meals we all said our numbers and picked out a ball, but unfortunately nobody got lucky. Then just as we were settling the bill, the thunderstorm suddenly got serious. Thunder and lightning is no lark when Gelsenkirchen is in the dark, so we definitely weren't going to waak through the *Stadtpark*. It was a mile or so back to the hotel. The rain was stottin' doon by now. So three taxis were ordered and we got back to the hotel safe and sound and dry. Iris and I were ready to turn in but the rest had a nightcap, and everyone had a good night's sleep.

We all met at breakfast and instead of the usual piped music we had the sound of chainsaws. Looking out of the window into the park we could see that council workers were clearing away fallen trees. At eleven o'clock we all met up again in the lobby to say our farewells. Vince and Caroline were getting a taxi to the station, and Chris and Sarah had some time to have a look around the city centre as their flight back from Düsseldorf wasn't till late afternoon. So Peter F. set off with Joanne, Pauline and Wilf to walk to the station, turning left immediately on leaving the hotel to go through the park. When they had disappeared from view, the rest of us remained chatting in the lobby, and a minute later we caught sight of our intrepid walkers again, this time walking past the hotel in the opposite direction. The park had obviously been closed for the duration of the tree-clearing work. Seeing them walking the other way was a wonderful Pythonesque moment. And too good an opportunity to miss. So I rushed out of the hotel main door and shouted:

'Hoo man, Peter! Just keep on waakin' straight aheed. Ye cannit gan wrang, bonny lad!'

And we hadn't gone wrong. It had been another brilliant trip. In many ways, so many things had finally come together, and the twin towns' clubs had met in a friendly. We had been made to feel very welcome in the *Ruhrgebiet*. The Geordies had come as strangers but left as friends.

Howay the Lads! *Und Glückauf!*